Singapore, Spirituality, and the Space of the State

Bloomsbury Studies in Religion, Space and Place

Series editors: Paul-François Tremlett, John Eade and Katy Soar

Religions, spiritualities and mysticisms are deeply implicated in processes of place-making. These include political and geopolitical spaces, local and national spaces, urban spaces, global and virtual spaces, contested spaces, spaces of performance, spaces of memory and spaces of confinement. At the leading edge of theoretical, methodological, and interdisciplinary innovation in the study of religion, *Bloomsbury Studies in Religion, Space and Place* brings together and gives shape to the study of such processes.

These places are not defined simply by the material or the physical but also by the sensual and the psychological, by the ways in which spaces are gendered, classified, stratified, moved through, seen, touched, heard, interpreted and occupied. Places are constituted through embodied practices that direct critical and analytical attention to the spatial production of insides, outsides, bodies, landscapes, cities, sovereignties, publics and interiorities.

Global Trajectories of Brazilian Religion, edited by Martijn Oosterbaan, Linda van de Kamp and Joana Bahia

Religion and the Global City, edited by David Garbin and Anna Strhan

Religious Pluralism and the City, edited by Helmuth Berking, Silke Steets and Jochen Schwenk

Singapore, Spirituality, and the Space of the State

Soul of the Little Red Dot

Joanne Punzo Waghorne

BLOOMSBURY ACADEMIC
LONDON • NEW YORK • OXFORD • NEW DELHI • SYDNEY

BLOOMSBURY ACADEMIC
Bloomsbury Publishing Plc
50 Bedford Square, London, WC1B 3DP, UK
1385 Broadway, New York, NY 10018, USA
29 Earlsfort Terrace, Dublin 2, Ireland

BLOOMSBURY, BLOOMSBURY ACADEMIC and the Diana logo are trademarks
of Bloomsbury Publishing Plc

First published in Great Britain 2020
This paperback edition published in 2021

Copyright © Joanne Punzo Waghorne, 2020

A catalogue record for this book is available from the British Library.

A catalog record for this book is available from the Library of Congress.

ISBN: HB: 978-1-3500-8655-5
        PB: 978-1-3502-8330-5
      ePDF: 978-1-3500-8656-2
     eBook: 978-1-3500-8657-9

Series: Bloomsbury Studies in Religion, Space and Place

Typeset by RefineCatch Limited, Bungay, Suffolk

To find out more about our authors and books visit www.bloomsbury.com
and sign up for our newsletters.

For my husband, photographer, and companion for all of my projects

Dick Waghorne
(aka William Richard Waghorne)

Contents

Figures

Preface

Rewinding Singapore

Our boat the erstwhile M. V. Chidambaram carried my husband and me from Madras to Singapore in August of 1974. In Little India, we stayed at another ill-fated site, the New Serangoon Hotel for three weeks. Just a decade ahead of disaster in both cases—the Chidambaram caught fire at sea in 1985[1] and in 1986 the hotel, then called the New World, completely collapsed into a mound of rubble in minutes in the worst post-Independence civil disaster in Singapore.[2] At the time we traveled, the Chidambaram still retained its fabulous glass tile pool from its days as a French liner, and we dined with elegance at the captain's table. Our passage through the Malacca Straits and the landing in Singapore felt so refreshing after a difficult year researching for my dissertation (Waghorne 1976), which involved serious visa issues when American research scholars were caught in a major spat between India and the USA—a long story. This voyage home would ultimately take us to Saigon, then Hong Kong, and via an American President line freighter—actually quite stylish—to San Francisco. So, in 1973–4, we proved for ourselves that the world is round, having taken the TransAsia highway in our VW Bug from Sweden winding through Turkey, Iran, Afghanistan, through the Khyber Pass into India. Again, ironically, this route would dramatically close behind us only five years later. In fall of 1974, Singapore was only a waystation for us as we were about to visit Saigon—just eight months later the city fell to/was liberated by the Viet Cong forces.

Although less than a decade from Independence at the time, Singapore nonetheless exuded a cosmopolitan feel—we were able to get hamburgers and drink beer across the street for a late breakfast. We saw evidence of massive reconstruction projects everywhere although Little India was untouched as yet. At the time I never imagined that Singapore would eventually become my major research site after years of work in South India. Although never as jinxed as our hotel or ship or the places on our journey, the route to *understanding* the Little Red Dot took me through warrens of theories, some embraced and many discarded, and years of travel both outwardly and inwardly—as the many gurus would recommend. This book is the culmination of those continual crossings between place and self (my own and others) and spaces built of imagination, myth, and tons of concrete.

I did not return to Singapore again until the summer of 2005 thirty years later—after completing a long project on new temples in what was now Chennai (Waghorne 2004). I had just taken my current position in the Department of Religion at Syracuse University not as a scholar of Hinduism, my role for many years, but rather in recent theory in the study of religion, especially the globalization of religions. My new role allowed me to return to my roots in the History of Religions and wander more freely among geographical areas. This was also the moment when ardent postmodernism began to give way to the realities of emerging new forms of connectedness—not in terms of old universals but rather in recognition of the new global economies of Asia—notably the liberalization of the Indian economy in the 1990s and the intensification of the digital age. I got my first global cell phone in 2007. Also important at the same time, the term "spirituality" emerged with the cover of *Newsweek*, September 5, 2005, announcing "Spirituality in America" and noting more people in the United States claimed to be "spiritual" than "religious."[3] My earlier return to Madras (now Chennai) in the summer of 2004 confirmed the extent of these simultaneous changes—still inchoate—from formal religious affiliations to "spirituality" focused on rising new gurus, and, most important for me, a rejection, at least rhetorically, of old social categories of caste, even creed, and often gender—a phenomenon Lawrence Babb had already disclosed in his work in Delhi (Babb 1986). A grand new Universal Temple of Sri Ramakrishnan in the heart of Chennai attested to the revival of interest in gurus and in the spiritual practices, including yoga, that would soon dominate the scene. Everywhere new centers and temples to the spiritual master Shirdi Sai Baba (1838–1918)—whose identity as a Muslim or Hindu was never fixed—had flourished. The head of a major complex told me that her beautiful temple to this master "tried to create a space of peace so that people would begin to realize that they needed to 'go inward' to find that peace that they needed." Old friends confirmed that gurus, who also built temples on the grounds of their ashrams, were the latest trend here. This was my impetus to return to Singapore in 2005 to see if the same trend toward guru-based spiritual movements and that slippery sense of "spirituality" percolated into this truly multiethnic nation.

In a more worldwide context, "spirituality" conjured a turn to the *inner* and the *inter*national—focus fell simultaneously on the *self* and the *world* often read as the inhabited planet and/or the cosmos—or what the rising guru Jaggi Vasudev called *boundlessness*. Chennai and Singapore shared a heritage as British colonial port cities both founded under the East India Trading Company. I contemplated a comparison of guru-led movements in both cities as steps towards *cosmopolitanism*—at that time an increasingly important trope often contrasted with *communitarianism* as new concern for the local. Colonial port cities had always spoken globalism—but with an imperial accent. But now, in the twenty-first century, I knew that the time-worn comparisons with the UK/US—as my earlier book had employed—did not reflect the growing dominance of Asia. This time my comparisons would remain within South and Southeast Asia—but anchored by common ethnic Tamil heritages and Hindu sensibilities which were my forte.

My reflections (*not* fieldnotes—I am not an anthropologist) from my initial weeks in the now remade Singapore in the summer of 2005 and again in 2006 reveal my sheer wonder at the transformation carried out in these three decades. Madras/Chennai had changed but not like this! Moreover, Singapore far outpaced my new hometown of Syracuse in upstate New York and even New York City. I openly wrote "coming from the grubby Newark Liberty Airport to Changi Airport tells a story that I wonder if many Americans want to hear"—*and* that was Changi Airport before the new terminals and Jewel Mall. When I returned and spoke of this in the classroom, my students often refused to accept such realities—one urged on an evaluation form, foreshadowing Trump to "send her back," in this case "to Singapore where she belongs." All the systems in Singapore, including transportation and education, had indeed transformed—as Lee Kuan Yew would title his autobiography—*From Third World to First*. At the National University of Singapore, Asia Research Institute, I met Bryan S. Turner who had just left Cambridge to take the position of head of the "Religion and Globalisation" cluster and the brilliant expositor of Singapore, Chau Beng Huat, and other younger faculty whose insights—combined with conversation with several active members of guru-centered movements—rearranged my sense of Singapore. Prof. Vineeta Sinha facilitated many of these contacts—I had the good fortune to review an early version of her first book for the National University of Singapore Press (Sinha 2005) and met her via email after that review. She had also considered such new movements (Sinha 2008), and provided an ideal companion and guide, Nagah Devi Ramasamy,[4] who was exploring the flourishing Satya Sai Baba Movement in Singapore in her graduate program (see Ramasamy 2008).[5]

In those hectic weeks during both summers, I encountered several movements that I ultimately did not include in this book but which formed a foundation for my work and whose presence often reemerged: Brahma Kumaris, Satya Sai Baba, Ramakrishna Mission, Sahaja Yoga, and the Sri Krishna Mandir (closely associated with the International Society for Krishna Consciousness [ISKON] then located in Little India). At that time, I also interacted with the Amriteswari Society and the very beginnings of the Shirdi Sai Baba Center—I continued to engage with both. But equally crucial were the conversations I had with so many Singaporeans whose life experiences often paralleled my own—literally half way around the world. I recall now with gratitude my long conversation with Swami Muktirupananda, then President of Ramakrishna Temple in Singapore, from whom I learned of the growing interest in the yoga classes that the mission had long offered. My many discussions with Sundar Gopal Das of the Sri Krishna Mandir—always with the good flavor of blessed food and the many events I attended at the Krishna Mandir in Little India—enhanced my experiences of Singapore. I still recall my conversations with a devoted follower of Satya Sai Baba, a professional whose confrontation with a priest—mine was with a nun—turned him from his Roman Catholic roots to Zen and finally to his guru in Satya Sai. I soon realized that unlike South India, and notwithstanding its past as a colony, Singapore did not feel like a postcolonial society. This continues to be hard to explain and easy to misconstrue, but I never heard apologies nor pat explanations for how things were done—nor assumptions about my own attitudes as a "Westerner." Nor did I experience either privilege or scorn because of my race or citizenship. I think it was because, even by then, this city surpassed London in per capita income and had emerged as the new "aspirational" model for growing urban centers in Asia. Singaporeans were denizens of the "First World" and knew it.

Even on the first days of my return to this city-state, I began to question my love affair with certain theories especially "global civil society" and "cosmopolitanism." I was entranced by the argument by political scientists, historians, and philosophers for "fading states" (Rudolph and Piscatori 1997), emerging global civil society (Keane

2003), Geoculture (Wallerstein 1991), and a new cosmopolitan connectedness (Appiah 2006). I had argued in several applications for funding:

> for those of us in the comparative study of religion, the almost breathless references by policy experts as well as political theorists to an emerging set of normative values, a new form of worldwide interconnectivity that transcends older universalisms, and new organizational structures that communicate fluently in innovative media cannot be ignored.

For me the emerging guru-led spiritual movements appeared to abet and embody such new forms of commonality and organizational structure outside of the traditional social and religious formations. My reflections note: "With a day-old eye, I see a carefully constructed system (is this a culture?) of public consciousness that in Europe would be the heart of the 'civil' in civil society"; but I soon learned that in Singapore such a public consciousness did not stand between the state and business institutions. The government of Singapore had carefully and consciously nurtured this. In fact, the government regulated the field we would call civil society—those associations formed by shared goals rather than familiar or ethnic ties. Social welfare, normally the work of civil societies, until very recently was in the hands of the state. All civil organizations had to register as "societies"—I would learn the details over the next years. Moreover, without proper registration, my shocked reflections record: "they cannot publicly congregate. In Singapore, no more than five people can congregate in public without a permit! Also, the group cannot get land to build. So, the many movements will shift to houses!" Then I noted prophetically: "issues of space are important here." I would also begin to question the need for explicit comparison with Chennai: "A certain irony, Singapore with its small size and tiny 4-million population yet an independent government system with its own ideologies and constructions of identity makes this city-state a contemporary equivalent of a 'primitive isolate' minus the primitive." Much later in conversations, fellow Chicago alum, Wee Wan-ling, would suggest that Singapore's size offers a "'test-tube' intensity." At this time, when even Anthropology moved into the city, I began considering Singapore as a field site, as a *place*. Here I acted more the ethnographer than the historian of religions, but both would radically merge in unexpected ways.

In the fall of 2006, I applied for a Fulbright-Hayes Faculty Research Abroad fellowship for study in Singapore under the exciting Visiting Senior Research/ Sabbatical affiliation with the Asia Research Institute in the Religion and Globalisation cluster. Titled "Re-placing Religion: Spirituality, Guru-centered movements, and New Cosmopolitan Communities in Singapore," my proposal argued that: "With their formation of new-style communities and alternative identities, the popularity of guru-centered movements amid the hyper-drive economy of this cosmopolitan city-state offers an especially rich perspective on the rise of religiosity in confluence rather than conflict with the new globalized economy." I further promised three "mappings" of guru-centered movements in Singapore: (1) "in the context of their transnational roots and the style of the transnational language that they create"; (2) "in the personal dimensions of these guru movements" for their followers asking "How do they understand and live the relationship between their ethnic/religious heritages and their membership in a guru-centered movement?"; and, finally, (3) "to place the guru-centered movements within the religious cityscape of Singapore with its broadly Asian cultural mix." The application was successful and I excitedly left for a fully funded research year from August 2007 to August 2008 kindly supplemented by a stipend from the Asia Research Institute (ARI) at the National University. With another grant—a short-term Senior Fellowship from the American Institute of Indian Studies (AIIS)—I was able to follow the Singaporean Ishas to the ashram in India and to return to Chennai in December 2008–January 2009 to follow some of the same groups in their South Indian context—particularly Shirdi Sai Baba, Art of Living, and Isha Yoga. My gratitude continues to the Fulbright program and the AIIS. The kindness and the intellectual stimulation at ARI and its faculty continue long after my tenure there—Lily Kong, who headed ARI at the time (now President of Singapore Management University) and remains a valued conversation partner, the head of my cluster; Bryan S. Turner (now Professor of the Sociology of Religion at the Institute for Religion, Politics and Society at the Australian Catholic University) and his successor Michael Feener (now a fellow of the Oxford Center for Islamic Studies); and, most recently, Kenneth Dean, Raffles Professor in the Humanities at the National University of Singapore who is mapping Chinese temples in Singapore with interconnections over Southeast Asia—an exciting project in space and place.

I recall with thanks the government of Singapore and the Asia Research Institute of the National University for their kindness and unfailing help with my research and the welfare of my husband and me. I have never received such welcome in any of my previous work abroad. ARI provided a lovely office overlooking the botanical gardens with a computer, telephone, email, and Xerox facilities. They provide excellent healthcare coverage and a monthly allowance to offset the costs of living in this expensive city. The public transportation and the taxi system made travels a breeze. My affiliation as a senior research fellow entitled me to a year-long employment pass for my husband and me, which functioned as a green card making travel easy. The government of Singapore does not waste the time of its citizens or visitors—all formalities took only a relatively short wait in a pleasant air-conditioned hall.

That year in Singapore meant more than just formally "researching" a specific topic. I had come to this city after decades of involvement with South India, especially Chennai and farther south into Trichy (Tiruchirappalli) and Pudukkottai. Those were places I *knew* in multiple senses (both *connaître* and *savoir* or, in Tamil, *teri*, "to investigate, test, ascertain" and *ari*, "to perceive by the senses.")[6] Acquiring factual knowledge-data, although never easy, nonetheless can conform to methodology, but knowing in a more sensual, instinctive sense—close to *affect* and the newer theories surrounding this—requires chatting, many everyday simple acts like buying groceries, and hours of walking or riding in cars, buses, trains—what I once would have called *wasting time*. I had logged years of that in Chennai, but not in Singapore. So, for that lovely year, I lived with my husband in Niven Suites, owned and run with finesse by the Tong family who also renovated the Perak Hotel, which would be my domicile for the many short stays during the summers that would follow this intensive year (for the last two visits I enjoyed Albert Court Village Hotel also old and renovated). Both are converted traditional shop-house designs—ironically, I chose my love of renovation and preservation over living in the high-rises that I defend in this book. But some of my choice was dictated by the rules then that the HDB flats were for permanent residents—and I could not afford the kind of private high-rise flats that feature in the popular movie, *Crazy Rich Asians*. At the edge of Little India, I sat many afternoons looking out the window of my room in the Perak at the streets below or walking down Niven Road to cross into Little India to eat or shop. When I am asked why this book took so long to write, I always answer that it took time to *know* the place, and then confess my love of *shopping* in one of the few places in the world where this is an acknowledged national pastime *without apology*. As I write this now, I admit that I would rather be in the TWG tea salon in Takashimaya on Orchard Road.

However, my location and involvement with daily life—albeit always part of tourist land as well—undercut any romanticism such locations might try to evoke. In Little India, my hotel was behind several bars that the word "raucous" understates—it's long gone now, but the Mohican Pub remains incised on my eardrums. Yes, a "Red Indian" in full feathers signaled the wild theme—Syracuse University rests on Onondaga land and this really rankled. The police would not intervene in part to satisfy the backpack tourist crowd. On the top floor of Niven Suites, our apartment backed onto a rather dilapidated building clearly used to house migrant labor from India, "guest workers"— their return from work after 11:00 pm meant shouting and noise. Again, I called the police many times but they could not seem to find the source of the racket, although I had no trouble. My walk home from the Metro often passed other bars that the term "seedy" did not quite fit, and the ladies outside were not walking the streets in the same sense as me. Singapore is not without its underside in spite of all of its polish and all of its concern for civil order. Gum may be forbidden but a lot else is tolerated that still sullies certain streets in certain areas. I write about the changes in Little India after a serious riot in 2014.

During that year as part of the Asia Research Institute, I attended ARI seminars and workshops almost weekly. Also, at the Hindu Center, I regularly took part in the "Hinduism Module 1," then ably taught by Kamala and Krishna Sharma to understand how Hinduism was presented from the inside by "an independent, non-governmental organization dedicated to the spiritual progress of Hindus in Singapore through education (Jnana), devotion (Bhakti) and service (Seva)."[7] However, I devoted the majority of my time directly to the project at hand and my final report reflected the distance between what I expected and what I discovered, and I turn to this now (here I borrow directly from that report from the fall of 2008). During my twelve months of research, my initial hypothesis that spirituality was "re-placing" religion in this supercharged economy proved to be true but in a much more nuanced way. So, too, my underlying notion that such spiritual groups erased old and reconstitute new communities approximating an emerging civil society also proved true but again with major complexities. Since all such organizations must register with the government online, the initial cataloging of groups was easy, but finding them and their meeting times was not. I lived within walking distance of Little India and found that most of these groups meet in this Indian enclave or posted notices of their meetings in temples and on pillars there. Once I made one contact, then others followed because many of the devotees belonged to multiple spiritual organizations, as well as their birthright religious affiliations, usually Hindu. For the purposes of classification, I selected organizations of living gurus and also groups formed around gurus who had attained Mahasamadhi (*mahāsamādhi*, they died as enlightened beings). The living guru-centered movements in order of the frequency of my involvement were: Isha Yoga (Sadhguru Jaggi Vasudev), Art of Living Foundation, AOL, (Sri Sri Ravi Shankar); Sri Kaleshwar (informal group); Amriteswari Society (Mata Amritanandamayi, "hugging guru"); Rajayoga Power Transcendental Center (Yoga Jnana Sitthar); and Sahaja Yoga Meditation (Shri Mataji Nirmala Devi). The organizations centered on gurus in order of my involvement were: Shirdi Sai Baba Spiritual Center (Shirdi Sai Baba, d. 1918); Sri Raghavendra Society (Swami Raghavendra 1595–1671); Krishna Mandir (Swami Prabhupada founder of ISKCON 1896–1977); and Ramakrishna Mission (Sri Ramakrishna, 1836–86). I spent considerable time with the Sri Kaleshwar group—informal—but their guru died and the group faded. As that year passed, and when I later returned, other groups took on increased importance often because of their openness and cooperation—especially Oneness headed by Amma-Bhagavan. So many leaders and members of these group willingly spoke to me and I especially thank now—I will use only first names to protect privacy—Deviji, Saro and her sister Devi, Sunil, Palani, Sagar, Arumugam, Isis, Vijay, Hyma, Gary, Maya, Elan and Reni, and many whose names I use in the following pages with permission.

The most important adjustment was to my theoretical perspectives. I did not find the kind of "de-ethnization" that I had expected in either these organizations or in the creation of new communities. While many of these organizations had both Chinese and Indian members, each group usually retained their ethnic identities and rarely socialized with the spiritual groups they attended. Yet all of the rhetoric of the gurus and of the members of these organizations continued to intone the open invitation for membership to all races and religious affiliations. This gap between rhetoric and practice became a major issue for my work. Moreover, with all of the claims to openness, I did not expect secrecy in these organizations. Before most officials and practitioners would talk with me, I was asked to undergo the basic multiday "course" which culminated in an initiation into the *kriya* or basic practices of the movement. This was how any new member joined the organization and claimed formal membership. I had to sign formal "Confidentiality Agreements" with Isha, Art of Living, and the AIMS program (yoga program of Mata Amritanandamayi) not to reveal exact descriptions of the practices. With all of the mention of openness and an unbounded outlook, I did not expect such issues with research. So, ironically, in my earlier research on Hindu temples, which are often formally closed to non-Hindus, I encountered complete cooperation and openness with my work, but with ostensibly "open" spiritual movements I found my research much more monitored and suspect.

Reflecting on this a decade later, however, I now understand both the suspicion and the requirement that I formally learn the practices and undergo initiation. With the rise of Contemplative Studies and Mindfulness at American universities, the argument that research requires *experience* along with data no longer seems marginal, especially with the University of Chicago Center for Practical Wisdom, or the Center for Contemplative Science and Compassion-Based Ethics at Emory University, or the

Contemplative Cooperative at Syracuse University among others. On the other side, the attacks—some justified—on specific gurus and spirituality in general continues. As I write in the pages that follow, *spirituality* remains controversial. For example, a very recent op-ed in the *Washington Post*, "For Marianne Williamson and Donald Trump, religion is all about themselves," argues that "both come from the quintessentially American conviction that the quickest and surest route to Ultimate Reality can be found within ourselves" (Burton 2019). Insightful but also part of the broad suspicion of the dangers of "inwardness"—here the use of President Trump magnifies the dangers.

When I completed my research in 2008 in Singapore and then 2009 in India, I thought a book would materialize within a year or two. But by then my grounding in global civil society and cosmopolitan discourse seemed inadequate in conversation with Singapore as a place and as an experience. I returned in the summer of 2010, attended some events as a member of Isha, but began to *look at* Singapore, that is the visual *effect and affect* of the place, and realized after conversations with Louis Ho and Wee Wan-ling as obvious, the very landscape and form of the city carried power—beyond the political. "Spirituality" was not confined to guru-centered organizations but also existed within the built environment of which they were only a part. The defining moment came with the opening of the Moshe Safdie's masterpiece, the ArtScience Museum, which I saw under construction that year. The museum opened in February 2011 and I saw the opening shows that summer of 2011. There I read a message—literally on the wall—asking, "Can building have a soul?" Suddenly two insights stuck at once: this museum and the entire Marina Bay complex had been urged by the government of Singapore in a search for *iconic* architecture that would mark the state. I realized that *iconic* carried the fullest sense of the term—as an *icon*, in both a religious *and* political sense. "Reading Waldon Pond at Mariana Bay Sands in Singapore" appeared in 2014 in the *Journal of the American Academy of Religion* and is now reworked as Chapter 5—my thanks to JAAR for permission to reproduce this. Now I had a new theoretical frame—spatial theory—with enough scope to bring Singapore into conversation with broader issues while maintaining its uniqueness—its life as a place.

Over the next years I continued to publish articles and chapters on the city-state (2013, 2014a, 2014b, 2014c), as well as an edited volume, *Place/No-Place in Urban Asian Religiosity* (2016), while expanding my own sense both of the city and of the increasingly important *spatial turn* in theory. While only one of these articles is reproduced here, some of the data and content are part of the chapters that follow. Here I recognize the University of South Carolina Press and Oxford University Press, and Springer Publications. As part of my own discovery of spatial theory combined with new urban studies I offered a series of graduate seminars around these themes: "Spirituality, Community, and Cosmopolitanism," (2010); "Making Space for Religion" (2013); "Cities: Sacred-Secular-Cyber" (2014).

I returned often to Singapore over the following summers and had the good fortune to confer with several fellow academics in Singapore's amazing government-aided institutes and universities. I thank Drs. Belinda Yuen and Sharon Siddique of the Lee Kuan Yew Centre for Innovative Cities in the beautiful campus of Singapore University of Technology and Design (SUTD) near Changi Airport. I first encountered both through their publications which re-formed my theory and thinking (Yuen 2011, Siddique and Shotam 1982). I attended seminars there and was invited to present my research leading to a rich discussion and valuable insights. I often taxied out to the Nanyang Technological University, Singapore (NTU Singapore) to meet with my fellow Chicago Divinity School alum Prof. C. J. Wee Wan-ling. At the Singapore Art Museum I enjoyed several conversations with Dr. Louis Ho, also a University of Chicago product. Housed at the Urban Redevelopment Authority, Dr. Limin Hee, Director at Centre for Liveable Cities, made time to speak with me. I knew her through her valuable edited volume (2012). My chief interlocutors from the spiritual movements provided deep insight, and this book could not have progressed without them. Vijay Rai of AOL and J. K. Thulasidhar of Isha Yoga both emphasized that their perspectives did not represent any official positions of either organization, but rather I found their outlook and interpretations so relevant to my own thinking as I worked over the years to understand this complex place in multiple senses. I also thank Tina Jabr of Isha Foundation for her early help and later comments. None bear responsibility for my ultimate perspectives— those are mine alone.

Finally, as I reflect on my relationship to this city-state, I find that I cannot come to "conclusions"—notice the book has no such ending. Singapore as a place, as a state, and as an experience has challenged my notions of democracy, of liberal politics, of self and society. But most of all the ever-changing built environment continues to challenge my imagination. This state, for all of its pragmatics, its aggressive commitment to economic progress, never eschews what I can only call the *mythical*—narratives carrying meaning beyond the secular and buildings defying reality like the recent headline on CNN, "A gravity-defying tower aimed at 'sustainable urbanism' has opened in Singapore," features a park seemly cut out from the center of this high-rise: "The dynamic tower frees itself from the canyon of stoic facades, integrating green space at unique vantage points and ultimately cultivating the public realm alongside a boutique, mixed-use program."[8] Just yesterday one of our graduate students attended a conference at the National University and emailed her stunned experience at an outing: "We visited the bicentennial exhibit on Raffle's landing, which was like a theme park ride . . . unreal. They simulated the rainy conditions of Singapore's modern Independence Day speech and had us stand in a room with umbrellas and an actual downpour (photo attached)"— my reaction: only in Singapore! Such leaps into sight and sound transported me back— after years of postmodern soul-searching—to my roots in History of Religions, to a new concern with myth and politics, and to that lovely fuzzy line between sacred and secular, real and imagined. Singapore is progress with panache. In the end, I love the place!

Joanne Punzo Waghorne, Syracuse, New York
National Day, August 9, 2019

1

Macrospaces and Microplaces

Singapore is an embarrassing success story. Celebrating fifty years of independence last year, Singapore's stunning achievements merited only scant attention in the American media and in academic circles. In one proud article in the Huffington Post, the Dean of the Lee Kuan Yew School of Public Policy at the National University of Singapore asked rhetorically, "Is Singapore the most successful society since human history began? Or, to put it differently, did Singapore improve the living standards of its people faster and more comprehensively than any other society?" (Mahbubani 2015). He catalogued the achievements in education, standard of living, health care, harmonious ethnic relations, home ownership, and the stunning increase in per capita income figured in US currency from $500 per year to today's $55,000. Currently Singapore ranks third in the world; the United States is sixth. Yet twenty years ago the famous architect Rem Koolhaas bemoaned Singapore's "blandness and sterility" (1995, 1017), and the stinging critiques continue. Recent blogs and online letters write of Singapore as a "Soulless Success" (Walmsley 2013), or again "Modern, clean and soulless" (Corke 2014), or the claim that overly clean "sterile" Singapore supposedly illustrates "what happens when everything goes right?" (Dover 2013)—a strange finale to handwringing fifty years ago by development studies over the tendencies in the "East" to follow "ways of life compatible with great serenity, great dignity, profound religious experience, with great art, but not with the accumulation of material wealth for society as a whole" (Ward 1962, 45).

As soon as "soul" comes into play, no scholar of religion can remain silent, especially after almost a decade of following the many religious-spiritual movements in this city. When I hear or read such comments, I ask, "What is the *soul* that Singapore supposedly lacks?" Summarizing the blogs, articles, and many informal conversations, the problems with Singapore seem to focus on the consciously *constructed spatiality* of the city: "utopian metropolis," without "stunning natural beauty, an ancient culture and a character all of its own" (Vittachi 2013), or Koolhaas's famous prediction that Singapore is "doomed to be a Potemkin metropolis" (1995, 1077). But what intrigues me the most in these critiques is that Singapore's *landscape* is—perhaps unconsciously, perhaps vaguely intentionally—presented as a *religious* problem. The very success of Singapore seems to be for some a miracle and for others a monstrous inversion of *development*. But pro or con, the very *being* of the city, its *landscape* and—to borrow a term—its *inscape* (Panikkar 1991), seems in question and often with presumed crucial consequences for the world.

Whether consciously religious nor not, Singapore has lived for fifty years under a grand narrative carefully constructed by the PAP (People's Action Party) but then plowed into the urban landscape by the bureaucratic apparatus of this highly successful enterprise. An insight from Wang-ling Wee in his *The Asian Modern* suggests that such slips into spatial language by critics may mirror the intentional focus on architectural form that marked the PAP's ceaseless creative re-forming of the state, less on the production of expressive ideology than on material construction:

> The aesthetic home of the PAP state's utopian impulses was not painting or literature—which cannot feed mouths—but building, the art we live in and do business in. Architecture in the form of extensive modernist public housing and a revamped downtown that reached towards the sky was the social art form that nobody could escape, and was needed if the new citizens of the city-state were to live well, materially.
>
> 2007, *kl* 259–61

So, while scholars for the last decades have argued against the grand imperial narratives of European colonial powers, postcolonial Singapore has made the cityscape into its own impressive narrative. The urban development board bulldozed old villages—the kampongs (from *kampung*)—and leveled the rainforests, replacing them with the gleaming high-rise, now iconic, HDB flats owned on long-term lease by most citizens. The structure of very modern flats, as Wee implies, subtly re-formed the citizenry with this assessment confirmed by recent studies (Appold 2011). By law the residents of each building must reflect the exact ethnic diversity of the nation. This social engineering purposely overturns the organic quality—social and biological—of places like nearby Malaysia or India, and mirrors the manufacturing of the landscape.[1] Very little about Singapore is natural—the bugs are brought under control each morning by uniformed spray patrols, and cleaning crews pushing very official-looking carts ensure that no palm frond or leaf is astray (fig1.1). Even the Religion/s have boxes—checked after a name on an application, summarized in textbooks, and marked in designated and limited spaces on the map. As Mark Frost concludes in his history of old Singapore, even history was erased and constructed anew: "Effectively, on August 9, 1965, Singapore's historical clock was set back to zero" (Frost and Balasingamchow 2009, 431), eschewing past histories, heritages, old social formations, and nature, or so the story goes.[2]

If the *soul* of Singapore depends on long-standing history, natural beauty, and ancient heritage—Singapore is now a soulless artifice of miles of concrete, and now steel and glass high rises, shopping malls, carefully managed parks, and controlled public space. But that is only to some eyes; for many others, "Singapore is now an urban prototype influencing the development and growth of cities and nations the world over. . . . To know Singapore is to know where the urban world is heading" (L'Heureux 2010, 6). However, Rem Koolhaas, without the starry eyes, tells the same story differently. In his innovative tome, *S, M, L, XL* (*Small, Medium, Large, Extra-Large*), Singapore "merits" a long chapter but with the denigrating title "Portrait of a Potemkin Metropolis . . . or Thirty Years of Tabula Rasa" (1995, 1010–89). Clocks restarted, land remade and reclaimed, Koolhaas smells a rat—or actually smells nothing. Recalling his

Figure 1.1 Official street cleaner pulls cart of fallen palm fronds.

first visit to Singapore with "sweetness and rot", but finding when he returned, "The smell was gone. In fact, Singapore was gone, scraped, rebuilt" (1011), a *tabula rasa* in the hands of the redevelopment authority's "dystopian program: *displace, destroy, replace*" (1035)—an almost satanic enterprise. In his stinging terms, the "Singapore model . . . is now poised to metastasize across Asia . . . an asymmetrical epicenter, there will be new Singapores across the entire mainland. Its model will be the stamp of China's modernization" (1087).

The drama of Koolhaas, the breathless praise of L'Heureux (both architects, the former a Dutch citizen teaching at Harvard and the latter an American citizen teaching at the National University of Singapore), and many of the speeches by the prime ministers equally border on the mythic—*not* in the sense of the untrue but of a carefully patterned narrative with deep import that live out of and on the borders of history, but unlike mere history or legend are "that small class of stories that possess both credibility and authority", at least to those bounded by the narrative (Lincoln [1989] 2014, 23).

I will return in more detail to this issue of contemporary myth in the next chapter, but for now to begin with a *tabula rasa* is a *creatio ex nihilo* from a pattern out of the human mind, or in this case from the PAP bureaucratic mind, which begins to sound like a cosmogony. Indeed, mythic terminology appears well into 2010 with Prime Minister Lee's speech at the opening of the new waterfront promenade, on reclaimed land:

> Marina Bay Story . . . Development is the result of ceaseless efforts over more than 30 years. Nothing but sea was here in the 1970s but even then we had a vision of building an extension to our city centre. Hence we reclaimed land, planned ahead and invested in development. . . . With each passing day, we are making Marina Bay a more beautiful and vibrant place. This mirrors our efforts all over the island, as we continue to build a Best Home for all Singaporeans.
>
> Lee 2010

The "we" and the use of capitals here is regal, confident, powerful with *nothing* but sea in the beginning. *SMLXL*, as well as *Singapore Transcripts*, also adopts such cosmological terminology. The introduction to *Singapore Transcripts*, a self-confessed "love story for Singapore," turns mythic:

> Singapore is a fully constructed landscape inside as well as out—new territory created from ocean bottoms or a nearby island, a flattened surface topography to make building that much easier and more expedient. . . . In this landscape of continual transformation, we see the traces of Utopian aspirations: a city that is at once an idea and in a process of becoming, a green garden manicured and constructed, a city of modest icons sampling the best of everywhere, encapsulated by a glistening blue sea; the lubricant for a frictionless city the envy of the world.
>
> L'Heureux 2010, 6

On the other side, the contrasting terms like authentic/inauthentic, artificial/natural have a moralistic edge. Koolhaas famously described Singapore's phenomenal growth as an unnatural fruiting, *metastasizing* across Asia—a cancerous growth, a disease, or perhaps a primordial sin?

I read much of this both caustic and dreamy language as the sign of boggled minds like mine. Even Koolhaas admits, "Our refusal to read Singapore in its own terms is frivolous: our most sophisticated reflections on the contemporary condition of city are completely disconnected from the operational. . . . Singapore is a paroxysm of the operational, therefore inaccessible to our imagination and interpretation" (1041). He is right in one sense: to walk in Singapore is never disorienting or even alienating but rather oddly over-oriented *yet* at the same time brash: entire shopping centers enfolded in plastic blinking lights but with well-marked signs, groves of giant steel trees in the new horticultural park where everything is labeled, and rows and rows of HDB flats, different colors and shapes but all carefully coded with large block numbers on their sides yet surrounded by trees and small parks. All the crosswalks are well delineated, crossing lights timed so that the only way forward is what I call *Singapore crossing speed*, actually a near run. This is what also holds and continues to puzzle me, Singapore as a *place* filled with oxymorons: a pragmatic utopia, a unique non-place (Augé [1992] 2008), a city-sized theme park, but also a delightful, often bland, sparkling place that *feels* so real and yet so unreal.

The recent call for papers at the conference at the Asia Research Institute at NUS, "Hard State. Soft City,"[3] introduced me to Jonathan Raban's famous *Soft City* about the supposed alienation of world cities like London. Describing his momentary confusion over the left-side/right-side direction of traffic, he refuses to cast his experience as yet another moment of alienation; rather, he now famously said:

> At moments like this, the city goes soft; it awaits the imprint of an identity. For better or worse, it invites you to remake it, to consolidate it into a shape you can live in. . . . In this sense, it seems to me that living in cities is an art, and we need a vocabulary of art, of style, to describe the particular relationship between man and material that exists in the continual creative play of an urban living. The city as we imagine it, the soft city of illusion, myth, aspiration, nightmare, is as real, maybe more real, than the hard city one can locate on maps, in statistics, in monographs on urban sociology and demography and architecture.
>
> 2

But the problem with Singapore—if I am right—is that an *imaginaire*/mythic dimension is already imbedded into much of the architecture and the very form of the city, what Steven Piles terms phantasmagoria: "a quality of life that is ghost-like or dream-like" (Pile 2005, 3). In Singapore, the state even provides its citizens with the dream-form in shopping centers like ION Orchard or the even wilder Bugis+ at Bugis Junction (Fig. 1.2), or the Gardens-by-the-Bay, or the lotus-shaped ArtScience complex (Fig.1.3). But, ironically, the state may provide the *imaginaire*, well-marked ways and planned communities, yet it does not guarantee permanency—in fact, quite the opposite. As many cabdrivers have joked with me, the one certain aspect of Singapore is continual redevelopment along with building cranes and redirected roads. A cabdriver recently provided a metaphor: the software and the hardware of Singapore always had to be updated. I heard the same imagery at a dinner, when someone asked me how I found Singapore this time. I told him it's constantly changing. He grinned, "Yes, it's always an unfinished project like computer software always updated." He loved this constant change while the cabdriver was exasperated as the road he had traveled the previous day suddenly had turned one-way in the opposite direction to accommodate the building of a new mass transit station.

The postcolonial world in this circle of South Asia and Southeast Asia has included other cities built *de nova*, in some cases on openly on religious models—Corbusier's Chandigarh (Prakash 2002, 71–95)—and many new nations aspired to five-year plans, but Singapore could actually implement this newness, a deep modernity, because the small detached island-like tip of Malaysia had no hinterland and could regulate migrants into its territory. With one ruling party with a firm electoral grip, a determined bureaucracy, and the iron leadership of Lee Kuan Yew, plans came into real form at the time of independence, at an optimal moment—the 1960s was a global age of city planning and development schemes (see Maki 1964). In Singapore, these took form,

Figure 1.2 Bugis+ at Bugis Junction fronted with a surface of honeycombed blinking lights.

Figure 1.3 Standing in front of the lotus-shaped ArtScience Museum. Photo by Dick Waghorne.

and continue to this day as old HDB flats that once replaced the kampongs are now themselves turned to rubble. And, at the same moment that I marvel at a fabulous and outrageous new shopping center, I equally despise the wrecking crane that will soon knock down a full block of colorful HDB flats that I regularly viewed from my hotels in and near Little India. Singapore promises political stability, and economic security with Asia's highest per capita income, and social harmony and safety, which I treasure as I walk alone downtown past midnight. But all these do not offer stability of *place* to particular persons—highways change, walkways disappear; benches come and go, favorite restaurants close, and eviction orders come offering a new flat no longer in center city but in another of the endless planned, and often lovely but outlying, high-rise developments.

A recent exhibit at the Singapore Art Museum, "An Atlas of Mirrors," includes a striking work by Melissa Tan hauntingly mirroring the come-and-go nature of Singapore. The artist transformed a chunk of discarded rubble, whose contours the artist incised onto a paper music reel, into a music box that captures "the subtle nuances and traces of time passed that have been left behind," preserving memory of the many feet that trod that now shattered pathway. Yet even this box "will in time reflect the physical attributes of the built surfaces that crisscross the island of Singapore ... as the paper starts to wear and its fibers become strained and tenuous" (Lingham et al. 2016, 139). Singapore offers orientation, a planned environment, but at the same time continual flux. Creation means destruction especially, and many of the "fractal realities" (15) in the exhibit reflect themes of absence, displacement, all converging in: "one instrument in particular—the mirror—brings us into that which is still so mysterious: the self"[4] in an old stairwell covered in mirrors, maps to places not really on maps, images of bulldozed environments, and sketches of old shop houses with traces of their migrant workers' discarded backpacks—new awakenings to the haunted world of seeping memory amid the staggering success of this city-state within Southeast Asia.

Just how singular is Singapore in respect to the knock-down, build-up world of Asia? Wan-ling Wee defends his own singular focus on this city-state: "Its smallness in fact offers a 'test-tube' intensity by which to consider the problematic of presumed non-Western or alternative modernities" (Wee 2007, *kl* 239–40), which I will rephrase for my purposes at the global corner of Religion & Place: Singapore challenges the problematic of presumed relationships between orientation/disorientation, authenticity/artificiality, myth/reality on the levels of both the person and community. But what models can we use to describe such a place? I have already hinted at the rhetorical structure of cosmology and the process of myth-making—long the hunting ground of religious studies, particularly of the History of Religions. Clearly arguing that the Singapore landscape mirrors a cosmos, elided with Utopia, must take account of averred secularity of the state. But there is more.

Given that, Singapore is compact and carefully constructed with all of the social and economic designs inscribed onto the landscape and built into daily life—"the social art form that nobody could escape" (Wee 2007, *kl* 259–61). Remembering that Wan-ling Wee, trained in religion and literature at the University of Chicago, takes his own models from textual studies, I suggest that Singapore *as a place,* in the terminology of religious studies, most closely resembles a *canon* in that order and borders continue to be accorded priority even as the landscape actually shifts dramatically—those shift, like the notion of scripture, and are folded back into the concern to keep to a blueprint, a plan, a closure. Although the term is usually associated with the scriptures of "Western religious traditions" and not an Asian city, nonetheless the model of a highly scripted text, where movement on the part of persons depends on "overcoming that limitation through ingenuity" through exegesis and interpretation between the lines (Smith 1982, 52), fits life in Singapore. When J. Z. Smith wrote his now famous essay on canon, he emphasized that submitting to a canon was an open choice, which then leads to other kinds of self-expression formed in other ways *within* the safe space of a highly ordered world. I think this describes Singapore *within a religious idiom* but I have found other idioms within *visual expressions*; both are valuable to begin to understand Singapore as a place and as a space.

Macrospaces and Microworlds

An earlier exhibition at the Singapore Art Museum provided visual clues—and literally a window into the city-state—in a brilliant exhibition, *After Utopia*, constructed in four major modules: *Other Edens, The City and its Discontents, The Way Within,* and *Legacies Left.*[5] The *City* module included a video project from Singapore—and another from nearby Malaysia—presenting the balconied facade of seemingly faceless government high-rise housing estates. As the Singapore video progressed, lights and life appeared inside these individual HDB flats, and the windows of each apartment began to open, giving a glimpse into numerous microplaces each with their own microstory (Fig. 1.4).[6] The artist described her project as an attempt "to rejuvenate a sense of neighbourliness, or the *kampung* spirit, among city dwellers, what it simultaneously reflects a dystopian reality—the congested, compressed urban fabric of contemporary Singapore (Fig. 1.5). The work . . . evokes the inescapable voyeurism of HDB living, where the high-density character of public housing estates ensures that simply looking out the window means gazing into someone else's home" (Siuli and Ho 2018, 66). For Castleman, the HDB flats are alive with isolated stories, but residents need to become aware and appreciative of each other's microworlds—*not* the planned harmony that the Housing and Development Board assumed this closeness would innately engender. Yet, ironically, if read another way, such flats attest to diversity, complexity, and subjectivity inserted into these well-manicured worlds. And, indeed, another module of the exhibit, *The Way Within*, marked the resurgence of subjectivity in Southeast Asia as a reaction to the loss of outward utopias:

> dwindling hopes in real reform have led many to turn away from sweeping notions of changing the world or society on a grand scale, in favour of focusing on and creating smaller, more personal micro-Utopias, effecting change one small step at a time. For artists . . . "Utopia" is to be found within oneself, and their works express their individual search for inner sanctuary—a reconciliation of the self with the world at large.

Figure 1.4 *Jurong West Street 81, 2008* from the exhibition *After Utopia* at the Singapore Art Museum. Author's photo used with the kind permission of the curator, Dr. Louis Ho.

In a recent conversation with one of the curators of this exhibit, Louis Ho, I asked why include Singapore among the failed Utopian visions of Southeast Asia—hadn't Singapore achieved its goals, hadn't the vision succeeded? He defined "Utopia," the framing idiom of the exhibit, as "an unrealizable concept that reflects on our realities." He reminded me that Thomas More wrote *Utopia* as a satire on the politics of his day. In successful Singapore, "the urban fabric, everything, screams affluence but . . . the way that this utopian dream lingers amid the everyday reality that people have to navigate becomes dystopia. We knock down, then we rebuild and that's how it is—the loss of short-term memory feeds into this dystopian framework." When I asked how to describe this binary/tension/dichotomy between an ideal often embedded into public space and the lived experience of Singaporeans, he supplied another term: "It might help to see the expression of the city-state as a certain *disconnect*—I am going to use that term—between a *top-down* and an *everyday* on the part of the people who have to inhabit these public spaces." In this context, we talked about how the loss of the "kampong spirit" has become part of the public discourse in recent years. For Louis Ho, the kampong was "about community not the family or individual—but in HDB flats the basic unit is the apartment." Louis Ho remembers moving from a kampong, which was leveled, to a small new HDB flat as a child; the move saw everyone's personal space

Figure 1.5 Older-style HDB complex with flags marking fifty years of independence.

eroded—a real tangible experience. In those days, he noted, the residents of the old kampong moved to the same or closely connected flats so that his father could keep old contacts alive, but this is no longer the case for new HDB residents who are too young to remember the living kampong, yet some vestiges live on.

Now even *kampong spirit* has a Wiktionary definition of "(*Singapore*) A sense of social cohesion in a community where there is understanding and compromise among neighbours, even as preferences differ from household to household."[7] This sounds like the term touted in recent government publications from the HDB. Reading the Housing and Development Board publications, especially the online and print publication of a full-color magazine, *Dwelling: Harmonious Living at Its Best*. Here the *kampong spirit* appears frequently but has the feel of nostalgia for an unexperienced past made *virtual* on the part of the top-down world. In 2015, "Little Pockets of Heaven" on community gardens noted, "community gardens are introduced in collaboration with local community groups. These projects are a way to revive the 'kampong spirit', where shared activities encourage neighbourly interaction."[8] However, the recent controversy over chickens in the flats became a prime test of how far the authorities would accept messier aspects of a revived "kampong spirit." The old kampongs not only kept gardens but also chickens which roamed freely, but very recently the government's culling of two dozen free-roaming chickens near an HDB complex caused a public uproar. In the *Straits Times*, "Culling of 24 chickens in Sin Ming ruffles feathers" (Feb. 26, 2017), a long-time resident commented, "I have been living in this area for 26 years and these chickens have always been around and they are harmless, they do not bother anyone and they are hardly noisy! If we keep removing all these ties to our past, what is left for us to show the next generation?"[9] The government scrambled to explain this extermination in terms of health rather than the original alleged noise complaint, and even as a measure to protect local indigenous wild birds from unwanted interbreeding.[10] Yet to many this seemed murder most fowl, ironically in the new Year of the Rooster.

I take the term *top-down* more literally as an overarching umbrella, perhaps a secularized version of Peter Burger's now discarded notion of *the sacred canopy*—the *macrospace* of the state? But micro*places* continue to elude, or perhaps sit ironically under, the umbrella of the HDB flats, those iconic structures of state planning and success. As suggested in the exhibit *After Utopia*, the turn inward remains strong even in Singapore, but *in a special sense* both external and internal. There are alternate spaces within the city—versions of the many little windows in the exhibit—that open into inner worlds, micro-utopias (?), that are classified as secular. The government defines spaces for official religious practice, the recognized temples, churches, etc., that are on the official maps, but such official public space is limited *and* circumscribed *and* confined to the specificity of Religion, which many of the spiritually inclined see as *external* practice—a social event, not *inward* transformation. Such informal religiosity, as Vineeta Sinha terms this, finds new space in "unconventional sites, many of which are commonsensically defined as 'secular' and 'profane' (former cinemas, community centres, auditoriums, homes, commercial spaces, etc.) in order to sustain everyday religiosity" (2016, 470). The inward-leaning movements may be popular but they are not popular religiosity, or folk elements, or even streetwise religiosity, but rather well-organized middle-class groups connected to large and small transnational movements. Often formally religious spaces do not suit them, not just in terms of convenience but as an expression of their sense that they operate as closely to secularity—in the sense of a pragmatic everydayness—as they do to Religion. These constitute many of the little windows into Singapore's alternate spaces.

I have participated in many gatherings in living rooms of HDB flats all over Singapore—meditations, elaborate ritual practices, prayers said around a smoking fire pit, and even a puja in a small temple built inside a living room. Policy in the HDB flats grants considerable freedom to the occupant-owners to mold their own private space, and these tinkerings often spill out into the hallways with plants and statuary and even innovative door grating. The government does not formally regulate such expressions of religious affiliation or "spiritual" practices within the "private" space of a flat. Singapore is not China (see Fisher 2016). However, in a conversation with Sharon Siddique and Belinda Yuen at the Lee Yuan Yew Center for Innovative Cities, both reminded me that the private space of an HDB flat continues to be a "gray area" in the context of religion. "As long as you are running a family space, for example, worshipping your connections to your ancestors and then inviting a few friends, this is not religion in the canonical sense of having to register as a religious society"—which is a complicated process to which I will return in a later chapter (also see Waghorne 2014, 194). Indeed, these gray areas where religiosity appears extend to many other seemingly secular spaces. Many of the groups meeting in HDB flats have formally registered as religious organizations and invite many participants, while others keep these get-togethers to a few friends and family remaining within the shaded zones of domestic not public space. Others like Isha Yoga are registered with ACRA (Accounting and Corporate Regulatory Authority) as a business[11] and most recently now as a nonprofit company. As will become apparent, domestic places in the hard sense become a physical expression of the self/family but also become places for remaking the self, yet a *feeling* still stands that these practices radiate outward to remake *something* in the world—not policy, not ideology, not roads or streets, but *something*, change of the larger consciousness in the world, an invoking of energy, a quieting of space for the transformation of the self-in-community. I have seen many such places in Singapore tucked into living rooms in numerous HDB flats. Many other such windows will open in the chapters that follow, not only in HDB flats but also in dull commercial buildings and some very glitzy plazas; but for now, let us peek into two *events* with HDB flats in the popular Ang Mo Kio district—both closely related to the process of making grand spaces within very small places. Both organizations, Isha Yoga and Oneness, are officially registered with the government. Oneness with the Registry of Societies "as a club, company, partnership or association of 10 or more persons, whatever its nature or object, and not already registered under any other law." In the case of such organizations, they register as a club/society not as a Religion.[12] Isha is registered as Isha Pvt. Ld. as a nonprofit company, Isha Foundation.

A Microworld *with Cats*

Most recently, I met an active volunteer in Isha Yoga in his small flat within one of the HDB high-rises in the planned district of Ang Mo Koi. I had already met him there the previous year just after experiencing Guru puja for Jaggi Vasudev, the founder of Isha held at the Global Indian School. This time I was early and sat in the open court in front of the housing complex decorated with flags and stacked with plastic chairs for the coming celebration of fifty years of independence (Fig. 1.6). Although well kempt with flower gardens as a common area for happy residents, I was the only sitter except for numerous lounging cats who had commandeered shelves under the unused and locked barbeque pits (Fig. 1.7) with a formidable sign declaring how and when a permit could be obtained—seemingly a perfect Koolhaasian illustration of Singaporean sterility. But this was no Potemkin village; there was depth and life behind these facades. Inside his flat, Thulasidhar and his wife Sharmila—both enthusiastic members of ISHA yoga and their guru Jaggi Vasudev—dedicated their extra bedroom to house a Sadhguru Sannidhi, which an Isha blog describes as "a live temple, a certain atmosphere that throbs in one space. The establishment of Sannidhi creates a powerful energy space within one's home. Particularly for those who have established spirituality as

Figure 1.6 HDB complex in Ang Mo Koi ready to celebrate the golden anniversary of independence.

the priority in their lives, creating Sannidhi has a profound influence on one's inner evolution."[13]

Although Thulasi works for a media company, and has a large TV and sound system in his living room, there is little else. Last year, with his wife, he had allowed me and a graduate student from Canada accompanying me to see the Sannidhi and graciously permitted me to take photographs. In that room below an enormous photo of Sadhguru Jaggi Vasudev in meditation rested a stone block with an image of feet incised into the granite. Usually termed a *padaka*, "footprint," a very ancient iconic representation of a holy teacher, Isha refers to this as Sannidhi (from Sanskrit *saṃnidhi*, "presence") and also Pada Yantra (Sanskrit, a mystical diagram, *yantra* of a foot, *pada*). Just above the Sannidhi was another smaller photo of Sadhguru fully awake, and in front a small votive oil lamp (Tamil *viḷakku*) burned (Fig. 1.8). The Isha blog described the

Figure 1.7 Cat sits happily under an unused barbecue pit.

culmination of the consecration ceremony for this Sannidhi that had taken place just a few months previously: "silence and the palpable presence of Sadhguru filled the room as people approached the Pada Yantra with flowers in their clasped hands to offer as thanksgiving," and Thulasi confirmed that the practices (which he later argued are not worship in the sense of devotion but a spiritual practice with the goal of personal transformation)[14] should continue each week, and that he was trying to invite friends over weekly for this.

Now a year later, adhering to South Indian custom, very familiar to me, as we sat in his purposely sparse living room, I asked Thulasi about Isha's activities in the recent International Day of Yoga, which I had come to Singapore to witness. However, our conversation actually continued a longer discussion about yoga from the previous summer when asked about spiritual movements within the *space* of Singapore. Earlier Thulasi described how practices, such as the guru puja I had witnessed that year, were "creating a space around you which is energized." Sitting just outside the room dedicated to the Sannidhi, I asked, "Where are we *now* when we create such a special

Figure 1.8 A lamp burns before the Sannidhi with portrait of Sadhguru Jaggi Vasudev.

space, are we sitting in Singapore, are we in Coimbatore [headquarters of Isha Yoga in India], are we nowhere, are we everywhere, where are we?" Laughing, he quickly answered, "We are in Singapore, no problem," and then explained:

What Sadhguru says is that for a guru there is no concept of space. If you are connected, if you are open ... but you are where you are, there are no two ways about it. You are physically a person. It's just like ... if you are aligned, open, receptive to access *it*, you can call *it* anything you want, some people call *it* God, energy, but in a sense what we are saying is that there is a high level of intelligence which is there, subtle, everywhere which is nature ... the whole set of the practices ... everything in Isha is to align ourselves to *it*. He always says, do not worry where *I* am, *you* be present where you are.

Summarizing, I said, "So we are grounded *and* connected." Thulasi agreed.

Sitting there on a bare floor with Thulasi, the Sannidhi in the next room, said to establish "a powerful energy space" within the home, promised an expansive presence within a very small architectural footprint. And, indeed, the Sannidhi literally holds the footprints, *padaka*, of the guru. While a very common way to invoke a guru's presence, here in Singapore the *padaka* allows me to reconsider the issue of space in Singapore. Padaka is a Sanskrit term meaning a footprint,[15] but also a step, a pace, and interestingly a form of recitation of the scriptures, Vedas. Here movement is embedded in the small space of stone block, captured but not confined, bordered but limitless, like the compact apartment in which it rested.

The Guru's Sandals: A Pied-à-terre for the Divine

I have seen the use of another guru's *pādukā*, not his footprint but his sandals, in yet another HDB flat also in Ang Mo Kio. The invitation to join the Shri Amma-Bhagavan weekly Satsang offered by a devotee at his home came via email. The Oneness movement in Singapore is headed by country coordinator Devi Naidu and trainer Cheah Kok Yew with youth leader Jidesh. The event was hosted at Kaushik's residence for which I attended with a program for an all-day event that would begin with "Aarathi" (Sanskrit *ārati*, honoring a divine image by waving lights) for Sri Amma-Bhagavan with devotional songs, then "Contemplation & Realization on Sri Bhagavan's weekly Webcast Teachings," followed by viewing his live webcast from the Oneness University in India,[16] then group prayer and a potluck lunch. Carefully following the program, I arrived in time for the Aarathi at a top-floor flat in a cluster of housing blocks designed, as many older HDB buildings, with entry doors along an outside corridor stretching the length of the building—an echo of the government estates in the *After Utopia* exhibit at the Singapore Art Museum with all of the windows and doors facing outward exposed to neighbors across the parking lot. However, looking out that day toward the multicolored flats across a generous-sized tree-lined parking lot, they offered only limited opportunities for voyeurism—more a matter of squinting than seeing. I spoke with Jidesh, who explained that he had recently settled in Singapore for a job in an American firm. He works in the architecture field, so we talked about the arts and crafts movement. I also met another recent émigré, Kaushik, also working for an American company based in Silicon Valley, who travels frequently to the US. He was raised in the Oneness movement after his once "secular" father had a profound experience with the guru. Both are newly settled in jobs in Singapore but neither intended at that time to settle here permanently. However, I met them both again at dinner five years later and they seemed more established in Singapore.

Although the external facade of this HDB block, the inside decor, likely the work of the flat's owner, included arches, doorways, and lovely flower-tiled walls. Our host, as most members of the Oneness community at that time, had constructed an altar in the parlor for Shri Amma-Bhagavan, the founding gurus of the movement: their names are often so hyphenated (Fig. 1.9). With the tiled wall as a backdrop, the eyes of Shri Amma and Bhagavan gleamed out from their large close-up photograph; above and behind a smaller photo of the divine couple enthroned hung another photo of Shri Bhagavan's sandals. A row of three pairs of sandalwood sandals—traditionally the *pādukā* made of sandalwood or pure silver are flat with a toe peg—rested on the altar table. The rich inner decor and the bland outer facade mirrored the event as it unfolded.

Here devoted followers of Sri Amma-Bhagavan, founders of the Oneness, which like many such movements also has its share of disillusioned members and critics,[17] gathered to watch their guru in a simulcast from his headquarters in India, Oneness University. In Oneness, at that time,[18] devotion to Amma-Bhagavan included only Aarathi, the waving of a lighted lamp, which is usually the last stage of a full puja. As Devi later explained, "When we prayerfully perform or observe the Aarathi, our head becomes illumined with God's glory and our heart enlivened with God's beauty. We can receive divine energy from the lamp with cupped hands passed over its flames and then touched to the forehead. Aarathi is performed in the beginning of a satsang and/ or as it ends with a gratitude Aarathi."

As some members took turns with the Aarathi, and others scurried to set up the complex equipment, I had the chance to chat with several of the attendees and heard versions of the founding of Oneness and the initiating miracle of the movement. The future Sri Bhagavan (born in 1949), then Mr. Vijay Kumar, was the principal of a school in Andhra Pradesh and wanted to experiment with a different and more natural form of education. These youngsters responded, and some became clairvoyant and began to receive messages about a coming age that is about to begin. A more complex and hagiographic narrative appears on the website as the "Phenomenon of the Golden

Figure 1.9 Two portraits of Amma-Bhagavan with sandals carved of pure sandalwood. Photo by Dick Waghorne used with the kind permission of the Singapore Oneness leadership.

Orb"[19]—a founding story of smallness and expansion, of little children given a grand vision—a revelation of microplaces holding macrospaces—interestingly apropos for this small flat.

At an early age Sri Bhagavan had a vision of a golden orb—which is figured as a light in the palm of the hands in an image set just above the official online story. Each day the future guru chanted a mantra with "deep intent to end human suffering being impregnated into this Golden Orb, thus charging it with His divine state of consciousness." In 1989 while he served as principal of an elementary school, the Golden Orb descended on the Lord Krishna who then "transferred this divine power by placing his hands on [the heads of] students of the Jeevashram School" who experienced "a variety of states of consciousness accessible only to the great yogis and saints of yore." The founders soon realized that this should be available to the world, and "thus came into existence the 'Oneness', which has ever since touched the lives of millions of individuals through the phenomenon of the Oneness Deeksha." The imagery both in this telling, and in the many devotional images of Amma-Bhagavan, moves from a golden orb to the vastness of consciousness, from the orb to the globe, from a school full of children to an imagined world full of enlightened beings— microcosms and macrocosms leading toward Utopia, as we will see, at the end.

As lights burns on an altar to the guru's photograph, we learned a new meditation technique called the Chakra Dyana Mediation to "Awaken … the Kundalini,[20] establishing a connection" with the "consciousness of Sri AmmaBhavan resulting in the realization of the teaching." This preparatory practice (Fig. 1.10) was coordinated with a video on the screen of Sri Bhagavan also meditating—he would close his eyes and then open them widely with his hands out to give *darshan* and then close his eyes again. Oneness does not demand secrecy so instructions for the mediation technique are widely available online.[21] As with many techniques, especially in Oneness, the goal is to invoke the flow of the *kundalini*: "With each exhale chant the mantra that is given in a slow, elongated fashion. Begin with the root chakra (Mooladhara) [Sanskrit, Mūlādhāra] and work upward to the Crown (Sahasrara) [Sanskrit, Sahasrāra].... Notice the dynamics of the energy in your body as the kundalini flows." Later as the simulcast connected to Oneness University, we sat together to hear the master's teachings. In all I counted twelve people in this flat, but, as we listened to the simulcast beginning about 12:30 p.m., I noticed that the ticker on the sidebar counting those joining the event kept soaring and finally recorded about 2,500 viewers worldwide. With some devotees here hugging the wooden sandals, *pādukā*, near their hearts in deep mediation—someone kindly gave me sandals to fully join in (Fig. 1.11)—others held photos of the guru, and all were listening more than watching. Again, I wondered where were we at that moment—as the simulcast ticker continued to whir and as the little computer opened to a large screen connecting a small town in southern India, Bathalavallam in Andhra Pradesh, to our small flat in Singapore and to the world of the Oneness movement.

Oneness is millenarian looking to the time when humans will be transformed. So Shri Bhagavan began his lesson by explaining that we should begin to prepare for the coming "shift" in human consciousness, which would be the end of the separation of you and me. Now "passionate people" would have the power to transform others—the

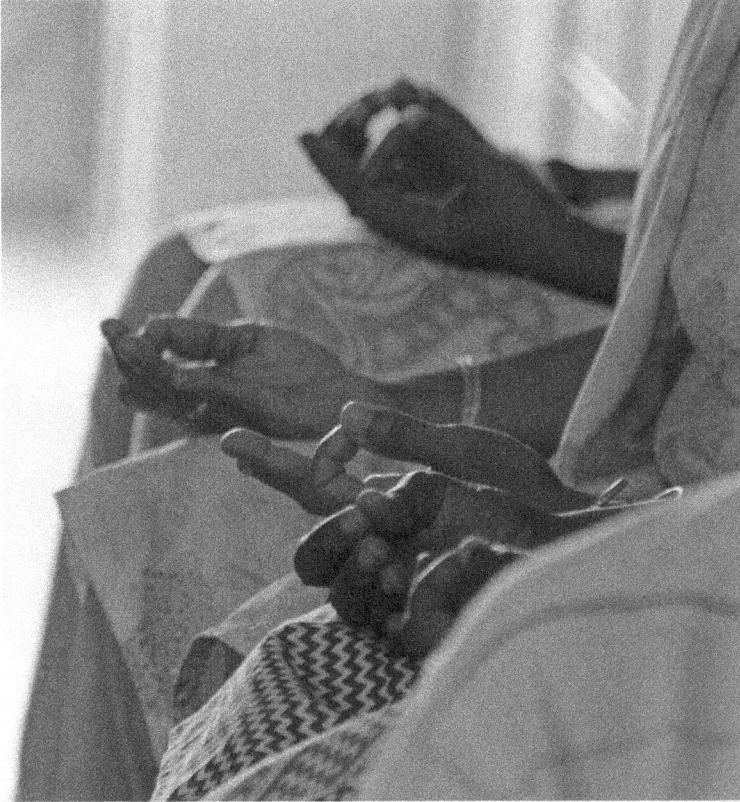

Figure 1.10 Devotees with hands poised for Oneness meditation. Photo by Dick Waghorne used with the kind permission of the Singapore Oneness leadership.

goal was 70,000 at that time in 2012[22] who had received Deeksha, an initiation that opens the potential for the transformation in a laying on of hands. Reminiscent of Christian practice, the Deeksha-giver cups their hands over the head of the receiver. I have attended Oneness events where we each gave and received Deeksha in turn. At the end of the simulcast, Bhagavan asked all of us to continue to join the webcast each week in our homes. The culmination of all of these practices would help usher great changes by 2035 that will initiate processes in human evolution: within a thousand years our bodies will need no food.

All of this unfolds within our consciousness as Kaushik explained to me a few weeks later over coffee at Starbucks. He began with examples from his own life. His father had some problems and was encouraged to attend an event with the guru, who was then called Kalki (the name of the last incarnation of God Vishnu yet to come). He came back "transformed." The next day he saw his formerly secular father singing *bhajans* (hymns) and dancing. "He told me his search was over." From that time Kaushik was raised in the movements and attended events with his father in and around

Figure 1.11 I hold the *pādukā* as instructed by the members of Oneness during meditation. Photo by Dick Waghorne.

Chennai. His own experiences deepened in a retreat when he was 17 years old, which "focused on success—why people try so hard but still things do not go their way." So the course was designed to progress day to day though examining examples based on values and ethics incidents in Gandhi's life: "These ethics are not based on religion, or based on any faith or belief or cult, and can be blended with your own belief or faith . . . you do not have to give up who you are or what you like. You do not have to convert; you can take these teachings and blend this with your own faith." He explained that the essence of this movement is based on inner change: "this course removes all the negative conditioning, so you can imbibe those teachings. This may be based on Hinduism but Hinduism is not a religion, it's a way of life." The experience taught him the need to change the *conditioning* from the past: "Wonderful things happening to me". After the course, he began to realize "all that is learned has to be unlearned, even in science this happens."

My later conversation with an active member gave me more information about the international spread of Oneness and the courses offered at the Oneness University, which was founded by Shri Amma-Bhagavan, and the many branch associations both in India and abroad. Oneness concentrates on teaching, not surprising since its founder began as a school principal. The movement offers numerous courses like the ones that transformed both the member and his father. The website lists "Social Work" as a category of their endeavors but the larger emphasis, as the name *university* signals, is on carefully designed programs, especially the "Journey into Oneness—A Transformational 14 Day Course Held at Oneness University." Those who have attended from Singapore lauded the program as personally transforming. Expensive and promising "wealth & abundance, flowering of intelligence & creativity, success, and discovering love & togetherness,"[23] the course becomes the target of criticism of Amma-Bhagavan and the Oneness movement.[24]

For some members, the emphasis on vastness of consciousness with flights into the imagination can seem edgy, but not for all. Members of Oneness hold very responsible professional positions and can maintain both faith in Amma-Bhagavan and the coming Utopian age together with daily life—in fact, that is what his courses promise: sharing his cosmic vision enables worldly success. I marveled at this *imaginaire* of a vast consciousness and a coming global transformation in which the Oneness members, gathered in this small place holding the *pādukā* of their guru, saw themselves as key participants—a Utopian vision undreamed of by the architects of the now seemingly bland utopian vision wrought in carefully numbered government-built and owner-occupied high-rises that cover Singapore.

Small Footprints, Vast Visions, Micro-Utopias?

The pādukā of Sri Bhagavan and the Pada Yantra/padaka of Sadhguru Jaggi Vasudev echo very ancient forms of a guru's presence bound tightly into the small space of a granite block or a wooden sandal. This ironic iconography of bounded boundlessness inhabiting nooks and small rooms in these concrete *blocks*—interestingly the official term for such buildings—in Ang Mo Kio seem to suggest *some kind* of mutuality between the Housing and Development Board's near paradisiac presentation of harmonious living in these brightly painted and numbered blocks—"Little Pockets of Heaven" as an article on community gardens proclaimed—and the power inherent in the footprints of a guru and the inner worlds of Isha and Oneness members. But does the one make possible the other? The *After Utopia* exhibition openly suggested, as did Louis Ho in our conversation, that the dystopia created from the impossibility of the governmental vision to heal that breach between the reality of daily life and the grand state visions of harmony, order, and plenty in Southeast Asia "led many to turn away from sweeping notions of changing the world or society on a grand scale, in favour of focusing on and creating smaller, more personal micro-Utopias" (Tan and Ho 2015, 49). The exhibit focused on artists, but most Isha and Oneness members earn their livelihood in business, engineering, or technology. Yet their altars are beautiful and visionary, and the practices that I have witnessed speak of spaces of vastness, perfection, and boundlessness enveloped in small objects of wood or stone that both bind and release the awesome powers within.

So, is this really a case of compensation: inserting a paradise of the mind into the failed and bland reality of life in an HDB high-rise? No one ever directly addressed that issue in my many conversations. I heard no complaints about the state—yes, from cabdrivers, and yes, in casual conversations on the streets, and yes, from academics—but not from members of these organizations. But do the Pada Yantra and the *pādukā* share *some kind* of affinity with the state that holds them? I would argue that these events within the HBD flats are coterminous in the same space with the state—they literally live within a government vision made real in concrete or, as a billboard advertising a coming Ion center proclaimed, "I am charisma cast in concrete." The value here of spatial theory, which will figure strongly in the next chapter, is moving away from questions of cause and effect and toward a consideration of the complexity of interlocking layers of shared dreams, ideologies, practices, and people in bounded places. What do the state bureaucracy of the HDB flats share with Isha and Oneness members: the willingness to work with a thin line between illusion and reality, mythic and rational thinking? Again, they share, as Jonathan Raban put it decades ago, a "soft city of illusion, myth, aspiration, nightmare." Moreover, the HDB editors of *Dwelling*—and the great architects of the HDB projects who will appear in the next chapter—share a concomitant commitment to pragmatics with the Isha and Oneness meditators—these seeming flights of fancy. The technics of *building* of harmony and peace are seen as totally pragmatic in both instances. Yoga and meditation claim to engineer a new self and open the windows into a boundless universe; HDB flats, supposedly, engender amicable Singaporean citizens living in their own little Edens.

2

Statecraft and Cosmology: Making the Macrocosm in Singapore

The image of Singapore as a highly structured state has stuck to its international reputation like chewing gum. The almost shockingly clean streets and numbered rows of housing blocks exude an overarching order. However, the state not only *builds* regularity but also *speaks* order. Signs on the subway trains exhort denizens to fight the dengue mosquito in their homes, watching stagnant water even in their plant containers. Recently subway cars were restyled with slogans for National Day 2016 such as "footprint decals asking commuters to 'Stand up for Singapore'" and the transport authority "also hopes the designs can encourage better commuter behaviour by acting as subtle social 'nudges.'" (Lee 2016).[1] Signs in the spotless public restroom illustrate the proper use of the toilets and washing hands. The Housing and Development Board continues to produce increasingly sophisticated pamphlets and magazines exhorting residents toward cleanliness and harmony. Government buildings, including universities, post placards or hang banners with maxims and missions. Indeed this "soft authoritarianism" would presumably produce and depend on what some might call *ideology*. However, the founding prime minister Lee Kuan Yew repeatedly abjured ideology for pragmatics. An editorial obituary in the *Straits Times* praised his "legacy of pragmatism" and his "willingness to change" as the key to Singapore's success (March 30, 2015). So, to take the founding father at his word, understanding the long process of making and speaking this state into life should not be traced by its political *ideology* alone—Singapore is not about concepts, or even dogmas. Yet living with those banners and signs, and existing in the newness of its buildings and the very constructedness of its environment, a visitor or resident sees some sense in the classic chewing gum cliché about Singapore: somehow nothing is allowed to gum up the works here either in acts of doing or of speaking. My argument: the state in its pragmatics continues to construct a *macroworld* that exists between concrete form, the constructed environment, and conversation. The trick is naming the nature of this overarching *world*.

State-speech can take the simple form of clever command signs, but, beyond this, another form of rhetoric functions, as the last chapter suggested, moving from ordinary discourse to *myth*—what Roland Barthes called *metalanguage* ([1957] 2012, 224)—in this ultracontemporary setting. Actually, one of the strongest clues that Lee and his People's Action Party continues to construct and inhabit *myth* comes paradoxically from its claims *not* to engage in ideology. Useful here is Roland Barthes's insightful description of "myth today" as contemporary metalanguage calculated, or at least consciously constructed, to be innocently consumed by readers/viewers as *real*. For

Barthes, this particular form of language—which "in fact belongs to the province of a general science, coextensive with linguistics, which is *semiology*" (219)—deliberately abjures clarity. Rather nebulae of meanings which Barthes calls "concept" fuses with a "form"—which can be an object, an image, a photo, a word—to become *myth*. Myth, unlike directives or dogma, by its very nature lacks clarity:

> In actual fact, the knowledge contained in a mythical concept is confused, made of yielding, shapeless associations. One must fully stress this open character of the concept; it is not at all an abstract, purified essence; it is a formless, unstable, nebulous condensation, whose unity and coherence are above all due to its function.
>
> 229

The function of myth is not to present a proposition but has "in fact a double function: it points out and notifies us, it makes us understand something, and it imposes it on us" (226). The kind of understanding here is not meant for reasoned or arguable discourse, but rather "depoliticization which is trained to *celebrate* things and not long 'act them'" (256). As "ideas-in-form" (221), contemporary *myth*, which Barthes locates in popular culture and everyday newspaper accounts, artificially rises above politics to disguise its deeply political function. Bruce Lincoln reads Barthes here as proclaiming myth as the "most ideological form of speech" (3–4). Myth, then, is actually ideology in hyperdrive but disguised as undebatable reality in concrete form.

But this is not the only sense of myth at work in Singapore. I have already mentioned the strong resemblance of seemingly innocent narratives, the prime minister's speech opening the Marina Bay park, that borrows metaphors from ancient cosmogonic myth. Consideration of cosmogonic myths opens into the era of Mircea Eliade, Joseph Campbell, and later Charles Long—the same time period that also produced Roland Barthes's *Myth Today*, and the independent state of Singapore. The founding father Lee Kuan Yew's life—as we will see—takes on imagery from cosmogonic myth, as does a whole series of retellings of the story of Singapore recently generated for its golden anniversary of independence in 2015.

I turn to *myth*, particularly *cosmogonic myth* that constructs "worlds" which are both, as Edward Soja put it, "real-and-imagined places" (1996).[2] Myth builds in the space between *place* and *discourse* and arguably on the edge of sacred and secular. But this cosmos is not totalizing; there are layers above-between-beyond this sacred canopy. The previous chapter introduced some of these *micro*places, but here I am considering *macroworlds*. There are alternate spaces/worlds in Singapore constructed by gurus who head popular "spiritual" movements. How do these spiritual worlds conflate, confound, or combine with what I am suggesting is a state-cosmos? But where to begin? Well, in Singapore . . .

First Take a Taxi

Taxis are special places in Singapore that move not only between traffic but also between—surprisingly—the sacred and the secular. Michel de Certeau may write of *walking* in the city as "a space of enunciation" (1984, *kl* 1494) and Nigel Thrift may counter that driving in the city with the rise of *automobility* "constitutes a different set of spatial practices" (2008, 75), but, in Singapore, movement through the city usually means the MRT (the subway), experiencing little of the upland terrain, or, considering the high taxes and fees on automobile ownership in Singapore, taking a taxi while looking out the window free from driving—*taximobilty*. However, taxis are not silent, and their spaces also become places of enunciation. Drivers talk freely about news of the day and transform their dashboards into mobile display windows. What would seem a very secular space often morphs into the religious with clear intent, as in one delightful dashboard display advocating Singapore-style pluralism with garlanded images of Jesus, the Qur'an, Ganesh, and more that I could not identify at high speed (Fig. 2.1). Most recently, while taxiing along the East Coast Road and the Pan Island Expressway on the way to Nanyang Technical University, I noted a Buddhist prayer wheel on the dashboard (Fig. 2.2). In a curious happenstance on the way back, my driver *proudly*—as he told me—displayed an eerily look-alike lotus-shaped stand with an arched niche but with a silver dollar sign occupying the place of the prayer wheel (Fig. 2.3). I have seen similar taxi minishrines housing other deities but not this dollar-deity. The driver openly told me that success/money was the real god in Singapore. Obviously, his deity stand—which, like the prayer wheel, turned as we drove—was mass-manufactured, so his sensibilities were more broadly shared. Taxis, like the housing flats in the last chapter, are yet another of the many microplaces—in this case, mobile—within the macrospace of Singapore.

Spinning dollars or spinning prayer wheels maintain a religiously based *form*—the lotus-shaped stand with an arch to house a deity is shared by Hindus and Buddhists—

Figure 2.1 Taxi dashboard becomes a visual paean to Singapore's multireligious society.

Figure 2.2 Miniature Buddhist prayer wheel sits atop the taxi's dashboard.

Figure 2.3 Revolving dollar sign occupies the place of a prayer wheel on this taxi dashboard.

but with very different enunciations. However, in this case, the *form* carries power in itself whether used "secularly" or "religiously." As Roland Barthes argued in France in the 1950s, what he calls *metalanguage,* which he associates with *myth,* can be fully deployed in popular culture for multiple uses, often to bolster nationalism, or— more importantly for this Marxist thinker—to enforce and encode bourgeois liberal consciousness in the broader (French) public. Such a language does not function as ordinary speech and cannot easily translate into discursive concepts; for Barthes, metalanguage in public life can be fabricated as much from visual as from verbal signs, as in the case of these taxis. I will return to Roland Barthes's seminal analysis of contemporary myth, but at this point the spinning prayer wheel and dollar, the easy swing from what could be called *sacred* to *secular* and back again, seem to speak to and within a larger context, the *metaspace*—perhaps a special *metalanguage*— of Singapore. Again, to repeat, when considering the spiritual/religious movements in Singapore, the pervasive presence of the state cannot be ignored—not even in a taxi.

A view from a taxi, especially on the proud expressways, becomes a panorama of Singapore on display, revolving rows of HDB housing blocks, new industrial complexes, a port stacked with containers, all on tree-lined roads in this highly planned state. Like the taxis with only a few models in service, the housing blocks share a common configuration, a difference in color and some design, but only a few choices of styles, until very recently (Fig. 2.4). But again, like *taximobility,* a certain kind of flexibility exists within the Plan here. While the *form*—this term will become significant in the discussion of *myth*—remains the same, modifications continue and are permitted in both. Like the little portable deity stand in taxis, an HDB flat can accommodate switching between *secular* and *sacred,* as the last chapter showed. But, taking this further, the Plan, the development framework—the carefully drawn "Concept Plan"— of 1971 modified in 1991 (Center for Liveable Cities 2017, 28–9)—operates something like a canon, or as we will see, like a *cosmology,* like a *myth.* Invoking Jonathan Z. Smith once again on the form of a scriptural canon, flexibility does not come with open change to the coded plan but rather through creative use and interpretation—a matter of time and occasion—but always spinning within the same spaces. To live in Singapore is to literally live, move, walk, ride within the Plan—code, canon, scripture, cosmos? —the ordered world. But, is this Plan sacred or secular—or does it matter? And in the case of Singapore, this nation-state also challenges the meaning of an ordered world— what kind of *cosmos* is this?

Although that spinning dollar revolves on the same axis as the prayer wheel, is it operating in the same cosmos, or does its irreverence, its sarcasm, move out into another space? I ask this because a lesser-known aspect of religious cosmologies, of the ordering of myth, is what Mircea Eliade, who wrote the once most influential book on cosmogonic myth and world-making, called "noncosmic religion" with its "primordial image of scattering the roof"—or perhaps bursting the so-called sacred canopy (Berger [1967] 2011). This second spinning also provides an image of the place of "spiritual" movements in Singapore not only as inhabitants and creators of those many microplaces within the city but also—both like the state and yet unlike the state—makers of macrospaces which paradoxically, to paraphrase Eliade, somehow claim to abolish all

Figure 2.4 The ubiquitous high-rise residences seen from a taxi along a pristine Singapore expressway.

situations, reject settling in the world, and choosing "absolute freedom ... the annihilation of any conditioned world" (1959, 178). Yet these macrospaces are also carefully constructed by a powerful leader—the global guru—around whom a massive system whirls, which nonetheless is *never* claimed to be the same as either a religious-cosmos or the state-cosmos. I will return to this guru-cosmos in the next chapter, but first the state.

Macrocosm—Prime Ministerial Style

The state in Singapore is in *some sense* a macrocosm into which life is set. This is exactly how Liu Thai Ker, who formerly served as chief planner and CEO of the Urban Redevelopment Authority, describes the massive effort to construct the now iconic HDB flats that cover the landscape and house the vast majority of Singaporeans:

> We could achieve so much because there was a very clear division of labour for the government and the people. The government has taken care of macro issues because it has the macro data—and the authority and resources—and so it's got macro responsibility. I feel that in Singapore we created a kind of 'perfect stage' for people to act out their life's drama.
>
> CLS 2014, 61

The state creates the *macro*world—a *perfect stage* for life's drama![3] In his *Conversations with Lee Kuan Yew*, Tom Plate, whose career began at the *Los Angeles Times*, adopts this same metaphor of drama—here as film to make sense of both the state of Singapore, "not as a bland corporation, but ... as a spectacular dramatic epic movie" (2016, 19). Plate imagines the founding prime minister, sitting in a director's seat, "barking out orders with his crisp, decisive can-do autocratic style ... Go head, you wishy-washy liberals—*Make My Day*"—clearly invoking a famous American actor-turned-president. Liu and Plate's converging imagery captures important aspects of this city-state. Lee and his fellow PAP compatriots did not spew a set of ideas, they constructed a stage, a place which is ultimately material/physical, but nonetheless a *plan*, a concept, a materialized story line that like a film or a drama is never static—like taximobility, like the spinning prayer wheel, Singapore *moves*.

But notice the complex interlocking planes here: *rhetoric*, a story which moves—I will show—into *myth*; and yes, this may be a drama, but, in the case of Singapore, the whole island is a bounded set, where daily life begins to meld with story, with imagination. However, the citizens here, as the former CEO of the Urban Redevelopment Authority asserts, are not the creators of their larger spatial environment; theirs is to act and to participate, to play well. I would argue that this kind of world-making moves well beyond the metaphor of drama or of film—this is a life-world with the power and the problems of a religious universe. What does this have to do with spiritual movements—a lot, as we will see!

Lee Kuan Yew, Founding Father

August 9, 2015 marked the golden anniversary of Singapore's emergence as a totally independent state free from the former colonial power and from its union with Malaysia. I use the wedding terminology because that is how the late prime minister Lee Kuan Yew described the "divorce," Muslim-style, of this "small island of 214 square miles at low tide" from the Malaysian confederation in his memoirs, *The Singapore Story*:

> The three readings in the two chambers of parliament (in Malaysia) were the three talaks with which Malaysia divorced Singapore. The partners—predominantly

Malay—had been marred by increasing conjugal strife over whether the new Federation should be a truly multiracial society, or one dominated by the Malays.

1998, *kl* 266

The breakup included Lee's now iconic news conference as "tears rolled down his cheeks," and his insistence that: "For me it is a moment of anguish" (*Straits Times* Aug. 10, 1965, 12). This deeply personal tone reflects the conflation of Lee's life with the story of Singapore both in his own reckoning and in public perceptions. When he died just a few months before the golden anniversary, the depth of the public grief literally poured out as thousands stood in the rain for his funeral procession. Some scholars that I spoke with thought the image-power of Lee had subsided, but found "very little questioned public grief when he died—I was shocked." Indeed, public comments turned mythic: "The past 7 days were hot and dry BUT on the very day of the procession at about 12ish when Mr. Lee's coffin left the Parliament House the rain fell heavily as if the heavens cried too. I noticed this and even a man remarked the same"; "So true of profound leaders, they inspire even at death, just like Jesus Christ"; "I am an Indian citizen, but the admiration and respect that I have for this divine human being is unparalleled"; and "the strict yet endearing fatherly figure and a hand that lead a united people marching forward is finally gone."[4] While interviewing a scholar at one of Singapore's research institutes, I suggested that the founding story of Singapore increasingly had the tone of a cosmology; the reaction came with a canny smile: "Oh yes and we have our creator god in Lee Kuan Yew."

While this "myth" of the founding father as reported at the time of Lee's death resonates with traditional mythic fare in other places, especially in Asia—the heaven crying, or the divine leader-father (Mittler 2014, 313–24; Borneman 2004)—its nature remains subtler and even more difficult to analyze in the case of Singapore. Not the product of ancient times or even the dark period of the rise of Hitler in the 1930s, the foundation story of Singapore dates from the 1960s and interestingly coincides with another wave of deep interest in myth by anthropology, analytic psychology, and the History of Religions that began in the late 1940s but surged into popular culture during the late 1960s. Unlike an earlier period just after Hitler's diabolical use of mythic forms that reinforced a call for rationality, the 1960s-rekindled interest in myth with Hindu "spirituality" at the fore (Oliver 2014) often blurred into advocacy. Interestingly, this was also the time of the Cultural Revolution in China (1966–77), where Mao's person indeed took on mythic proportions along with his Little Red Book, which the People's Liberation Army openly called a "spiritual atom bomb" (Cook 2014, 1). But, with a focus fixed on India and Hindu spirituality, this grand political myth in China, perhaps unseen and unacknowledged in certain circles at the time, did not deter the growing advocacy of the positive power of myth. Here such narratives, *myths*, are "literature of the spirit" that "helps you to put your mind in touch with this experience of being alive" (Campbell 1988, *kl* 1 and 7).

This was the age of the scholar-master—collapsing Joachim Wach's much earlier distinction between a teacher/university student and a spiritual master/disciple (Wach [1925] 1988, 1). Joseph Campbell and Mircea Eliade, in particular, willingly and sometimes by popular conscription, became key figures in a popular revival of myth—

prefiguring the rising sense of spiritual-but-not-religious sensibilities still apparent with Campbell's posthumous but persisting bestseller, *The Power of Myth* (1988), which exhorts: "Read myths. They teach you that you can turn inward" (1988, 5). Sadhguru Jaggi Vasudev began his intensive reading during his college years at this same time, as did Sri Sri Ravi Shankar. While lines can be traced from the counterculture period of the 1960s beginning in the United States to the rising global popularity of gurus in the 1980s and beyond (Singleton and Goldberg, 2014), even widely dotted lines do not *specifically* connect this academic-popular world of the mythophile[5] to Singapore or its founding father. For this Euro-American group that later spawned "Practitioner-*Pandits*" (Goldberg 2010, 237), *myth* remained positive and pointing inward, aiding human potential, revealing hidden depths of human consciousness as part of the much-touted "subjective turn" (Heelas and Woodhead 2005, 2–5). I will return to this "turn" in detail in the next chapter.

During this same decade of the 1960s, sociologist of religion Peter L. Berger reemphasized the communal, not the individualizing, aspects of myth in his equally influential *The Sacred Canopy* (1967). Here cosmogonic myth, *the acts of cosmization*, remained central to the process of "world-building" so essential to the otherwise fragile and biologically incomplete human beings who are "congenitally compelled to impose a meaningful order upon reality" which "presupposes the social enterprise of ordering world-construction" (Berger [1967] 2011, *kl* 22). Although this Austrian-born émigré included an internal component of world-making, the enterprise had none of the inward-seeking, romantic tone of Campbell. "Always a collective enterprise" (16), the constructed cosmos for Berger—more closely paralleling the tale of the state in Singapore—was about community and cohesion, intolerability of chaos, and warding off the frightful sense of marginality. In other words, institutional programs are endowed with an ontological status to the point where to deny them is to deny *being* itself—the being of the universal order of things and, consequently, one's own being in this order (24). Religion, as the title makes explicit, formed that sacred canopy:

> The sacred cosmos, which transcends and includes man in its ordering of reality, thus provides man's ultimate shield against the terror of anomy. To be in a "right" relationship with the sacred cosmos is to be protected against the nightmare threats of chaos. To fall out of such a "right" relationship is to be abandoned on the edge of the abyss of meaninglessness.
>
> *kl* 26–7

Berger's most influential sense of cosmogonic myth is coterminous with order, with the human necessity to be part of the Plan and, moreover, to meld oneself with the social role: "Society assigns to the individual not only a set of roles but a designated identity. . . . the individual is not only expected to perform as husband, father, or uncle, but to be a husband, a father, or an uncle—and, even more basically, to be a man, in terms of whatever 'being' this implies in the society in question" (14). But, for Berger, the socialization process includes a consciousness of, even a discomfort with, the total assumption of the social role. In the end, even this internal dialogue takes place within a social environment: "society now functions as the formative agency for individual consciousness" (14–15). So, for Campbell, *myth* frees, but for Berger myth *binds*. For neither is this narrative form sinister in the 1960s. In the case of both, their material derived from the ancient or so-called primitive world, although Berger later re-formed his approach (1969).[6] The issue arises when myth as part of the contemporary world comes into play.

Mircea Eliade ended his *Sacred and Profane* ([1957] 1961) with a long meditation on the modern world and "profane man" who now resides in desacralized human existence but who "still retains a large stock of camouflaged myths and degenerate rituals" (204–5). Eliade recognizes "the various political movements and social utopianisms whose mythological structure and religious fanaticism are visible at a glance." Then he turns directly to Marx whose "classless society and the consequent disappearance of historical tensions[7] find their closest precedent in the myth of the Golden Age" (206). At Chicago as a graduate student during these years, recognizing such camouflaged myths became second nature but so did a certain naiveté about historical motive or consciousness within this process. Rather, as Moshe Idel proposes, central to the master's work, unveiling the camouflages for deeper meaning did not include historical context but rather a search for revelatory insights: "In order to reach a higher form of existence, one must be able to recognize those revelations, which are sometimes expressed by signs" (Idel 2010, 160). In his last lines of *Sacred and Profane*, Eliade concludes "nonreligious man had lost the capacity to live religion consciously" and then relinquishes any analysis of modern mythic form to "problems proper to the philosopher, the psychologist, and even the theologian" (213)—an abnegation which, as an Historian of Religions à la Charles Long, I am *not* willing to accept.

Meanwhile, back in Singapore during this same time period, Lee Kuan Yew built a state and a strong narrative of its creation—but dark criticism of his motive and modus operandi have emerged, especially since his death. Lee openly opposed communism (although the PAP had a left wing prior to its brief merger with Malaysia in 1963–5) and now stands accused of using an Asian version of the Red Scare. Revisionist historian Poh Soo Kai charges him with engineering the jailing without trial of his political opponents by accusing them of an attempted communist takeover in the (in)famous Operation Coldstore during the height of the Cold War period (Poh 2016, 257–72; see also Chau 2017, 30–1). Lee's well-known series of radio talks, *The Battle for Merger*, later published (1961), stated his case for the original merger with Malaysia as a concern about the communist threat which would lessen in a larger national unit. Indeed, the copy in the Syracuse Library was filed under "Communism—Singapore." Lee, according to Poh, then, recast the story of Singapore's independence with himself in the starring role in his memoirs, interestingly titled *The Singapore Story* (1998).

Increasingly, those crippled by Lee's rise to power, as well as a some of the younger generation of Singaporeans, view the grand narrative of the formation of Singapore as a pernicious *story* at the core of state power which shut down historical nuance and became a state *myth*. The longtime and long-incarcerated dissident Poh Soo Kai's *Living in a Time of Deception*, released after the founder-father's death, is introduced as "a gift of history to Singaporeans," whose "mission is to undermine orthodoxies and pieties" (Poh 2016, 49)[8]—note here the use of religious imagery. When Poh Soo Kai and others now seek to debunk the founding "myth" of Singapore, *myth* for them is sinister and a matter of statecraft, not spiritual inner engineering. Their unwillingness to assent to a certain version of history meant exile or years of imprisonment. The voices and the tears of these perpetual exiles saturate the documentary, *To Singapore, with Love*,[9] currently banned in Singapore (Buncombe 2014). Their leanings are openly left—but with a complex relationship to more official communist circles—their sensibilities resonant with that other far darker discussion of mythology from the 1950s by Roland Barthes concerned with social and political implication of "myth for postwar France." Closely related was Ernst Cassirer's *Myth of the State*, his 1946 analysis of the rise of Hitler. Both openly connect contemporary myth with statecraft and also with the rising media technologies of consumer capitalism.

However, while few—although shockingly some—would refute the evils of the state myth of Hitler, and many later berated the hollow materialism of the 1950s, the successes of Singapore—even with its constructed state myth—nonetheless remains more problematic to condemn. I have heard strong arguments that the astounding success of Singapore makes its middle-class citizens, supposedly the wellspring of the democratic desires, less willing to risk their current booming consumer economy by demanding more political free choice that could endanger the long stability of PAP rule (Kuhonta 2017, and Chua 2017, 157) and, by extension, the dominance of Lee Kuan Yew's successful Plan. Once again, as Tom Plate puts it, "We in the West may quarrel with the way it was achieved, but the achievement somehow seems to dwarf the critique" (2010, 39). Indeed, as many who grew up during the Cold War remember, democracy's defense was always its economic success—i.e., West Germany as a showcase, the iconic Nixon–Khrushchev kitchen debate was *not* as a dispute over ideology but over the ability of communism vs capitalism to deliver the goods.[10] Now successful Singapore, with its "soft authoritarianism" (Plate 2010, 16) *and* economic success, stares us in the face.

Erasure and Construction

In the many retrospectives of Singapore published and created for its golden anniversary, current and retired officials openly admit—in fact, celebrate—the careful construction of the land and the social engineering that transformed a city from a place where "diesel vehicles with loud engines and even louder horns spewed thick fumes all over the city ... latrines and uncontrolled pollution sources tainted the Singapore River, where dead animals could be seen floating on foul waters" (CLS 2016a, 2) into "a liveable city-state with a world-class built environment" (CLS 2015, 2).

Dr. Limin Hee, now director of the Centre for Liveable Cities, first introduced me to these many remembrances, suggesting that these stories all seem to have a common structure of chaos overcome by hard work, and good organization leading to a newly ordered prosperous nation. The series of well-designed full-color *Urban Systems*

Studies Books and *Singapore Systems Studies Booklet Series* produced by the Centre are publicly available in print edition or online as free PDF files.[11] Among the Urban Systems Studies, I will spotlight the following four publications: *Land Acquisition and Resettlement: Securing Resources for Development* (CLS 2014); *Built by Singapore: From Slums to a Sustainable Living Environment* (CLS 2015); *Cleaning a Nation: Cultivating a Healthy Living Environment* (CLS 2016b); *Urban Redevelopment: From Urban Squalor to Global City* (CLS 2016c).

Wan-ling Wee in *Asian Modern* provides a rich analysis of the many discursive constructions of the "Singaporean nation-state formation," using writing and speeches of Lee Kuan Yew and early stalwart cabinet ministers Dr. Goh Keng Swee and S. Rajaratnam (*kl* 782–1200). On the other hand, the Centre for Liveable Cities publications are especially designed for the Singaporean public and the many visitors to the Singapore City Gallery at the Urban Development Authority in which the center is housed. They are unabashedly patriotic and intent on presenting the accomplishments of Singapore in its fiftieth year. Most of these studies are based on oral histories, and include firsthand accounts by many of the now retired senior officials who once headed key organizations in charge of the massive redevelopment process. These short vignettes have the feel of storytelling by old wise chieftains-turned-technocrats. In this sense, each booklet is less designed for scholarly debate than as Roland Barthes argues—albeit irreverently—more like *myth* with: "it points out and notifies us, it makes us understand something, and it imposes it on us" (226).

On the surface, the publications abound in pie charts and colorful statistics and do not read like classic cosmogonic myth. There are none of the deities and powers, which Charles Long—once a colleague of Mircea Eliade—introduces as a key component of the many cosmogonic myths listed in his now classic *Alpha: Myths of Creation*, also from the early 1960s:

> Man's world is an ordered world of meaning, but the ordering principle is interpreted as a revelation which comes from a source outside of his ordinary life. It is this source which is given (revealed) and (it) defines any future possibility of man's existence. The thirst for a plenitude of being is always a religious craving.
>
> 1963, 11

These tales of the formation of the new state of Singapore have no such external power; the successful production of the state evolves from good planning and clear laws but does set the course for the future. Consider the *Land Acquisition and Resettlement: Securing Resources for Development*. The creation and ordering of the land appears as a frequent motif in creation myths, with the gods finally in control, usually after battling with the forces of chaos. However, in this short book, the progenitors of Singapore do take control and order the land by pushing the Land Acquisition Act through Parliament, "Following intense debate and scrutiny" (CLC 2014, 13):

> The pace, nature and primary purpose of land acquisition and resettlement in Singapore have evolved over the decades, in response to changing priorities and challenges. While compulsory acquisition and resettlement are often controversial

and sometimes cause hardship to those affected, they have been core to the success of Singapore's national development over the decades.

CLC 2014, 1

The gloss here is over the controversies and even the very notion of compulsory acquisitions, which provided the founders with broad—almost unlimited power—to tame the old system and to create anew on re-formed soil. This story arguably also exhibits Long's "thirst for a plenitude of being" but defined in a different register.

Again, "The CLC Liveability Framework" chart giving the "Integrated Master Planning and Development" that precedes this overview of land acquisition imparts the look of a classic bureaucratic production. The chart contains three overlapping circles—"High Quality of Life," "Completive Economy," "Sustainable Environment"— and then lists the important ingredients of success: "Dynamic Urban Governance," which includes building a "Culture of Integrity," working with market forces, as well as involving the community as "Stakeholders"—hardly the stuff of classic myth. However, note the need for moral order and the intimate involvement of the populous amid the discussion of market forces and competitive economy. This is not a purely mechanistic world order but assumes that a change of consciousness must accompany the building process—an inner and outer *re*-formation.

This story and others share a crucial impetus, *the crisis*, that engenders the production of creation myths, which Long strongly correlates with new beginnings of any kind that question the old order: "The novelty may appear on the historical level in connection with the discovery of a new plant, animal, or technique" (1963, 21). Moreover, Charles Long, more than Mircea Eliade, insists that mythic thinking remains a key part of the contemporary world:

> Specific myths or mythological structure may be superseded, but it is our position that *mythic thinking as a specific mode of apprehension of the world* is present in man in spite of the particular world-view of his time . . . but it is precisely the mode of apprehension which we have called mythic which allows man to respond to the new and novel situations.
>
> emphasis mine, 1963, 17

This switch from *myth* as a particular ordering of the world to *myth* as *a mode of apprehension* particular to new situations—as Long puts it, "the manner in which man understands his ordering of the world is as important as the specific form of order" (1963, 18)—opens mythic thinking to the contemporary world. Moreover, Long suggests that mythic thinking "allows" for the needed transition from one mode of life to another—perhaps providing the best means for this reordering process to take hold within a given society. And Charles Long was never willing to disentangle myth from religion: his working definition of religion matches the underlying modality of myth, the *crisis* situation:

> Thus religion is related to crisis situations. These are the generic situations of birth, puberty, and death; and, in addition, there are those crisis situations which are

particular to the culture and history of a people. From this point of view, we may define a crisis situation *as a situation in which a person or a culture is in transition from one mode of being to another and therefore is threatened with nonbeing.* As such, a person's response to this situation carries with it more intensity than his normal living habits. His experience of himself and of the otherness in life is heighted.

emphasis mine, 1963, 9

That heightened sense of self and others arising from a crisis situation resolves in a religious response and a turn to mythic thinking.

This is precisely the intense situation that leaders of the PAP both experienced and reinforced at the moment of independence—that tiny island standing alone as Prime Minister Lee declared "with grim determination ... 'We must survive. We have got to survive'" in a broadcast speech to the new nation just hours after the final separation from Malaysia (*Straits Times*, Aug. 10, 1965, 12). Chua Beng Huat, in his very recent *Liberalism Disavowed*, argues that the PAP government used the emotionally charged sense of crisis to mold a new national identity in a religiously and ethnically diverse population—i.e., we all must hold together to avert an always impending disaster. As Chau puts it, "The collective anxiety drives the underlying determination of the PAP government and Singaporeans to succeed; failure is not an option ... economic success only aggravates the anxiety as the current success is always ephemeral against the permanence of vulnerability-and-survival" (2017, 33). In a Longian world, such a constant state of anxiety is ripe for mythic thinking and, ironically, for religiosity—but here in avowedly secular state?

Even in this early stage of his work Charles Long opens both *religion* and *myth* to broader contexts, and later to an acute awareness of the power of "signification"—the creation of "an arena and field of power relationships" (1986, 2) that grants to some the right of signifying others. Long's later work confirms, "Religion will mean orientation—orientation in the ultimate sense, that is, how one comes to terms with the ultimate significance of one's place in the world" (7); but, unlike in *Alpha*, in *Signification* Long is acutely aware of who and what determines the setting of these acts of orientation. Colonization, new cultural contacts, and an emerging world of "new forms of human creativity" (1986, 6), but also of unequal power relationships placing peoples into environments not of their own making. Myth-making is not innocent, and reactions to crisis depend upon those who define the nature of the crisis and manufacture the solutions. In the case of Singapore, at the beginning, the crisis was real with the Vietnam War occupying the US and ethnic religious riots dominating Singapore in 1964 just prior to its solo run as a state. But, although a postcolonial state, People's Action Party quickly displaced the former colonial masters while not continuing to portray the British as the villains, as was the case in India. Even the Communists recede from concern by the time of the golden anniversary volumes. Rather, chaos and disorder appear to come from within—both the need for a continued change in consciousness in the populous *and* circumventing and taming those who obstructed progress. The latter in these publications have morphed into mostly nameless agents without specific identity.[12]

In *Built by Singapore: From Slums to a Sustainable Built Environment*, Lim Kim San, the founding chairman of the HDB, recalls those crisis years with his officers:

> I told them: "You see how urgent it is." The smell and the conditions were terrible, really terrible.... From then on, we started working. I told them: "We have a job to do and we better get going. Do it well"... There was no such thing as having to wait for a committee to decide on anything which has got to be done. They will come up to me and I will just say yes or no.... And things were done quickly rather than having things on paper and having a formal meeting. We all just sat around and discussed, right up to 9pm, and then we would adjourn and have dinner.
>
> 2015, 11

Here the crisis justified working within a small circle circumventing "red tape," i.e., normal bureaucratic procedures. Likewise, the Land Acquisition Act gave the government broad powers to take land for public use, without "any process for landowners to challenge the government's decision to acquire their land" (CLC 2014, 13). Commenting on this in *Land Acquisition and Resettlement*, Lee Kuan Yew argues:

> It would have been uneconomic and impossible to develop if we had had to acquire the property under the ordinary machinery of the Land Acquisition Ordinance with a right of appeal in the case of every award contested, to the High Court, with two assessors who are both trained and accept, as part of their ethos, the right and sanctity of private property. This becomes all the more compelling when vast sums of public revenue are being spent on developing huge areas ... would not have been possible if the concept of private property and all the rules and regulations that have been elaborated over hundreds of years were complied with.
>
> CLC 2014, 14

But more than just property-holders demanding compensation, the booklet on the next page places these landowners in the role of demonic forces—in the classic sense not only of obstructing progress but of willfully harming the people:

> Members of Parliament (MPs) at the time referred contemptuously to them as "an iron ring of landlords and landowners" and "the handful of rich landowners who do nothing but suck from the poor" and "hold posterity up to highway robbery" through actions that are "disastrous to the community" and cause "chaos and financial difficulties." In such a context, acquiring land from this group was seen by the majority in Parliament as fair.
>
> CLC 2014, 15

In both cases the crisis allowed extraordinary actions to thwart the forces—both legalistic and personal—holding back the creation of a new world.

Classic cosmogonic myth remains an "expression of man's cosmic orientation ... his apprehension of time and space, his participation in the world of animals and plants, his judgment concerning other men" (Long 1963, 19–20), what would be called the moral as well as the physical order of the world. Again, in Singapore, the government's conscious aim to set moral order interestingly ran closer to mythic thinking than bureaucratic. Another booklet from the Center for Liveable Cities ties cleanliness with sanitation and with the kind of public morality that Mary Douglas of *Purity and Danger* would love. *Cleaning a Nation: Cultivating a Healthy Living Environment* declares unabashedly:

> The story often told about the cleaning and greening of Singapore is that it was done mainly for the purpose of attracting international business and investments. In the city-state's early days as a newly independent country in the late 1960s, Singapore's rapid industrialisation and economic development plans were carried out in conjunction with its cleaning and greening efforts. However, it is less well known that the political leadership prioritised public cleanliness for the well-being of citizens, so that they could enjoy a higher quality of life. The simple wisdom that health leads to happiness had been applied to the entire nation.
>
> CLC 2016, 1

The story begins with the era of chaos, "living spaces were cramped and unhygienic, and public health standards were low. Many people suffered from cholera. Mosquitoes—the vectors for malaria—bred in drains" (2). To make matters worse, the "Broom Brigade ... unskilled labourers who had worked under the British administration" went on strike. Immediately the new government proceeded to enact new labor laws and to divide the state into new districts to localize public cleaning and to relocate and license the many food hawkers who plied the streets without any health inspection. Finally, a national campaign began when the Ministry of Health "recognised that the lack of cleanliness was a 'people-orientated problem' requiring mass participation of the public, which had to be addressed if Singapore was to be a 'garden city.'" In October 1968, the first annual "Keep Singapore Clean" campaign was launched, which became a national event, later with Tree-Planting Day "to foster morale and national pride through the promotion of greenery in common areas." In addition, the government imposed the now iconic Singaporean fines "on individuals who littered, and competitions that rated schools, markets, community centres and government offices on their cleanliness were held. The cleanest premises were rewarded, while the dirtiest were publicly named" (6)—a classic case of public shame and public rewards.

Cleaning a Nation narrates an admirable campaign that indeed produced one of the cleanest cities in the world. I have enjoyed the litter-free environment and safe drinking water everywhere. However, the path to this goal involved far more than physical engineering, and the booklet openly argues for the necessity of social engineering—put in terms of "social capital" and civic pride and "on community ownership, emphasising that sustaining the environment is everyone's responsibility. Fostering this sense of civic duty continues to be the state's on-going mission, to influence Singaporeans to take ownership of keeping Singapore clean" (36). The effective handling of the potential SARS epidemic in 2003, however, shows the particular Singaporean style which leans heavily on personal public behavior enforced with public posters and slogans. For example, the "Singapore's OK" (SOK)" campaign hinged on the collaboration between the Public-People-Private (3P) sectors, in order to expand its outreach. NEA actively encouraged stakeholders of food establishments, schools, condominiums, markets, construction sites and workers' dormitories to embark on the voluntary scheme and show their commitment towards public health by displaying an SOK decal.

41

Included was the "Happy Toilet" program complete with its own decal and sponsored by the Restroom Association of Singapore.

Linking happy toilets to myth leads directly to Roland Barthes's *Mythologies*. Such public printed material, which the various agencies of the government of Singapore produce in quantity, carry a similar combination of intimately personal yet highly public, broadly nationalistic but with class-infused values, as the magazine covers, detergent conferences, cuisine, sports events that Barthes examined in mid 1950s France and named as contemporary *myth*. The anthropological/religious studies scholarly cohort who celebrated myth in the 1960s confirmed the capacity of mythic thinking to tap the deeply personal while unfolding cosmic order—but in grand narrative tones. Barthes turns this conversation—his work went unacknowledged by these experts at the time—toward the utterly mundane of daily life captured in mass culture. The fragments of French cultural life exposed by Barthes sometimes feign a grand tone but in a grainy voice which Barthes mocks and yet underscores in a series of humorous essays collected in the first part of his *Mythologies*—the second part is his long critical essay, "Myth Today." This linguistic (here semiological) magic by which the micro becomes the cosmic resonates with the many signs and slogans in Singapore. Consider his "Saponids and Detergents" on the first World Detergent Conference in 1954 which, in Barthes's terms, "authorizes the world to commit itself to the euphoria" of the new cleaning agent, *Omo*, "the foamy" as opposed to the merely *deep* cleaners: "Foam can even be the sign of a certain spirituality insofar as the spirit is reputed to be capable of producing everything from nothing, a great surface of effects from a tiny volume of causes" (34). Ah, those glorious bubbles have the scent of Happy Toilets with their ties to moral and civic progress and in turn to a higher-order, truly successful, Singapore.

The elevation of this level of the mundane/intimate to an essential in public life expresses, I think, the PAP's elevation of pragmatism over ideology. The publications of the Centre for Liveable Cities present a leadership willing to get down in the dirt—photographs often show Lee and others on the ground with people or traveling in a truck, megaphone in hand—not pondering the skies. Peter Ho describes Prime Minister Lee: "But he was not, and had never been, a starry-eyed optimist. His approach was best captured when he said, 'The good things [in] life do not fall from the skies. They can only come from hard work'" (CLS 2016, 42). And yet, like Barthes, I also see the cosmic embedded in the newly re-created discursive *field*—new-land and new-language. But unlike Barthes's popular cultural artifacts characterized by Andrew Robinson as "the type of discourse which is particularly typical of right-wing populism and of the tabloid press" (2011), these studies are official productions—state-talk not the work of private (i.e., private enterprise) journalists or magazine editors. We are in a world here where bourgeois values may indeed prevail but not primarily as corporate productions—although some argue that Singapore INC operates in the same register. However, as much as happy toilets brings a smile, I cannot analyze the Singaporean state myths with the same eye as Roland Barthes, nor with the same critical/cynical force, because the process—openly admitted as constructed—produced civil-minded, if somewhat overly self-censored, denizens who were not tricked into a new cleaning agent that never really delivered, but rather into taking measures that kept SARS in check in Singapore in 2003, and virtually eliminated malaria, dysentery, and food poisoning—all too common in other nearby nations. Yet the process—the newly embedded moral compass—did have a price.

Again, that dilemma with Singapore: success and a well-functioning public world make charges of falseness and duplicity difficult. What would it mean to demythologize this state, to undertake the "political act" of semiotic analysis and establish "the freedom of language from the present system and unveiling the constructedness of social realities" (Robinson 2011)? Indeed, much of the rhetoric of the state arguably speaks in the register of *myth*—Singapore may be constructed of sand and stone and concrete but also of very potent metalanguage well expressed in those billboards for the new Ion center, "I am charisma cast in concrete." But there is a twist here; perhaps my dilemma with the stories of Singaporean's foundations are also shared with Barthes. As Jonathan Culler argues with Barthes's vignette on French wine, "The mythologist is concerned with the image of wine—not its properties and effects but the second-order meanings attached to it by social convention" (2001, 25). The dilemma with *myth* as a metalanguage is that the material out of which it is constructed is not false nor pure delusion, but exists in the world, as Graham Allen puts it: "something can at one and the same time be literally itself and the medium through which ideology propagates itself" (2003, 34). This back and forth, "this constant game of hide-and-seek between the meaning and the form" (227), between words and form, is what makes *myth* for Barthes and what makes Barthes's insights particularly apt for Singapore: the macrocosm of Singapore is constructed out of a seesaw of form and concept, the land constructed literally as "ideas-in-form"—*the* classic subject of the semiologist (Barthes, 221).

Barthes, like the myths he analyzes, is both highly accessible and yet slippery to grasp. Even at the end of his tour de force, he bemoans his own work as a "mythologist's," and his tenuous connection to the larger society. For he, as the analyst/decoder/demythologizer of myth, "is condemned to live in a theoretical society" (272). He ends *Mythology* with this haunting discussion of any who take up this process of revelation:

> For if we penetrate the object, we liberate it but we destroy it, and if we acknowledge its full weight, we respect it, but we restore it to a state which is still mystified. It seems we are condemned for some time yet to speak *excessively* about reality. This is probably because ideologism and its opposites are types of behavior which are still magical, terrorized, blinded, and fascinated by the split in the social world, And yet, this is what we must seek: a reconciliation between reality and men, between description and explanation, between object and knowledge.

How to read this? What is the analyst's goal—to demythologize Singapore—what would it mean to deconstruct this cosmos? The metalanguage of myth continues to exert a force on consciousness. Charles Long—who remains well aware of semiology and who titled his 1986 book, *Significations*—does remind the analyst that, at crucial times of change, mythic thinking gets thing done, again with loss and with gain. And Barthes's last section of "Myth Today" is ironically titled, "Necessity and Limits of Mythology" (271–4).

But now what specifically *does* a Barthes-style analysis of myth uncover in the PAP-Lee Kuan Yew creation myth/s of Singapore, in the foundations of this new cosmology? At the end of his complex essay, in the section, "Reading and Deciphering Myth," Barthes begins to ask how myth is received. He looks to eschew the purely analytical to become a "reader of myths":

> The first two types of focusing are static, analytical: they destroy the myth, either by making its intention obvious or by unmasking it: the former is cynical, the latter demystifying. The third type of focus is dynamic, it consumes the myth according to the very ends built into its structure: the reader lives the myth as a story at once true and unreal.
>
> 239

Barthes aims at this point to understand the process "*in the eyes of the myth consumer*" but his very choice of words and tone does not exude empathy. This move into the consumers' consciousness, while seemingly close, is *not* an act of phenomenology in the religious studies sense of Ninian Smart[13]—Barthes's analysis loses none of its hard bite. But, in this section, he does name some of the technologies that allow myth to work its magic on its consumer. Turning Barthes's pregnant prose into a list—a risky business which Robinson tries more extensively[14] (2011)—I can only abstract some of the pithy statements (there are many more) that resonate with Singaporean-state metalanguage and then reconsider the same studies and material above in a Barthesian mode:

> 1. Myth transforms history into nature: "We reach the very principle of myth: it transforms history into nature. We now understand why, *in the eyes of the myth consumer* ... what causes mythical speech to be uttered is perfectly explicit, but it is immediately frozen into something natural; *it is not read as a motive but as a reason*".
>
> 240

Turning history into nature may be the ultimate act of creation for the PAP government. In Singapore, this could be read literally—and the question asked, why were so many "unsanitary" shop houses and kampongs torn down and replaced by HDB flats with their tree-lined parkland and open spaces. Consider *From Slums to a Sustainable Built Environment*—the title tells the tale: old buildings/slums are removed and instead an *environment* is created. Indeed, they must move from the shabby to the pure—divested of their dirt and their particularity. The urgency that excused, even lauded, the circumventing of debate and bureaucratic process, naturalized into a real need with an erasure of any motives aside from the pure necessity to improve. Viewing the current Singapore landscape from on high, the HDB blocks look organic, in spite of their clear constructedness—their similarity and coloration seem to sprout from the soil (Fig. 2.5). New buildings increasingly have plants emerging from their roofs, propagating on their porches, or drifting from their walls (Fig. 2.6). The new Gardens by the Bay recreates the very tropical rainforests that the government eliminated to build highways and more and more HDB housing developments. The wildness is now literally caged but great fun to see from the scary, but, of course, safe surrounding cantilevered walkway (fig 2.7). Yet the image remains the same, the whole of Singapore is a constructed *natural* environment.

But this naturalness, this greening, remains strongly associated with good citizenship and nationalism. Describing the ultimate effect and affect of the greening process, Eunice Seng concludes in her recent dissertation:

> From this moment onwards, it seemed no longer possible for the citizenry to imagine the development of green open space beyond the framework of national identity. In no other post-colonial, Asian city was the twin conception of "home" and "land" more instrumental in defining its architecture and urbanism.
>
> 2014, 167

But while the process was happening, who questioned the need for total redevelopment, and why did Lee Kuan Yew have *A Chance of a Lifetime* with the "physical transformation of Singapore"? And if some did object within the government, their voices are not included among the oral histories in the official studies.

2. <u>Myth depoliticizes speech</u>: "Myth always comes under the heading of metalanguage: the depoliticization which is trained to *celebrate* things and not long 'act them'".

256

Figure 2.5 A highly planned city seen from atop the Marina Bay Sands Hotel. Photo by Dick Waghorne.

Figure 2.6 Vines spill down the newly constructed School of the Arts, Singapore.

Figure 2.7 Encased within a giant clam shell greenhouse, a massive cement mountain rises covered with plant displays viewed via hanging walkways. Photo by Dick Waghorne.

By depoliticization, Barthes meant the removal of any traces of abiding contestation, of unresolved contingency—abolishing "the complexity of human acts" (256). Take, for example, *Urban Redevelopment: From Urban Squalor to Global City*, which shifted the Singapore story from housing development to the growth and enhancement of its city center, starting with the now familiar trope of saving the populous from a degenerate area:

> Many of Singapore's problems in the 1960s emanated from the city centre. The housing shortage was extremely acute then, with three quarters of the population crammed into the small downtown area, and many families squeezed into shared accommodation in decrepit shophouses.... Valuable land that could be used for commercial development was instead taken up by run-down shophouses that were essentially housing slums.

> 2016c, xi

Impressive, this study summarizes and reviews fifty years of the redevelopment of the city center—now both a commercial and prime tourist area. On the surface, the study maintains a balanced factual chart-rich view giving the ups and downs of the long process—but a Barthesian eye glimpses the mythic dimension, especially at certain key points in the texts. The study charts the quick short-term development of the downtown as first charted by a UN-sponsored "town planning expert Erik Lorange," who drafted a basic long-term framework "alongside short-term action plans on the precinct scale" (14). Over and over again, repetition of tropes, "action-oriented" and "effective," validates the rapid government acquisition of the land and the "resettlement" of residents. For example:

> Singapore's first decade of self-governance brought about rapid change and development. The establishment of an effective system of governance—including the setting up of action-oriented agencies with greater legislative muscle—enabled more effective implementation of urban renewal and infrastructural construction programmes.

> 18

Again, this study quotes Prime Minister Lee on the need for extraordinary measures in a time of crisis: "When we were confronted with an enormous problem of bad housing, no development, overcrowding, we decided that unless drastic measures were taken to break the law, break the rules, we would never solve it" (2016c, 10). Put in Barthesian terms, this depoliticized retelling openly admits the *elimination* of the give-and-take not only of political debate but even of bureaucratic processes. However, the study seems far more sophisticated, and includes officials admitting that "clearing people and business is a very painful experience and if we can, we should try everything to help ease their problem" (26), and empathically discussing measures taken to ease the transition. But again, Barthes might counter that such a statement is yet another slippery technique, which Robinson summarizes as "Inoculation—admitting a little bit of evil in an institution so as to ward off awareness of its fundamental problems. For instance, admitting the existence of 'a few bad eggs' in the police so as to cover up the abusive nature of official police practices" (2011). The fundamental problem is that no voices of the dislocated are included in the oral histories here, only the reembraces of the administrators, and dissension is always soothed in the end.

Urban Redevelopment focuses on the "Central area" and begins, as did the government, with precincts N1 and S1. Precinct N1 "consisted mostly of reverted properties in the form of two-storey shophouses, single-storey temporary workshops, and other structures in dilapidated condition. By 1967, about 75% of the land area in the precinct was made available for urban renewal through land acquisition, affecting 2,216 families and businesses which were relocated to public housing estates with relative ease" (2016b, 22). I cannot attest to that case, but even today new local voices are emerging on the resettlement of residents in Precinct S1, "situated adjacent to the heavily populated area of Chinatown which consisted of overcrowded slums overrun with squatters" (2016b, 22). That area, now a spillover upscale tourist area from the more crowded Chinatown, includes the Singapore City Gallery and the offices of the Urban Redevelopment Authority. The glorious new Buddha Tooth Temple is just a short walk across the street at the very edge of Chinatown proper.

Urban Redevelopment describes the resettlement of the disposed in newly designed HDB flats as a creative attempt to keep the basic community together:

> The URD experimented with a "strata-zoning" approach that allowed for trooped instead of a traditional mono-functional zoning approach. This allowed affected communities to adapt more easily to their new high-rise environments by maintaining the relationship between homes and businesses, and also helped to optimise land use. The same approach was eventually applied to private developments through the Sale of Sites Programme, creating bold, iconic mixed-use developments such as the People's Park Complex.
>
> 27

The study then offers a section on "Resistance to Urban Renewal," especially in the case of ethnic groups who claimed that racial discrimination was the heart of the resettlement program, particularly in the Malay areas of the city. The voice of Alan Choe, head of the Urban Renewal Department, dominates here, recalling those early days when he and the prime minister trooped out into the streets in the back of flatbed trucks:

> He went personally [as part of a] convoy. The whole lot, we went in about three, four convoys. I was in one of them, sitting in one of the rear trucks. They are open like a van. We went through the Kampong Glam area to try to convince the people ... North and South. Chinatown, we do it; Indian area we do it ... I said this because at the end of the day, when we talk about urban renewal, who are the key persons involved? Without a doubt, it's the Prime Minister of the time because that was a political platform. He promised and he wants to live up to it, that he would clear the slums and he will not compromise.
>
> 29

Notice that there was never any intension of allowing dissent to end the resettlement program or to halt the demolitions or the construction of new HDB blocks. A political platform here does not imply debate, only reveals and confirms the Plan. If read carefully, the section catalogues the long-term effort with "deep sense of empathy"—a Singaporean version of the US politician's I-feel-your-pain? —to change public opinion not alter the decision, and with the happy ending:

> Singapore's pioneer post-independence government shared a deep sense of empathy with the populace, which helped them ensure that policies would address the everyday needs of the residents. With strong leadership and an unwavering commitment to the people, difficult policies such as urban renewal and resettlement could be implemented with unparalleled success.
>
>   30

However, this "unparalleled success" with urban renewal has not gone uncontested. Jean DeBernardi, working with Taoist movements and temples in Singapore, demonstrates "the city state's program of urban renewal has pushed Chinese popular religious culture to the margins" (2016, *kl* 2673). Taoist ritual practices such as street festivals, ancestor worship, divination, and spirit possession are "practices that modernists and political reformers regard as peasant superstitions ill fitted to a modern urban setting" (*kl* 2692–4), and her material suggests—although not directly—that choices for urban renewal included deeply rooted fear of spiritual disorder, or actually disorderly deities. She uncovered another side to this supposedly happy ending notably in that very S1 precinct where former residents with strong Taoist roots supposedly adapted into their new high-rise environments that mimicked the multiuse environment of their old shop-house world. *Urban Redevelopment* fails to mention that moving meant the Taoists' gods also lost their residences, particularly on Duxton Road and Amoy Street. DeBernardi describes the loss: "When the government redeveloped Amoy Street in the 1970s, some buildings were torn down, and others restored as heritage buildings ... a popular Teochew porridge restaurant stands next door to the former premises of Xuan Jiang Dian's mother temple" (*kl* 2883–5). And again, the bitterness remains for the Chng family whose temple was relocated. The family once "supported former Prime Minister Lee Kuan Yew in his ascent to power, but after he won office, the government appropriated the buildings on Duxton Road and relocated its residents. The temple moved to a new location in the Geylang district, an ungentrified area of Singapore that includes a down-market red light district" (*kl* 2849–51). In order to keep the memory of lost and inappropriately relocated temples, former residents— lead by an educated Singaporean working in the tech industry—have taken to the Internet and Facebook with "Taoism-Singapore" and "Diaspora of Amoy Street." Most importantly, a project from a local university undertook a final project boldly named "Reclaim Land: The Fight for Space in Singapore," interviewing Singaporeans "who through their daily actions reimagine a new geography of Singapore, one of their own, one that gives birth to the question: Whose city is it anyway?" (*kl* 2828–9). This politics of who defines "superstition" becomes a matter of cleaning up slums. Again, *Urban Redevelopment* ignores the longing of the dispossessed residents and whispers of their gods-in-possession—muting them both in substance and in word—and transmuting the entire process into a grand success.

3. <u>Myth becomes unquestionable, contingencies become fact</u>: "A myth is at the same time imperfectable and unquestionable; time or knowledge will not make it better" (241) and "myth is read as a factual system, whereas it is but a semiological system".

242

Suddenly another function of all of those graphs and pie charts that abound in the *Urban Systems Studies Books* and *Singapore Urban Systems Studies Booklet Series* becomes an ironic clue that these are indeed modern *myths*. A crucial conundrum is seemingly solved—how could such a booklet be named a *myth* when so many facts are embedded in the text? Singapore is extremely transparent in its publications—and its rules—but we are not privy to the processes, only the results. This almost desperate turn to the factual could be read à la Barthes as the ultimate mask that hides political choices and arguable decisions, and presents them as clear facts: there *were* problems, they were solved. And a disturbing Barthesian question emerges: is the point of these impressive charts to convey information or project *an image* as "an abnormal regression from meaning to form, from the linguistic sign to the mythical signifier" (227)?

Although Barthes's emphasis on popular cultures and his warnings about essentialism and hidden political agendas prefigure post-structuralism, Barthes sees "'Myth Today' as the beginning of a new phase of work focused on the idea of a science of criticism, more precisely structuralism and semiology," as Graham Allen discloses the central influence of Saussure and structuralism in Barthes's *Mythologies* (33–40) and in his later "project to establish a structural account of narratives" (48). Indeed, when *Mythologies* was printed, Claude Levi-Strauss was about to publish *Tristes Tropiques* (1956) followed by *Anthropologie structurale* (1958). At this point Barthes was a structuralist seeking broader patterns but ironically came close to erasing the narrative element in myth by focusing on the image—the concept-in-form. Barthes elides the story line, the *history*, to concentrate on the production of the image/concept seemingly glossing the spaces in between, the tensions, the twists and turns—ironically the same sin that he accused the constructers of myth of doing—erasing history.

However, neither Barthes nor the PAP remained still. In Singapore, as CLS publications affirm over and over again, "time" and "knowledge" did "make it better"— as my earlier point in the taxi ride—change, turning, movement become a major modus operandi of the state—Singapore moves, the government learns. Another urban systems study, *From Slums to a Sustainable Built Environment,* telling again the story of the HDB flats, features a remembrance from Johnny Wong, Group Director: "Engineers could always try new things in HDB. There was no dedicated research centre back then, but one can say the whole HDB is a 'big research centre'" (CLC 2015, 48). A key feature of the PAP pragmatism is precisely this claimed ability to adjust. As the reflection by Peter Ho states, "Singapore: Always a work in progress," but this in the same volume in which Lee Kuan Yew states flatly that no one deviates from the Plan. And as Allen confirms, Barthes soon moved into post-structuralism, arguing it was "because I formulated my sentence so that this would be seen by those who pay attention to ambiguities and ellipses" (quoted in Allen, 20, 2003). *Mythologies* ends with just such ambiguities. But, as much as the PAP government may laud its ability to change, in the end Singapore remains a structuralist paradise: the plan will change but only for another bigger and better PLAN. Toilets may be happy here but not loose ends. Ultimately Barthes's initial analysis of *myth* as rendering discourse unquestionable remains but with the proviso that discourse here functions more like a whole film, not just a frozen frame.

> 4. Myth erases history: "... Myth is constituted by the loss of the historical quality of things: ... things lose the memory that they were once made ... A conjuring trick has taken place: it has turned reality inside out, it has emptied it of history and filled it with nature, it has removed from things their human meaning so as to make them signify a human insignificance".
>
> 255

Myth and the erasure of history turn to a place where Eliade and the general chorus of praise for myth meets its most severe critics at the corner of Politics and Power. Recall that political dissidents in Singapore consider the official retellings of the origin, development, and eventual success of Singapore, a *myth*. As the introduction to Poh Soo Kai's *Living in a Time of Deception* claims:

> A government that controls the writing of history as vociferously and menacingly as Singapore's indicates just how much it has to justify its use of the Internal Security Act to come into power and to maintain its rule. It has tied itself completely to the founding myth of the PAP".
>
> Hong Lysa in Poh 2016

I consider these negative aspects of myth-making to be crucial for understanding the nature of *contemporary* myth. Those who argue the political and social implication of erasing a complex history for this certain kind of narrative are engaged in a serious project that echoes Ernst Cassirer's critique in his *Myth of the State*—written originally in English at Yale University and published in 1946. Although much earlier in *Sprache und Mythos* (1925, later translated into English[15] and also published in 1946), Cassirer understood myth and language as rooted in the power of metaphor and ultimately now "have become a light, bright ether in which the spirit can move without let or hindrance" into "self-revelation" (1946, kl 1284-1285), at the bitter close of World War Two the misuse of the power of myth roused his ire. And this is the point that his work foreshadows Barthes and remains unnervingly relevant today.

There is *consciousness* about *modern* myth, as Ernst Cassirer argued so forcefully just a few weeks before Hitler's Third Reich collapsed. In *Myth of the State,* Cassirer reviews the functioning of myth related to the state from Plato to the early nineteenth century and the slow changes toward the mid twentieth century. Then, in the last chapter, "The Technique of the Modern Political Myths," Cassirer powerfully distinguishes features of the modern construction of myth and its earlier antecedents:

Myth has always been described as the result of an unconscious activity and as a free product of the imagination. The new political myth ... are artificial things fabricated by very skillful and cunning artisans. It has been reserved for the twentieth century, our own great technological age, to develop a new technique of myth. ... It has changed the whole form of our social life.

1946, 282

Prefiguring Barthes, but with even more intensity, Cassirer described the new artifice of myth working at a level of deep-seated emotions to "change the function of language from the semantic to 'the magical word'" and "these new-fangled words are charged with feelings and violent passions" (282–3). Magic in connection with mythology in lieu of rational debate—and here he also prefigures Charles Long—emerges in times of crisis and "always occurs if a pursuit is dangerous and its issues uncertain" (279). Cassirer argues for the primacy of this primordial power diabolically commandeered: "They undertook to change the men, in order to be able to regulate and control their deeds" (286). For him, the military rearmament of Germany with the rise of the Nazi Party "was only the necessary consequence of the mental rearmament brought about by the political myths" (282).

His description of the power of this new "technology" of myth-making to obscure content and facts and debate outshouts Barthes: "What characterized them is not so much their content and their objective meaning as the emotional atmosphere which surrounds and envelops them. This atmosphere must be felt; it cannot be translated nor transferred from one climate of opinion to an entirely different one" (283–4). Throughout *Myth of the State*, Cassirer mounts a passionate plea to "carefully study the origins, the structure, the methods, and the techniques of the political myths" (296), which were too easily dismissed as Hitler rose to power. He also exposed the intellectual groundwork that provided the needed political tools and names for Heidegger's work *Sein und Zeit* that subtly taught "we cannot emerge from this stream and we cannot change its course" as an example of the attitudes that lead to then current state of affairs in Germany—again eerily relevant today:

But the new philosophy did enfeeble and slowly undermine the forces that could have resisted the modern political myths. A philosophy of history that consists in sober predictions of the decline and inevitable destruction of our civilization ... have given up all hope of an active share in the construction and reconstruction of man's cultural life. Such philosophy renounces its own fundamental theoretical and ethical ideals. It can be used, then, as a pliable instrument in the hands of political leaders.

293

For Cassirer as a Jewish exile in Britain and Sweden, before finally settling in the United States, the construction of the modern myth of the German state was a matter of life and death.

In Singapore, for some, the situation was nearly as dire: not death but exile and imprisonment. To challenge the founding story of Singapore continues to have consequences in spite of other areas in which the ruling PAP have moderated their views:

> There is one area where the PAP government appears to be intransigent in using heavy suppression—the reinterpretation of Singapore's political history. Historical reinterpretations which raise doubts about the veracity of the Barisan leaders as communists have been actively countered by the government, which insists on the objectivity of the official history. The careers of some young revisionist historians in Singapore have ended before they began as they have been unable to secure academic positions in local universities.
>
> Chau 2017, 180

Here the issue appears on the surface as debates over the "objectivity" of the official history, but the heavy suppression that Chau describes belongs to another realm of rhetoric—the very foundations of a world appear at stake. Revisionist historian Poh Soo Kai decries the tenacity of this origin story by invoking religious imagery: "However, the politics of merger and separation have been so distorted that it is difficult to dislodge the notion that Singapore's history as an independent state started in 1965, the way a lotus emerges from the mud, pure and clean" (Poh 2016, 245). Poh refers here to numerous references to the emergence of the divine from otherwise muddy waters: "As the lotus opens each petal to the air, not a stain or spot of mud remains externally"— so says one of many current New Age Internet sites.[16]

The Overarching World of the State

Myth works at a deep level of consciousness; all the theorists agree but they do not agree on the level at which myth—particularly cosmogonic myth—functions or *should* function. Is the modern state construction of myth the key to the good society—to the well-functioning state? Or is it, on the other side, the demon that destroys democracy, free will, and real choice? Singapore could be considered, as does Wan-ling Wee, as a tiny state that offers a "'test-tube' intensity" to issues that move beyond its seemingly limited borders, in this case to examine the relationship between a modern state and the production of a macrocosm—the umbrella of ideology constructed in *form* fashioned of the rhetorical and the built environment. My argument here is: the *process* of construction as well as the *form* echoes, evokes, and feeds on the same social and mind power of myth, especially cosmogonic myth. The larger question is: does this imply a religious project in spite of the state's strong commitment to secularism? That answer is more complex and will involve the discussion of Religion vs Spirituality in the next chapter.

Whether religious or not, however, the reconstruction of Singapore was not confined to the concrete form but also to the re-formation of the denizens of Singapore into citizens again with stupendous success. The intensity of the project, the sense of urgency and fear of failure, the initial concern and then the stoking of a constant crisis mentality marks the creation of this Little Red Dot Singapore with cosmic proportions.

Throughout the Centre for Liveable Cities' recent publications, the Singapore government deems the entire world watching their project as they morph now into a leading global city. In this sense, the dark nebula that surrounds this success is threatening. Critique questions order, purpose, and legitimacy. In the strenuous opposition by PAP, Barthes or Cassirer or Long would divine the presence of the mythic.

But the debate within Singapore lives within a larger discussion: those who defend myth see it as a move toward boundlessness while others continue to acknowledge the social power of mythic language to bind and to confine in both a positive and negative sense. As the next chapter will explore, these are tensions between *religiosity as spirituality* and *religiosity* as necessary commitment to community and social bounds, and *spirituality* as unbounded. The argument is vast. In the erasure of history, Singapore's PAP founding story returned to myth. The irony is that Eliade writes of myth as erasing history with little regret—mere profane history *should* be erased for a taste of the cosmogonic where the world is made new, reborn, and reworked in a constant back and forth between myth as destructive and myth as creative. Destruction and reconstruction as regenerative processes are ultimately positive, just as the gods dismember the monstrous body "in order to create the cosmos" (100). Eliade saw myth less as a social glue and more as source of revelation—of the human ability to transcend profane time, ordinary history, for cosmogony, "the supreme divine manifestation, the paradigmatic acts of strength, superabundance, and creativity": a "thirst for the real" (80). His seeming lack of concern for the conscious social levels of religion, his eschewing of the ethical in preferences for the occult and the yogic—the magical— abetted the accusation of his fascism: "The collapsing of opposites can dissipate the power ethical imperatives, the foundational demands to cure the world . . . what matters most for religious communities is what really can be done, not what exists in some platonic stratosphere of the spirit" (Wasserstrom 1999, 78). Joseph Campbell was even more insistent that myth rather than a recipe for social stability was a vital step, not toward bounded social obligations but toward ultimate enlightenment:

> The function of ritual and myth is to make possible, and to facilitate, the jump—by analogy. Forms and conceptions that the mind and its senses can comprehend are presented and arranged in such way as to suggest a truth or openness beyond. And then the conditions for meditation having been provided, the individual is left alone. Myth is but the penultimate; the ultimate is openness—that void, or being, beyond categories—into which the mind must plunge alone and be dissolved. Therefore, God and the gods are only convenient means—themselves of the nature of the world of names and forms, though eloquent of, and ultimately conductive to, the ineffable.
>
> 221–2

Singapore PAP, on the one hand, builds a cosmos in the here and now, one closely attached to an ethic of citizenship and of harmonious community living, with responsibility and duty. At the same time history is erased, Lee argues, just as in the case of the Land Acquisitions Act, out of necessity to build a sound, ordered world without disjunctive seams. The state also leans toward myth that subverts *another kind* of ethics—disavowing, as Chau has argued, the sensibilities of liberalism. Moreover, there is little room for boundlessness in the Singaporean cosmos except boundless ambition for success in every aspect of life.

I end with another taxi ride. I asked my driver if he knew Albert Court and the old hotel there. Yes he did, and he drove me through the back streets with ease. Finally, he confessed that coming here was always emotionally difficult: his ancestral home had been recently demolished to make way for the LaSalle College of the Arts, a stunning and now iconic architectural work that opened in May of 2009. He now lives as do most Singaporeans in an HDB flat. The construction of LaSalle, as a speech by the prime minister put it, "reflects the increased interest in the arts in Singapore. As the economy develops and our society matures, the demand for more intangible, less material satisfactions increase, and with it also demand for arts education" (H. L. Lee, 1995). LaSalle, although a private church-related college, is strongly supported by the state as part of the increasing public-private cooperation in education. Now the Singapore government undertakes demolition to pave the way for a truly grand house for the intangible—*interesting*.

3

Macrospaces—Guru Style

In March of 2017, over 3,500 people assembled to hear Sadhguru Jaggi Vasudev speak for over four hours in a grand space at the Singapore EXPO Convention & Exhibition Centre. The rows of gold-framed chairs with blue velvet in the S$200-seat level contrasted with the vaulted steel-beamed hall (Fig. 3.1) for "Mix, Mingle, & Mediate with Sadhguru in Singapore."[1] This massive government-owned and constructed complex is managed by a private corporation SingEx Venues, under the government bureau MICE (Meetings, Incentives, Conferencing, Exhibitions), which is under the STB (Singapore Tourism Board), which is under the (MTI) Ministry of Trade and Industry. I sat in my own blue velvet seat and stared at the massive ceiling, after walking from the MRT station for what seemed like a mile through corridors. I passed a huge book fair, a "flower fest," a Chinese wedding party, and several eateries, before finally reaching the conjoined Halls 1 & 2. We all had convened within a world constructed by the Singapore state and meant to impress. Neither homely nor intimate, the atmosphere seemed design to overawe, although EXPO advertized to bring the kids to PlayLAH@ Singapore EXPO—for the coming Chinese New Year.[2]

The event with Sadhguru marked the recent release of his *Inner Engineering: A Yogi's Guide to Joy*, which the global speaking tour that included Singapore was meant to highlight. Isha volunteers sold books at a discounted rate in the lobby (Fig. 3.2) and announced, just prior to Sadhguru's entrance in the auditorium, that the *Guide* had become a *New York Times* bestseller—the claim appears on the cover of the well-designed hardbound book published by a division of Random House. At the end of the event, Sadhguru left the front stage to autograph copies for his excited audience at the very back of the hall—as he said, for those who could not really see him but only his image on the massive screens.

The core of the event was his astounding unfaltering call-and-response talk delivered spontaneously from 4:00 p.m. to past 8:00 p.m. Prior to the talk—and as punctuation during the event offering some respite to Sadhguru and his audience— videos came on the huge screens at the front of room. The opening video reaffirmed that the Isha Foundation was "non-religious" and nonprofit and showed his project in Tamilnadu, *Gramutsavam* (Tamil-Sanskrit, *grama* + *utsavam*,[3] "village festival"), to revive rural culture and arts. Another video midway into the program highlighted his massive *Alai-Wave of Bliss* program, featuring Sadhguru dancing with large crowds of people mostly in Tamilnadu. Volunteers then burst into song in this cavernous hall and encouraged the rather staid Singaporean audience—with only slight success—to join

Figure 3.1 Blue velvet-covered chairs, now empty, await participants to take their seats in Hall 1&2 of the EXPO center.

in the Tamil folk-song-style dancing.[4] Somehow the Expo center could accommodate the talking and the videos, but the wave of spontaneous dancing dwindled in this enormous space with thousands of close-spaced seats.

Perhaps coincidentally, or perhaps not, many of Sadhguru's directives to acquire real joy through inner construction of the Self fit the outward and highly constructed environment of the Expo center. Although Sadhguru often extolls natural beauty in his own poetry, his Inner Engineering program conjoins the deliberate use of techniques with often humorous lessons. He stresses *not* concepts or beliefs, but *techniques*. This "spiritual master with a difference," as his Facebook page proclaims, told his Singaporean audience that beliefs in ideologies, philosophies, and scriptures were outdated; we needed to step forward. Sadhguru began by asking us if the ancients were smarter than us. Many in the audience shouted, "Yes!" But he said, "No! Now is the smartest period of all times and we need to move ahead." Over and again, his point was that each of us could take control of our own lives, could become joyful by turning inward, the one dimension that we did control: "When it comes to our inner nature, there is only one governing principle: borderless unity. Our physical and social worlds are governed by

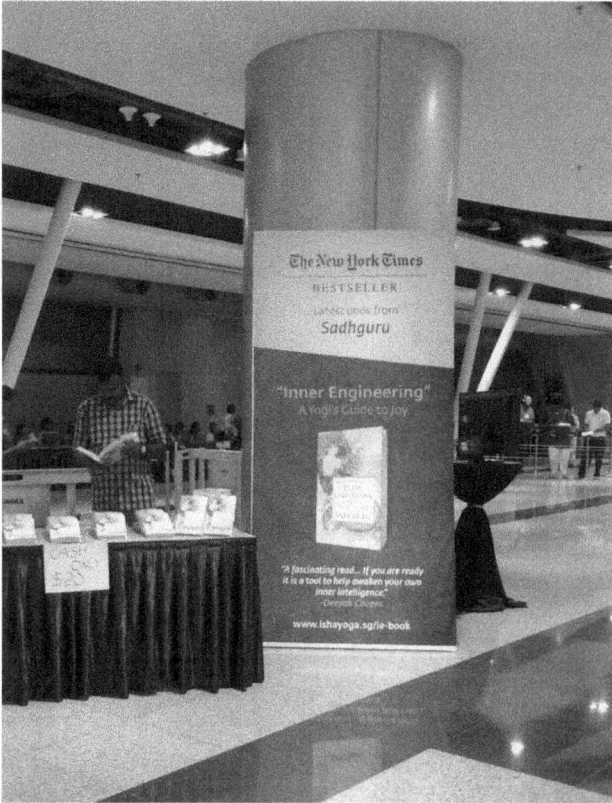

Figure 3.2 Volunteers from Isha Singapore sell Sadhguru's new book in the lobby.

boundaries. Our inner world needs none" (Vasudev 2016, *kl* 529–33). Submitting to religious "authorities," including scriptures and priests, is becoming a thing of the past. He had scathing words for turning spiritual yearning towards the Heavens—especially heavens that promised a paradise with tantalizing virgins. What good would they be since in heaven we have no body? Then he told a joke of a man and his wife from Texas who finally traveled to the Holy Land, but she died there suddenly of a heart attack. When people there offered to bury her for much cheaper than transporting her body back home, he refused finally because "In Texas people stay dead."

At this point, I had a startling moment: I began to countenance the concerns of the critics of spirituality from *within* religious traditions. Sadhguru did not seem to understand how seriously many Texans might hope for resurrection or confirm "faith" as the core of Christianity. He seemed unaware—or was he?—of the very meaning of "Muslim," one who submits to the will of God and who understands the Qur'an as the living word of God. As I watched people near me, they did not seem deeply impressed, clapping sparingly. In a conversation prior to the formal event, the gentleman in the next seat told me he was a Sindhi whose father had escaped Pakistan during the

Partition and fled to Indonesia, which had just achieved independence in 1945. He told me that Isha in his home city of Jakarta was very small, mostly because of the Islamic influence. I asked about Jakarta and he said this was a mixed religious city with a lot of Christians and, in spite of news reports, he felt quite settled there. I did not talk with him afterwards but wonder how he heard Sadhguru's statements living in Indonesia with the world's largest Muslim population.

The issue of not submitting to authorities belied the *visual* setting of the hall and the guru's *rhetorical style*, which confirmed his own authority, although he always tells Ishas—members of his organization—and his readers that he offers no "tenets or teachings" but only signposts "on a journey that can be made by no one but you" (2016, *kl* 111). In the front of the hall, spotlights shone on a special chair, used by kings and spiritual masters, *gaddi* (Hindi, "throne"), the same setting which I have seen Sadhguru occupy on other occasions, especially at his ashram in Coimbatore for Mahashivaratri (Fig. 3.3)—to which I will return. In front of this dais, a section of premium seats with golden chairs covered in auspicious red offered the only real close-up view of the guru. My section in blue was

Figure 3.3 Lights shine and brass bell and other decorations on the wall behind the *gaddi*—the ever-present video camera in front will soon project Sadhguru's image on two huge screens on the sides.

behind these. From here, his face appeared the size of a cameo, and I found myself, like most of the audience, watching the huge video screen instead to see his face clearly. As Sadhguru spoke, he often punctuated his comments by asking "Isn't it?"—a common English translation of a Tamil formula, *illaiyā*, to which the only real answer can be affirmation. Often, he entreated his tepid, or perhaps just restrained, Singaporean listeners for a louder response. His brilliance shone alone on that dais in an astounding performance; we meditated together only for the last half hour of the program.

There are multiple ways to understand this seeming double-talk over scriptures, rituals, and religious authorities. In the chapter on "Energy" in the *Guide*, a significant section, "Sacred Science," reconsiders temples in South India, emphasizing the difference between those consecrated via "pratishtha" (*pratiṣṭhā*), "by using rituals, mantras, sounds, forms, and various other ingredients" from those sanctified by another form, "prana pratishtha" (*prāṇa pratiṣṭhā*), that "uses your own life energies to consecrate something" (2016, *kl* 3102–3). Jaggi Vasudev does not belittle sacred space or acts of consecration; in the very book that marked the event, Jaggi Vasudev declares:

> If I were given the necessary support and opportunity, I would like to consecrate the whole planet! This is what I am good at: turning thin air into a very powerful vibrant space, turning a piece of metal or stone into a divine reverberation. It is my dream that someday all of humanity should live in a consecrated environment. Your home should be consecrated; your street should be consecrated; your office should be consecrated. All the places where you spend your time should be consecrated.
>
> 2016, *kl* 3116–19

However, here in Singapore, his speech *seemed* an especially strong rejection of "Religion" defined as ritual, scriptures, priests, and even the gods. Later conversations confirmed that others had the same impression and were also confused.

At a dinner, a week later, I spoke with Devi Naidu, an active member of the Oneness Movement mentioned in Chapter 1, who has provided keen insights on spiritual movements during my time in Singapore. She attended the event with a group of friends. Citing his temples at his ashram in Coimbatore, I expressed my surprise at the contradiction between what he says in Singapore and what he does in Coimbatore. She told me that some of her companions in the back of the room had said exactly the same thing, and she explained to them that night as she was explaining to me now. She thought that Sadhguru knew that he could not speak openly of Religion in Singapore, and so this is why he spoke the way he did; he had adjusted his points for the place—for Singapore. I heard the same augment sometime later, from Vijaya Rai, a highly articulate lawyer and my instructor in Sudarshan Kriya of Sri Sri Ravi Shankar of Art of Living.[5] I shared my concerns about Jaggi Vasudev's seeming hypocrisy, but she did not agree. She reminded me that gurus have great insight and can sense the tone of an audience— as soon as they feel the ethos of the room, they will shape their message to the time and place and people. Sadhguru likely sensed that in Singapore mention of Religion or of ritual was not wanted. Unlike India, people in Singapore have passed the need for deities/gods and are seeking something else beyond that; but in India the gods are needed and expected so he builds temples there. She reminded me again and again that consistency of message was *not* the modus operandi of gurus but rather to fit the message to the place and the time!

Religion/ Spirituality, Secular/Religious?

Experiencing Sadhguru Jaggi Vasudev in that cavernous space at the Expo center on the Sunday afternoon just before Chinese New Year, I am bound to ask what happened. The last chapter suggested that there are alternate spaces/worlds in Singapore constructed by gurus who lead popular "spiritual" movements. Did Sadhguru create an alternate space, a macrocosm, a newly consecrated arena that evening? Was this a borderless world? As with many similar large-venue gatherings from other guru-centered movements—to which I will return below—volunteers had organized this with business-like acumen. The atmosphere was thoroughly *conventional*—literally echoing many academic and business conventions but with friendly sari-/*kurta*-clad volunteers with folded hands in traditional greeting stationed all along the long walkway. When I got to Hall 1, everything was carefully arranged. I was guided to the right line for my P1 ticket, and interestingly I queued just behind a Muslim woman who also had a P1. Volunteers checked my passport and, finally at the desk, I received my formal credentials, then dropped my bag and moved, like many, in search of food (Fig. 3.4). I finally found a Coffee Connection on the far horizon. I spotted a woman bringing back a huge slice of cake and smiled; she saw my badge and we began to chat both at my table and then at hers with her friend. They were both en route to a rejuvenation program at the ashram in Coimbatore and had stopped here for the program before going on. Both were Australians, the more talkative being ethnic Chinese whose father was Catholic and mother was Taoist. Her friend was a European-Australian who had just lost her husband and needed solace. We chatted about Sadhguru, the Chinese-heritage woman describing herself as deeply curious and spiritual and a seeker; she saw an ad for Inner Engineering and was drawn to it because the intersection of science and religion fascinated her.

The presence of those from Australia, as well as the man evidentially taking the seat next to me from Jakarta, marked this gathering as multinational and multiethnic, with a global feel. However, the venue offed few hints—with the one exception of the gaddi in the very front of the room and a kolam (Tamil *kōlam*, a welcoming decorative painting with rice flour) in the highly polished entrance hall (Fig. 3.5)—of the *spiritual*, let alone the *religious*. The very spatial configuration seemed to belie a Hindu, religious, or even spiritual atmosphere, but the very awesome construction with the steel-beamed ceiling and shining floors spoke *Power*. In *some sense,* this was an alternate space—with its own grandeur—a macrospace in Singapore shaped by a guru and his highly committed volunteers, but ultimately this venue remains a product of Singaporean governmental planning and pride. The Expo center reflects what Barthes would consider a *myth* told in concrete, marble, and steel—a new government-cum-business project, "an iconic landmark in the eastern part of Singapore," as the official website describes the center with its mission "to grow, nurture and reinforce Singapore's reputation as a dynamic business events destination"[6]—a thoroughly secular venue except for that Barthesian suggestion of *myth* at work.

Figure 3.4 An Isha volunteer waits to guide participants into the hall.

My proposition at this point is that there is something both very similar and yet different in the kind of *space* that the state built and the kind of macrospace that Sadhguru summoned within its walls. Earlier, in Chapter 2, I asked: how do these spiritual worlds conflate, confound, or combine with what I am suggesting is a state-cosmos—with its *myth,* its cosmology? But the first step is to recall that in the context of the 1960s-theoretical framework that reasserted its importance, *myth* was deemed both *liberatory*—a highly personal journey to the self as with Joseph Campbell—*and,* at the same time, *binding* as in Berger's *Sacred Canopy* effecting an ordered world, *or,* in Cassirer's darker sense, inducting the Fascist state. In turn, I proposed that these dual aspects of myth are closely related to another much-discussed difference—between Religion and Spirituality. I will move beyond Isha Yoga later, but for now Sadhguru's performance both echoes some of the modalities of the state myth at the same time that he confounds it: his rhetoric and practice at points seem an embodiment of the academic descriptions of spirituality. Moreover, he and other Hindu-based gurus abjure their connection to "religion" at the same time that they perform new rituals, create new texts, and even build new "temples" in India that nonetheless resemble counterparts in "traditional" religion. Important here,

Figure 3.5 A traditional South Indian kolam created with flowers marks the entranceway to the lobby in this otherwise ultramodern structure.

the state of Singapore also echoes, evokes, and feeds on the same social and mind power of myth, especially cosmogonic myth with all of the connections to religion—as Charles Long and others would argue—in the face of the state's strong commitment to secularism. Neither the state nor Sadhguru would openly call their carefully constructed spaces and their highly developed practices *religion*.

Paradoxically, *perhaps not*, as Sadhguru cautioned his audience in Singapore against the authorities of religion, he was about to consecrate a "112-feet tall ... statue" of Adi Yogi Śiva as the first teacher of yoga during the Mahashivaratri celebrations at his ashram in India the following month. The guest of honor at the rites for this controversial structure[7] was Prime Minister Narendra Modi, who would officially "unveil" the statue—*The Hindu* reported the event minute by minute (February 24, 2017). In his widely reported speech, the prime minister appeared to carefully avoid terms associated with *religion*—like Singapore, India is officially a secular state—but then the prime minister pours holy water from a copper pot (Sanskrit, *kumbha*) at the base of Adi Yogi in a typical gesture of consecration for a Hindu temple as the culmination of his visit. Yet on the Isha video[8] of the prime minister's early morning visiting to the Dhyanalinga temple that day, a staid voice declares that this entity in the sanctum "does not subscribe to any particular belief or faith and does not require any ritual prayer or worship, just sitting silently for a few minutes within the sphere of the Dhyanalinga is enough to make even those unaware of meditation experience a state of deep meditativeness" (5:50–6:04). It seems that in India, as both Devi and Vijay argued, Sadhguru appears to invoke God/gods and consecrate holy images with the full consonance of the chief executive of the Indian state with the added presence of the governor of Tamilnadu, and other "VIPs."[9] Here a confluence between the state and the guru and spirituality exists in full view of the press and the public—but the status of "religion" in this triad still remains ambiguous. I will return to Coimbatore with Sadhguru Jaggi Vasudev on his home turf.

Defining Spirituality vs Religion

In the first decade of the twenty-first century, the media reported the rising presence of "spirituality" signaling some drastic changes in the religious landscape—in America and worldwide. Reminiscent of the screaming black and red *Time* cover forty years before, "Is God Dead?" (April 8, 1966), a stunning *Newsweek* cover in gold, showing a young woman, arms raised, eyes closed, surrounded by glowing white aura, announced "Spirituality In America" (September 5, 2005). An almost simultaneous *Straits Times* issue headlined "GOD and US" under the sky-blue banner declaring, "Choices Galore" and "God? YES, Religion? NO," interspersed with advertisements for movies and a multicolumn blackened square with the white words "Liberating" above a radiant silver car (July 16, 2005). Ever since Jeremy Carrette and Richard King published their *Selling Spirituality: The Silent Takeover of Religion*, which was understood—incorrectly the authors have claimed[10]—as a full-throated denunciation of the then rising spirituality movements, academics entered the debate passionately in defense or denunciation of the book. Carrette and King warned of "a silent takeover of 'the religious' by contemporary capitalist ideologies by means of the increasingly popular discourse of 'spirituality'" (2005, 2). Set in the context of the contemporary Anglo-American scene, their concern with money changers in the temple of religion paralleled other caustic critiques of the unholy alliance of "spiritual" movements and money (Ward 2006, Goodchild 2002, York 2001, Lau 2000). On the other side, Mark Heelas and Linda Woodhead emerged as early defenders of the spiritual—mostly in the United Kingdom, taking over from earlier more appreciative works on rising spirituality in America in the 1990s (Wuthnow 1998, Roof 1999).

Heelas and Woodhead in *The Spiritual Revolution* immediately define two modalities of the *sacred* (their preferred general term): *life-as religion* and *subjective-life spirituality*:

> One of the great virtues of the language of 'life-as' and 'subjective-life' is that it enables us to sharpen up the distinction between 'religion' and 'spirituality' by distinguishing between life-as religion and subjective-life spirituality. The former is bound up with the mode of life-as—indeed it sacralizes life-as. Thus, the former

involves subordinating subjective-life to the 'higher authority' of transcendent meaning, goodness and truth, whilst the latter invokes the sacred in the cultivation of unique subjective-life.

5

Heelas and Woodhead passionately—with their own subjectivity barely below the surface—connect the rise of spiritual with the "subjectivization thesis," invoking Charles Taylor (2002) and others, and understand this "massive shift" as "a turn away from 'life-as' (life lived as a dutiful wife, father, husband, strong leader, self-made man, etc. to 'subjective life' (lived in deep connection with the unique experiences of my self-in-relation)" (2005, 2–3). For those who cling to religion, "what matters is living one's life-as a member of a community or tradition—whether it takes the form of a kinship system, a feudal system, a nation-state, or a particular religion" (2005, 3). Strong resonances of Peter Berger's *Sacred Canopy* become obvious: "Society assigns to the individual not only a set of roles but a designated identity. In other words, the individual is not only expected to perform as husband, father, or uncle, but to be a husband, a father, or an uncle" ([1967] 2011, 14). Heelas and Woodhead clarify that life-as religion and subjective-life are not synonymous with religion and spirituality because they do *not* include "spirituality" as part of, or as an increasing new pseudonym[11] for, religion, which is often the case, as with Catholic spirituality. However, they posit a "spiritual revolution" in progress in "the West" and claim that their clarification of life-as religion and subjective-life spirituality "renders it rigorous enough to be tested empirically."

Their test case is the small city market town of Kendal in northwest England, my case is a large globally connected cosmopolitan city-state, avowedly multireligious and multiethnic, in Southeast Asia. My goal is *not* to trace or prove a spiritual revolution. Rather, the Heelas–Woodhead delineation of self-development versus submission to a higher authority as members of a "community or tradition" forwards comparisons between the *macroworld* of the gurus and the *macroworld* of the state. Note again that Heelas and Woodhead add to their understanding of life-as, "whether it takes the form of a kinship system, a feudal system, a nation-state, or a particular religion" (3). So, they have made the move—or the slip—from *life-as religion* to submission to the authority of *either* a state or a particular religion—the same elision I have inferred about the state in Singapore and religiosity/sacrality. Within Singapore, the state imagines denizens as playing on/within an ordered stage; Jaggi Vasudev invoked the dimension of the "self" again and again both in his new book and on his own platform that evening in the Expo center. However, in this context, heed Chua Beng Huat's long discussion of the disavowal of Western liberalism with its overarching emphasis on individual rights by the PAP (Chua 2017, 157–75) and recall the Centre for Liveable Cities' *Urban Systems Studies*, where Lee Kuan Yew asserts over and over again that rapid economic progress "would not have been possible if the concept of private property and all the rules and regulations that have been elaborated over hundreds of years were complied with" (CLC 2014, 14). Individual rights that supersede the state and the needs of the whole are not protected in Singapore nor even lauded. Nonetheless, Sadhguru exhorted his Singaporean audience to take control of their lives, to become joyful by turning inward, the one *dimension* in everyone's control—thus turning to spatial imagery. He adjured submitting to religious "authorities" in the form of scripture or priests or dogmas—but note that on a second listening, he did *not* mention state or governmental authority here, although he does in India.[12] Here he did *not* elide subjective-life with political, individual self-determination, with a bill of rights. His was no declaration of independence from authority as citizen but only as persons acting, as Vijay had suggested, to suit the time and the place. What, then, is the interplay, the conflict, the intersection between the macrospaces—the overarching world—into which Ishas and other members of guru-lead spiritual movements enter when they attend a program or mediate during Sathsang? And *where* is the ever-present marketplace, the space of commerce—the raison d'être for the Expo center and that moneyed world and so much a part of the state's near sacred story of economic growth—which so disturbed the critics of spirituality?

In Singapore, these questions of space and authority take on an added dimension affected by the governmental regulation. Interestingly, most of the movements like Isha in Singapore use commercial, community, or educational spaces for meetings and programs, and Isha has just recently established a more permanent Isha Yoga Centre in Techplace II, a large commercial complex listed as a light industrial building.[13] Sporadically, Isha will use the multipurpose hall of a local temple, most recently for a program in Singapore for the goddess Bhairavi[14] installed in the newest temple at the headquarters in Coimbatore—I will return to these instances of "templing" in guru movements in a later chapter. Isha and other organizations work within the state regime of Singapore—both its ethos *and* its legal statutes governing not only temples but also all voluntary organizations. The Singapore cosmos—that I considered in the last chapter—forms an overarching regime, an affective atmosphere that subtly cajoles residents, but *official* regulation of religious activities also exists. While freedom of religion is guaranteed by the constitution and denizens can meet for religious/spiritual purposes in their own flats, the government carefully regulates and monitors public displays of religiosity. When a yoga, meditation, or "spiritual" group want to hold public events, solicit donations, or advertize, they are usually required to officially register as a "society" with a government agency called the Registry of Societies (ROSES)—a very long process, which until recently was under the Ministry of Community Development, Youth, and Sports, but now falls under the Home Ministry, whose major function is the "safety and security" of this city-state.[15] Most of this information is openly available on the massive website of the Singapore government (see Waghorne 2014, 192–6). Isha, however, is not a registered society, but nonetheless enrolled with another government agency as Isha Pvt. Ltd.—under ACRA (Accounting and Corporate Regulatory Authority)—and now in part as a nonprofit company, Isha Foundation.

The category of *Religion* is even more regulated, with very little available space for applicants proposing to construct a new temple, mosque (*masjid*), or church (see Sinha 2005). In the case of Hindu temples, these are regulated by the Singapore Hindu Endowments Board (SHEB) and mosques fall under the purview of the Majlis Ugama Islam Singapore (MUIS)—both government agencies again in the context of an avowedly secular state (see Sinha 2011, 233ff).[16] In fact, in Singapore, religious *places* are carefully demarcated but spiritual movements are left to wriggle within and between secular spaces. The PAP remains firmly within the secular realm—their brief experiment with teaching religions in the public schools as a character-building enterprise failed[17] (see Chua 2017, 58–60, Waghorne 2014, 195–6). Most guru-centered movements firmly reject categorization as a *Religion*; I was constantly questioned as I took courses and attended meetings about my title "Professor of Religion," which earned me little credit and some delicate scorn.

However, guru-centered movements, especially the increasing powerful Isha and the Art of Living,[18] while properly registered with the government, make claims on certain forms of public space that transcend, and act between, categories that the state regulates. Ironically, much of this shadow presence strongly resembles (and differs) from the same myth-like, real-and-imagined, space of the state—they are both playing, I propose, in the same spatial atmosphere perhaps best described by Henre Lefebvre and developed for the contemporary American and global context by Edward Soja as *Third Space*—I will return to this in detail in Chapter 5—but in this context *Third Space* describes that domain where both the conceptual and the actual meet, and where the imagination moves along with fantasy working with "reality." Again, like Barthesian notions of *myth*, *Third Space* remains ambiguous, slippery, undefined yet powerfully *present*, "a space that is common to all of us yet never able to be completely seen and understood" (Soja 1996, 56). The last chapter argued that the government of Singapore under the PAP created and constructed, through its own mythic rhetoric, a realm, a "stage"—although named as secular—with the same powers and energy as a religious cosmos.

Carefully watching and listening to Sadhguru's performance, some of the same modalities as the state-myth appear. Later, more examples and vignettes will complicate this, but Mix, Mingle, & Mediate in the Expo center reveals some striking parallels to the macrocosm constructed by Singapore's long-term ruling party as well as some crucial contrasts. Both rely on a rhetoric of pragmatics over hard and fast tenets—a keen sensitivity to time and place. Recall that the PAP extols order and planning but at the same time credits their success—especially in the hands of Lee Kuan Yew—with an emphasis on technique, nimble change, and a do-what-works modality. But such pragmatic technologies nonetheless have an overarching power. They turn to a myth-like *style* in a Barthesian sense—that aims *not* at consistency but a "nebulae" of meanings, "concept" fused with a "form." PAP aims to impress with concrete achievement more than debatable principles. Jaggi Vasudev's very term *inner engineering* and his constant refrain, "the function of the guru, contrary to popular belief, is not to teach, indoctrinate, or convert" (2016, 71), and "a guru is—a live road map. GPS: Guru Pathfinding System!" (*kl* 104–5): both play in the same field as business and everyday life. But while the PAP lives in the concrete—and literally builds in concrete—the gurus, especially Jaggi Vasudev, builds out of "vibrational energy," out of thin air. And, most importantly, both of these worlds—seen and unseen—whirl around a founding figure—the *guru* and the *minister*. Sadhguru *consecrates*, Lee Kuan Yew and his PAP *construct* but both make claims on space—public space *as well as* inner space with personal involvement. Do not forget the PAP slogans and the calls to change habits, *and* Jaggi's demands that his audience respond loudly. In the most recent National Day celebration the MC asked the audience to "Clap, clap, clap to wipe out mozzies" as giant puppet-mosquitoes collapsed onstage.[19]

Sadhguru consecrates. What does it mean to "consecrate" a home, an office, a street? Note, this is not the set-aside space of a temple or church but firmly placed within commercial and domestic space. What kind of macrocosmism does this create? How does this intersect—if at all—with the state cosmos? And equally important, how does this intersect with Religion? Sadhguru's "very powerful vibrant space" appears to transmute the secular sphere including the business world and the malls into *consecrated* spaces—usually only for specific times. And he is not the only guru engaged in such an enterprise. Unlike Hindu or Buddhist/Taoist temples, or mosques or churches—*sacred places* clearly mapped and allotted to the various religions by the government— "spiritual" movements occupy a much broader and more ambiguous spatial sphere. On one level, they create a vast inner world that strongly resists boundaries and expands to encourage a consciousness that englobes the universe—I will return to a much-used visualization practice with this aim. However, when this inner world goes public to teach, celebrate, or expand, movements like Isha in Singapore slip into meeting rooms in office buildings, malls, community centers, and educational and civic institutions. For example, the venues for Isha Yoga's Sathsang,[20] monthly meeting, during the times I have attended, has moved from the Gujarati Cultural Center in Little India, to the Multipurpose Hall of the Chai Chee Technopark, to the Global Indian International School, to Samtas Hall in the Management Development Institute of Singapore at Queenstown, to the Smart Innovation Center, and now to its own center in the Techplace II. I have also attended Isha programs at the far edge in the Island at the Woodlands Community Center. Art of Living used to hold all of their programs in the Chan Brothers Building opposite Bugis Junction shopping center before also securing a more permanent space in a shop-house on a commercial street at the edge of Little India. I have joined various events for other guru-centered/yoga groups at the Civil Service Club, Ceylon Sports Club, the Chinese Chamber of Commerce, and the bottom floor of the Ion Station mall.

So, what is the *macrospace* that gurus conjure within Singapore and how does it "fit" within this city-state with its own functioning but unacknowledged cosmos? I will provide another highly public event—and earlier: "Practical Wisdom for Personal Excellence" in Suntec City International Convention Centre (April 15, 2008), again a government-sponsored convention center. The massive multiuse complex near downtown allows for shifting spatial configurations and Sri Sri appeared in an auditorium assembled from portable bleachers with comfortable seating accommodating an audience of over 3,000.

"Art of Living Foundation Singapore invites you to a public talk by His Holiness Sri Sri Ravi Shankar"

I discovered this lecture on "Practical Wisdom for Personal Excellence" April 15, 2008 not through the usual posters, which appear all over Little India in Singapore, but by cell phone from my friend Saroj.[21] When I arrived in the cavernous Suntec Singapore Convention & Exhibition Centre, I found the large auditorium with poster boards that announced the lecture in English and Mandarin. The general audience sat in padded bleachers. The S$50 and S$100 seats occupied a ground area with individual chairs. I would guess that about 20 percent of the approximately 3,000 attendees were not Indian-heritage, perhaps more.

Most people sat reading the elegantly printed programs prepared for the evening. Events for the Art of Living (AOL) always draw a much more ethnically diverse population. I have seen monthly meetings and some events attended equally by ethnic Chinese Singaporeans and Indians, while Isha's constituency remains mostly within the Indian community, often from a new population of recently settled engineers, IT professionals, and banking executives mostly from South India.

A richly decorated divan, likewise reminiscent of a royal *gaddi* (throne), awaited the guru's arrival. Potted flowers and a waterfall, audible from where I sat, filled the stage. Two very large screens hung on both sides of the stage. Soon video clips appeared from the massive celebration of the twenty-fifth anniversary of the founding of Art of Living (on February 17–19, 2006).[22] Then the MC, dressed in a purple sari and speaking with an Australian accent, talked about the charitable work of the Art of Living Foundation. Finally, Guruji arrived, sat on the gaddi, listened to a choir singing Hindu *bhajans* (devotional songs), and then rose to speak. We were permitted to record and to freely photograph, unlike events in Isha Yoga.

He began by asking "What do we want? What is it that I want in my life? Do we get time to ask this question?" He wondered why we are so miserable because "you never put your eyes on something that is beyond what you see." Then he asked, "How can I make you smile a little more. You do not smile because you have never asked, 'What do I want?'" He then turned to our lack of self-confidence, "If the self is there, you have confidence." However, "We believe in weaknesses more than our strengths . . . we doubt love and believe in anger" but "Each one of us is a fountain of love." Then his talk moved to metaphors from science, saying that we needed to attend to our "dark matter. What you see is just a tiny space of energy, which you do not see. Can you image a vast space, you feel the breath in your lungs, feel the air, there is air, in the same way you are able to see [space] full of dark matter. Whole universe is dark space, dark energy, creation came out of light but now dark space is dancing energy everyday—this unseen energy." Again, the theme of tapping unseen energy arose.

The most interesting moment came during the question and answer period when someone in the large audience asked him, "How can the Art of Living make its courses acceptable to people of other religions such as in Malaysia and Singapore?" In his answer, Guruji (as he is usually addressed) declared that his yoga programs change neither the culture nor the religion of practitioners, "It's about life, it's about meditation . . . religion is about your name, your marriage, your death . . . this doesn't touch that aspect at all." Then he began joking about the popularity of Chinese food among many non-Chinese, telling his laughing audience, "Just by eating Chinese food you don't become Chinese . . . doing yoga, you do not become Indian." And yet, like Isha Yoga, the Art of Living promises deep personal *transformation*.

Later the AOL website reported the event in the following brief summary of Sri Sri Ravi Shankar's visit:

> That evening was guruji's main event in Singapore, the public talk. The event was named, 'Questions & Answers with Sri Sri Ravi Shankar', which was held at SUNTEC city Convention Halls 602&603. For the first time ever, AOL Singapore had a speaker of Parliament as a special guest for guruji's talk. Speaker of Parliament

Mr. Abdullah Tarmugi and his wife were at guruji's public talk as special guests. As usual guruji was welcomed into the hall by the Chinese Lion Dancers (a Singaporean trademark). The talk drew a huge crowd of 4,000 people. [I was later told 3,500.] Guruji taught many new techniques, answered many questions from the audience and did a meditation. The audience were left in bliss at the end of the talk.[23]

I have already related some of the content of that lecture and question and answer, but Guruji's *style* remains crucial. He lectured much like a seasoned professor in a large class; he moved around the dais from side to side usually leaning on the steel handrailing on the stairs (Fig.3.6). He spoke directly to those below but remained conscious even of the back row of the bleachers and would ask, looking up at them, "Are you with me?"

Figure 3.6 Guruji leans on the railing in the hall at Suntec City as he speaks directly to his devoted audience. Art of Living does not restrict photography and I thank them for freely allowing all to photograph.

His informal talk lasted less than forty-five minutes, and was filled with lively jokes, but repeated his teachings easily found on the Art of Living website or publications. So, while his audience listened attentively, they seemed to be here as much to see and be in his presence as to hear him. In the last hour, Guruji led meditation with all present. He spoke giving quiet instructions as we meditated in our seat for about twenty minutes as the light dimmed. Then, as the choir sang *bhajans*, he moved out into the audience. I was seated at the end of a row of chairs and was almost trampled as others ran to him to try to touch his feet. He seemed oblivious of my presence even as I stood almost face to face with him—but there was such a crush.

While Guruji engaged the audience "live," however, most people encountered him via the massive screens at the right and left sides of the stage. The videographer did not simply film the guru, he played with the image, changing backgrounds and creating arresting portraits of Guruji. At one point, the videographer cleverly switched to a blue background with a shadow around the guru's profile—very effective (Fig. 3.7). As I will later show with Sadhguru, Guruji adjusted his robes, very conscious of his image both onscreen and in the flesh. His clothing appeared carefully chosen for maximum but subtle effect. He wore white robes with an embroidered border over a long white shirt. The effect at first glance evoked an Indian holy man, but, on second look, the shawl draped over his right shoulder shaded into a Roman toga. The blued shadowed image on the screen turned Guruji's profile, with his classic beard and shoulder-length hair,

Figure 3.7 The videographer projects Guruji in profile with a blue background altering his live presence speaking in front of the auditorium.

into a simulacrum of the ubiquitous Warner Sallman "Head of Christ"[24] and portraits of Jesus in films like Ben-Hur. However, at the same time I could recognize ancient Indian images of the Buddha, especially in the drape of his garment if not the color.[25] Many in the audience would be aware that South India likely supplied the cloth for the ancient Roman toga: elegantly draped white fabric with rich borders survives in the formal attire of South Indian gentlemen. By visually invoking Jesus, the Roman period, and even the Buddha, Guruji's videographer created an aura of ancientness about him, at times providing an ethereal blue backdrop that erased the present. Yet at the same time, Guruji stood "live" in one of the most modern convention centers in the world.

Interestingly neither Guruji nor Sadhguru Jaggi Vasudev belongs to a clear lineage of masters, although Sadhguru claimed late in his career to have had a teacher in a previous life. I heard a rumor in Pudukkottai that both Jaggi and Ravi were college classmates in Bangalore. Both are rumored to have been teachers at one point—Ravi an English teacher, Jaggi an itinerant yoga teacher—but, true or not, these stories say a lot about their current roles as teachers. Both are understood to be self-made men who were educated at universities; who studied the sciences and the classic European humanities; only Sri Sri claims to have studied classical Sanskrit texts.[26]

Occupying Global Space

Unlike the Singapore state which always has an eye turned toward global opinions, world rankings and a sense of its position at the crossroads of trade, gurus, especially like Jaggi Vasudev and Sri Sri Ravi Shankar, aim for the whole world, their boundlessness defined not only as a meditative space but also a geographic expansiveness. I have heard Sadhguru described as "very ambitious" in the sense that "he wants the whole population to be transformed by this and touched by this and to be as blissful as he is." To mark the twenty-fifth anniversary of Isha, Sadhguru launched the *Anandha Alai, Wave of Bliss* throughout Tamilnadu; courses ran consecutively throughout the state. The Wave culminated with over a thousand recent initiates seated cross-legged as they listened to Sadhguru in Chennai.[27] Guruji Sri Sri Ravi Shankar's celebration of the silver jubilee of the Art of Living in Bangalore two years previously reportedly attracted "2.5 million people from more than 140 countries gather[ed] to meditate, to celebrate human values and to commit to building a One World Family."[28] While claiming to neither convert nor proselytize, Isha has centers from Coimbatore to London, Lebanon to Tennessee. Art of Living website includes a world map dotted with bases from Canada to Argentina, Portugal to Korea, Russia to New Zealand.[29] Building a One World Family or initiating Waves of Bliss are acts of sweeping global expansion.

Sri Sri Ravi Shankar and Sadhguru Jaggi Vasudev forcefully eschew language associated with *religious* conversion that demands what Heelas–Woodhead call *life-as* religion—a total recommitment that *does* change, as Guruji put it in Suntec City, "your name, your marriage." In the context of South and Southeast Asia, this sense of *religion* translates to your birthright socioreligious identity, the kind found on an identity card in Singapore. Guru movements, on the other hand, stand accused of laying the ground for a complete victory of another kind of shadow religious identity: full membership in the worldwide consumer society, especially in the anglophone world. Srinivas Aravamudan argues that gurus have long engaged in "proselytization" thorough the century-long rhetorical conjuring of "Guru English"—constructing a new spiritual vocabulary amenable to consumerism, mining "religion matter . . . one of the vast areas of standing reserve for commodification" (2006, 268). Now, under the term *spirituality*, respected savants within Religious Studies have risen up against "selling spirituality" to "raise awareness of the ways in which popular discourse about 'spirituality' tend to displace questions of social justice, being increasingly framed by the individualist and corporatists values of a consumer society" (Carrette and King 2005, x). Others warn, "this media-orientated consumer spirituality is inseparable from the desire to be diverted, entertained . . . and become one's own designer product" (Ward 2006, 185).

If the gurus' methods of spreading their message operates in the same *space* as advertising and their modus operandi mimics corporate style, then these masters shift religiosity into a new *space* destabilizing older domains of the social cohesion/cultural continuity conveyed by Religion—the subversion of *life-as*. Such gurus carve out a space of operations that slips in between markers of religious identity. My move here into spatial metaphors is deliberate and related to Guruji's fascinating unrehearsed response on religion: "While yoga is about 'life,' religion is about name, marriage and death." This is not a statement of doctrinal difference, this is rather topological—a matter of demarcations and intersections expressed, as I will show, primarily in visual forms within the very commodity culture that gurus stand accused of abetting.

I have many vignettes of lectures, convention-like meetings, and "courses" that are the platform from which guru organizations engage the broader public. True to their rhetoric, these events are never billed as invitations to convert to another Religion, but members always distribute brochures of the many "courses" offered by the organizations. I turn to one more example of major public appearances in which a guru took the starring role: the nationally televised nightlong celebration of Mahashivaratri (the great night of the Shiva) at the Isha Ashram near the industrial city of Coimbatore in South India (March 6, 2008). Here Sadhguru appeared on his own turf, and much on his own terms, within India. And here Vijay's and Devi's argument that gurus craft their messages to place and time took another turn—adding yet another layer to issues of the space of the state and of spirituality and religion. The interweaving of identity, religion, spirituality, and the media of national and international television was especially complex. But the first step back to India for Ishas in Singapore—and at the same time towards an expanded consciousness—begins at the monthly Sathsangs. Note how topological imagery of the expansion of consciousness melds with movement materially out toward India—but not just an India on the map but one that is also both *real and imagined*.

Heaven on Earth

The least public and most intimate meetings of guru movements are always held in a public hall, but nonetheless restricted: the Sathsang (*satsang*) remains open *only* to those who have taken the basic course, and hence are now "members." In the case of

Jaggi Vasudev, Sri Sri Ravi Shankar, and Amma-Bhagavan of the Oneness movement mentioned in Chapter 1, the headquarters of their organizations are in India where they have constructed grand temples and ashrams and universities.[30] So, the eyes of their Singaporean members turn across the Indian Ocean to another shore—and for some to the Isha USA center in Tennessee, a farther shore. But first let's listen to the voices and experiences of members gathering at the monthly Sathsangs for Isha. At every monthly Sathsang, those initiated into Isha Yoga and also those who have completed the online course always do their *kriya* (Sanskrit *kriyā*, practices) communally—a progression of yoga poses, breathing exercises, and chanting designed by Sadhguru Jaggi Vasudev.[31] The programs for the Sathsangs have varied over the years that I have attended in Singapore, currently from 2007 to 2018, but most have included these basic elements: the communal *kriya* (always), testimonies, "a time set aside with Sadhguru," visualization or another special practice, watching a recorded question and answer session set at the ashram or the center in Tennessee on the video monitor, and a shared potluck meal. In my intermittent decade-long (usually every summer) participation in the Sathsangs and in my conversations with my fellow participants, Ishas move between a sense of being-in-place both in Singapore *and* at the main ashram in Coimbatore, but also simultaneously transcending *place*. My descriptions here will combine the many times I have attended the Sathsang while in Singapore to protect the identities of participants and to remain within reasonable parameters of confidentiality.[32]

The first Sathsang that I attended after completing my weeklong Inner Engineering course included the communal *kriya* and reports from those who had attended programs at the ashram. I particularly noticed the "time set aside for us to be with Sadhguru," and when I asked, one of the leaders explained that Sadhguru sets the time according to the zones so that at that moment we were actually *there* to feel his presence—not to speak telepathically or verbally communicate—but to be in his company. A feature added at the next meeting and at most other Sathsangs was a guided meditation by Sadhguru through a CD. I would experience this same visualization exercise in changing forms over the following years. Sadhguru asked us to imagine ourselves in the garden gradually rising above the ground and little by little moving up and up and finally moving horizontally to another part of the world, a forest where we then moved down into a clearing and spotted a thatched hut and inside found our "Spiritual Master" who then filled our whole body with the "light of creation." Then we were asked to imagined three *wishes* (I cannot recall the exact term)—projects that we wanted to accomplish, a short-term, mid-term, and long-term. We were to imagine these fulfilled and feel and express the deep gratitude for this grace. At this moment, and even before, some people began to laugh loudly with delight; I also heard crying, and then others shouted, "shambo, shambo" and even "Shiva shambo." Sadhguru then guided us back into the garden and the shouting stopped.[33] We had traveled far from somewhere to somewhere but now we were back in Singapore.

Usually at this point in the Sathsang, Meditators (or Ishas), as they are called rather than followers or members, are asked to share their experiences with their own practice or other Isha programs. They speak in choked voices of regained health and increased energy: "My practices have become so precious to me . . . the number of things I can fit in and balance has tremendously increased."[34] Another Isha had returned to India to take her ailing mother to the Inner Engineering program at the ashram: "I was not expecting such a dramatic change would come in a few days, but I had complete faith in Sadhguru and complete faith in the program." Many who attended programs offered personally by Sadhguru at the ashram relate profound spiritual episodes: "I could not stop crying, a feeling of love, of gratitude and relief, and acceptance." Another young man breathlessly related an experience when Sadhguru led a program at the Isha center in Tennessee: "I could see everything so brightly ... I was God and God lived through me and everyone else was also me." Speaking of his experiences at the ashram in India, a tearful meditator proclaimed: "Everybody is so joyous, it's a heaven on earth."[35]

In these testimonials, eyes are turned toward the centers—mostly the main ashram in South India—where heaven resides on earth. All who hear are reminded of the expanse of the organization and the power of the guru. To anyone used to hearing "testimony" in churches, or who reads of evangelical conversion experiences during mass revivals, this sounds startlingly familiar: the healing, the changed outlook on life, the new beginning, the sensitivity to others and to the world, a new closeness to the divine within. Yet important here, while the same format in an evangelical church would attest to a deep turn toward Jesus as a personal saviour *and* to commitment to Christianity as a religion, Ishas never understand these experiences in this way. The space of the Sathsang is expansive, moving Ishas into the presence of Sadhguru and to experiencing travel that takes them both within themselves and yet somewhere beyond, moving them to that "heaven on earth," the Isha Yoga Center near Coimbatore, India. And, thither I went in 2008 during my full year in the city-state, to experience the Mahashivaratri.

Mahashivaratri in the Velliangiri Hills

Saiva temples throughout Tamilnadu in South India remain open for twelve hours of vigil, often including music and chanting, to celebrate Mahashivaratri, the great night of the god Shiva.[36] The festival has recently gained mass popularity in many temples and even online. Sadhguru Jaggi Vasudev's own rejuvenation of Mahashivaratri was awash in the new media as it revived the old. At the central ashram in India, officially the Isha Yoga Center, his spectacular celebration conjoined traditional elements with both classical South Indian music and Vedic rock from famous players, all televised for a broad audience. Here the grand arched steel and glass ceiling of the Expo center gave way to South Indian thatch, the village palm fronds, held together by hemp cords and bamboo poles in a massive structure built, as is traditional for celebrations in South India, within a few days and then removed quickly. Incidentally, the seating and configuration of both Suntec City and the Expo center are also easily changed, although the steel beams and portable bleachers may seem less transient.

I attended this spectacular event with my photographer-husband and several other Ishas from Singapore in March of 2008. My Isha yoga Teacher (this is a special status within Isha requiring extensive training), Tina, had arranged for our accommodation in the guest cottages on the ashram grounds.[37] As we drove from the busy business-centred Coimbatore to this ashram, the view from the narrow road became idyllic as the white hills—the literal translation of the Velliangiri range (Tamil, *Veḷḷiyaṅkiri Malai*)—emerged on the horizon. Sadhguru located the Isha center here in the foothills with the conviction that these mountains had sheltered seers in the past. Later, during the Mahashivaratri, he described the setting as "a space, which is 100 percent dedicated to the spiritual process ... being in such proximity ... to the Velliangiri peaks which is referred to as the Kailash of the South"—a southern version of Shiva's celestial mountain home.

We arrived two days before the event, giving me time to talk with many volunteers and permanent resident renunciants. Here among the guests at the cottages, the global reach of Isha was apparent. I met two Euro-American women, one from Michigan and the other from New York City. Both had met Sadhguru in the United States. The Michigan woman had resided here for over two months and worked at the Isha Home School run by the ashram, a residential school.[38] The woman from New York had met the Sadhguru for one of his talks and had had a transforming experience. Her mother is an Episcopal priest and very open. She still considered herself a Christian and said that she now understood so many of Jesus' well-known statements so much more deeply than before. This New Yorker emphasized that Isha was not a religion but a science, a technology for transformation. I asked both if they now thought of Jesus as a guru, and they thought a bit and said, "Yes!" I also met with a volunteer, an American woman of Telegu heritage from Cincinnati. She had just finished her BA from Northwestern in biology and made the decision to come here and undergo Teacher training. Her entire family belonged to Isha, but she became so enthralled with Sadhguru that, in spite of her family wanting her to go to medical school, she came here thinking, "If I do not do this now, I may never have the chance." She reported that, in the US at that time, mostly South Indians followed Isha. Only recently has it spread beyond the Indian community. She also noted that, in India, Isha extended only in Tamilnadu and then in Bombay via English and Tamil. At that time in 2008, Isha had had no Hindi-speaking Teachers and offered no courses in North India. So, ironically, Sadhguru was settled at the Isha Institute of Inner-sciences in the hills of Tennessee in 2006,[39] before his organization reached North India, according to this Cincinnati Isha. She planned to return to the US as a formal Teacher of Isha yoga. I soon realized that the international ethos at the cottages was part of a complex multileveled world here in the Velliangiri hills.

The innovative architecture and the complex organization of the ashram would be a story in itself, but several incidents and conversations on my rounds revealed certain sensibilities—a developing ethos that seemed to hover over this "heaven on earth." My experiences at the Dhyanalinga Yogic Temple, the focal point of the ashram, revealed that the temple operated at dual levels. An elliptical dome constructed of brick and mud mortar, this temple contains only a single huge *lingam* (Sanskrit/Tamil, *liṅgaṃ*, pillar, the aniconic image of Shiva) in a base shaped not as the traditional *pitha* (Sanskrit, *piṭha*, seat, representing the female element) but as a coiled snake with the most delightful smile (so it seemed to me). A series of little niches, meditation coves, are arched into the walls around the circumference of this amazing structure. I visited in the morning for the offering of sound, and then the next afternoon for meditation, and finally to offer a brass and copper deepa (Sanskrit, *dīpa*) with a cobra on the rim echoing the temple, a unique craft item purchased at the adjacent store. When I reached the stairs, someone immediately took me aside and arranged my vessel with a flower and neem and adding the wick, which I filled with ghee. Trying not to spill the ghee, I climbed down the steep stairs and, at the temple entrance, someone brought a tray with a matchbox. I carefully lit the deepa and entered the temple. The swami, one of the permanent renunciant residents of the ashram, a tall man of European heritage, directed me to circumambulate the *lingam* and leave the lamp with the others at the corner—an innovative form of offering in this temple without priests. It would be returned to me the next day.

Later, I noted the architectural elements of the temple, especially the entrance Sthamba[40] (Sanskrit, *stambha*, a pillar with its fours sides covered with Hindu, Buddhist, Christian, Sikh, Confucian, Taoist, and Jain emblems and the Star of David, reminding me of the covers of World Religions textbooks). When I asked about these emblems, I was direct to a much-harried swami in white on the other side of the veranda. He emphasized that they did not represent the religions, suggesting that the temple was not an amalgam of religions, but rather this Sthamba "was meant to indicate a welcoming of everyone." He then proffered a distinction between religion and spirituality, saying that religion was "about the group." Religion was only meant as a "preparation for spirituality," but had now become a matter of group consciousness. I heard echoes of this all weekend.

Later, inside the temple, I noticed a pattern of local visitors and possibly Indian tourists dressed in silk saris and men in relaxed business attire using the temple as a typical temple: they prostrated and circumambulated, but seldom sat for long. On the other hand, the meditators sat in the niches or on the floor for long periods in meditation—about a third to a half of these meditators were non-Indian, while many of the others looked by their clothing to be nonresident Indians living aboard. The distinction between the two uses of the temple played out later during the Mahashivaratri and many times throughout our stay. The distinction became bitterly clear to me in reverse at the snack stand called the Pepper Pot Café. I wanted some cookies and water and stood there with a rupee note in my hand as several people pushed in front of me while the woman attendant ignored me and served them. I finally said something in Tamil and she condescended to take my money.

On the evening of the Mahashivaratri, a large *pandal* (Tamil, *pantal*, "awning"), a temporary pavilion made of the traditional palm fronds, now stood in the center of a fenced area. The event again was divided into two tiers—those seated within the *pandal* and those outside who could watch the event on large video screens set up in the field with concession stands around the perimeter. That area had a carnival feel—with families making a picnic on the ground of packed red dirt (Fig. 3.8). None of these folks looked poor: the tickets had to be purchased in advance and were costly by Indian standards, so, obviously, many families chose to see the event "live" but via televideo. They were segregated from those within the *pandal* behind ropes and fenceposts which stayed in place until the early morning. As I walked behind along the border, many stood along the fencing posts looking into *pandal* to catch the performances live.

Taking our assigned seats inside the *pandal*, I began to chat with a businessman seated behind, who promptly told me that religion was about fear, fear of loss of life and wealth,

Figure 3.8 Families wait just outside the *pandal* to see Sadhguru on the screen erected there but also to catch a glimpse of him in person on the stage. Photo by Dick Waghorne used with the kind permission of Isha Yoga.

etc. He said that this was what Sadhguru says. I asked him what the difference was with spirituality, and he said that was about answers to life's serious questions. Once again, I found in this casual conversation a shared sensibility, though *never* part of the teachings during the Isha courses: ordinary people have *religion* but he and others in Isha had *spirituality*—something different. Just as we settled in, Tina came to take us to much better seats very close to the dais just behind the major donors—a much better seat for photography which we much appreciated. Earlier my husband had kindly received special permission to photograph the event provided that he submitted the card for review; we readily agreed. In front of the stage at the center of the *pandal* an enormous TV camera on a long arm swivelled, almost snakelike, around the room (Fig. 3.9) Sometimes I could feel its eyes on me—this happened especially as I fought sleep late in the night. The entire event was broadcast on Aastha TV and Aastha International as well as RAJ music and RAJ digital, and webcast live to Isha centers globally.

The Mahashivaratri at the ashram was a carefully staged event. I say this not as an accusation but rather in appreciation. Sadhguru's very savvy staff of renunciant

Figure 3.9 Ultramodern TV camera swings eying the audience and the performers contacting with the traditional thatched roof overhead. Photo by Dick Waghorne used with the kind permission of Isha Yoga.

brahmacharies[41] had very carefully arranged the stage to carry multiple messages to suit a widely divergent audience, which included ardent meditators, curious wellwishers, spectators, and devotees of Jaggi as a traditional guru. The arrangement within the *pandal* reflected this. Along the center of the *pandal* and leading up to the seat reserved for Sadhguru at the side (only a few rows in front of me) was a long trough running below the seating in the *pandal* and opening to the public seated outside. At the end of this subterranean walkway, an altarlike table stood to collect the offerings of flowers, mostly lotuses, that people brought for their guru, sitting for much of the performances just above this table. Later in the night this walkway opened and a steady stream of devotees filed up to the front: some offered flowers, some simply offered their obeisance (Fig. 3.10).

The stage set was a masterful evocation of traditional and very contemporary imagery that could be read on multiple levels. If the large TV camera could be ignored, the atmosphere might be described as *studied traditional*. Everything onstage was constructed of natural common material: bamboo, straw, and wood. Three small

Figure 3.10 Devotees of Sadhguru offer lotuses to him as they would a more traditional guru. Photo by Dick Waghorne used with the kind permission of Isha Yoga.

pavilions made of bamboo with rounded thatched roofs that seemed to evoke the dome of the Dhyanalinga Yoga Temple stood onstage. These became the setting for the music performers and also for Sadhguru when he offered his discourses and meditations; at the far left (audience view) was a wooden platform for the larger musical ensembles. All of the smaller decorative elements inside the pavilions, hanging and large standing bronze deepas (Tamil, *viḷakku*), are items in common use in South Indian temples and homes. Just inside of the central pavilion was a wooden chair the size of a gaddi but constructed of rough-honed wood that was at once simple yet regal—such seats are commonly used in Tamilnadu for major renunciant gurus and were once used by kings. The same style wooden gaddi with a more modern flare would be echoed a decade later in the Expo center in Singapore.

Everything was on time. Sadhguru arrived dressed in a traditional while dhoti with a shawl arranged on one shoulder with the other bare, and wearing a saffron turban. He greeted the audience with a namaste (hands folded in greeting) and ascended the stage—I spotted him arranging his robes before the light hit the stage. I noticed that he changed his clothing later in the night, but this first attire, unlike Sri Sri Ravi Shankar's robes, remained within the same South Indian idiom as the stage setting. Nods to European or American styles and contemporary technology did not occur within overt religious forms but rather within the music and Sadhguru's many references to physics and neurosciences throughout his discourses, which punctuated the flow of events during the night.

During the long night, Sadhguru would sit in the first row of the audience for the musical performance, but rise and take his place on the gaddi for his discourses, or move to the front of the stage to lead everyone in chanting mantras or in short meditation sessions. To begin the event, he rose and began chanting in a wonderful clear voice the mantra appropriate for this night, "Om Namah Shivaya" (Sanskrit, *Om Namaḥ Śivāya*, "adorations to Shiva"). Speaking in slow, deliberate, flawless English, which an announcer later translated into equally flawless textbook Tamil, Sadhguru began a discussion of Shivaratri. He explained this night was "significant to all those on the spiritual path and to all those yet to take the conscious step toward their spiritual nature." This dark night just before the new moon creates "a natural upsurge in the human system." He urged his audience "to make use of the assistance that nature is providing for one's spiritual growth." And, to assist everyone to stay awake, to keep their spines erect during the night, Isha would provide "some of the best voices in the country to keep you awake. This is my vision, my blessing that this night should not pass without your moving at least one notch higher in your awareness and your wellbeing."

The music was calculated to do just this. After a classical South Indian performance, the music began to rock. American drums shared the stage with the Indian *mrudungam* and *tambala* in "Vedic rock"—religious lyrics set to a fusion of rock, jazz, and Indian popular Bollywood music. As the night wore on, the energy level of the performers, but also of Sadhguru, increased. After some sets, he moved back up onstage and began to chant-sing, "Shiva Shankara." The sheer emotional energy of his voice rivalled the best *otuvars*[42] and priests that I have heard in temples. Unlike the rather somber audience almost a decade later in Singapore, the audience enthusiastically joined the chanting. The young woman beside me, a very educated middle-class person, began to shake almost uncontrollably in her seat. We were pledged to keep our eyes closed but I could feel and hear others among this well-healed section of the floor also in ecstasy—which also commonly happens during Sathsangs in Singapore when Sadhguru chants. But a later conversation with another Isha gave me the impression that some meditators were not comfortable with such displays; again, some Ishas are likewise uneasy with such open displays of rapture in Singapore. That night, Sadhguru pointedly encouraged exuberance, even making fun of a comment posed from the online audience that this celebration was not serious, and he later joined in the dancing (Fig. 3.11).

For the final prayer, he appeared again onstage but wearing a long-sleeve shirt and with flowing embroidered shawls (Fig. 3.12) His face mirroring passion, he looked the perfect devotee of Shiva.[43] However, other elements spoke of a closer relationship. The gaddi located inside the central pavilion had hanging brass votive lamps mirroring where the deity inside a temple would be placed. During the night, a questioner, again online and read by an announcer, asked, "Are you Shiva?" Jaggi Vasudev's answer was that he was not devoted to Shiva, he never worshipped at temples, but Shiva was always

Figure 3.11 Sadhguru begins to dance as the event reaches a crescendo. Photo by Dick Waghorne used with the kind permission of Isha Yoga.

present in his life. No, he was not Shiva, but only a strand of hair on the deity's head. Toward the end, many began to dance—including me, much to the horror of some proper ladies behind me. Then the Isha brahmacharies also began to dance, and finally Sadhguru took to the stage and danced in a pose striking like the Shiva Nataraja, Shiva in his cosmic dance. There was nothing staid about his event, nor anything unmanaged. More than a decade later, the Mahashivaratri on this night remains one of my deepest experiences.

The next day I had the opportunity to reflect on the event with a knowledgeable person at the ashram. I directly described my impressions through the night: Sadhguru's very brilliant manipulation of Shiva images allowed both his person and the event to function on multiple levels. I saw both devotional persons who understood Sadhguru as a divine figure and others who read him as providing spiritual guidance and a source of energy. However, I no longer thought that this division always mapped onto class or educational differences. Multiple signs pointing *both* to his potential equivalence with Shiva *and* his visual claim to traditional guruhood seemed apparent.

Figure 3.12 As the dawn rises, Sadhguru offers the final prayer. Photo by Dick Waghorne used with the kind permission of Isha Yoga.

Much to my surprise, my interlocutor agreed that the powerful invocation of spiritual imagery was done with full consciousness in order to further Sadhguru's mission to attract people at all levels of perception: "I would not even stop at consciousness, I would say there is a science behind this." My kind conversation partner averred that some people at the ashram would be "uncomfortable with my saying this, but many others would agree." In the end, "you get to touch so many people so deeply . . . if I have something important to say, then I need important means to touch them." This committed Isha openly admitted that some may see this as manipulation but "I would say that of all the people who came last night, many people would have transited from where they are . . . because of this entire grand staging." Then our discussion turned to those devoted people who streamed through the burrow. "Sadhguru is not unwilling to be engaged on those terms . . . there is a certain channel that opens up which Sadhguru can make use of to make things happen." Suddenly I realized that even the two levels of approach to the guru, and likely to the Dhyanalinga Temple, were pointedly allowed to coexist within the broader ethos of spirituality.

Jaggi Vasudev remains deeply embedded within South Indian religious imagery at the same time that he conjoins traditional religious practices and spirituality on one level, yet affirms their difference at another. He who does not pray in temples—even tells of his early refusal to attend temples with his parents—has designed, built, and consecrated his own. While his meditators, and even some of his Teachers and Swamis, see a clear distinction between religion and spirituality, he willingly accepts the role of the guru for those who are devoted but are not Isha meditators. He actively utilizes the visual and aural vocabulary of Indian devotional and ritual practices to attract people to take that first step, as he puts it, "into boundlessness."

One of his earliest disciples, Swami Nisarga, describes Sadhguru in his introduction to *Mystic Musings* as "very unorthodox, if not wild and totally devoid of conformity" (Vasudev 2003, iii). On the one hand, his nonconformity attracted many of his early educated Indian disciples as well as those non-Indians who joined him from the US and elsewhere, while on the other, his fascinating play of tradition enticed another population, who themselves remained in between. As Swami Nisarga says, "Even in a time when there is great versatility in people's understanding of the word 'spiritual', it is hard to fit Sadhguru into the category of Spiritual Master in the established sense of the word" (i).[44] Understanding these newer-style gurus like Jaggi Vasudev and Sri Sri Ravi Shankar becomes an inescapable art of knowing the power of their appeal, the force of their form of transformation, and the space that they occupy.

The Grays of Religion, Spirituality, and the Contours of the State

Turning to the language of natural science or psychology in their discourses, gurus like Sri Sri Ravi Shankar and Jaggi Vasudev nevertheless claim much of the terrain on which "Religion" operates: the enhancement and transformation of life through a carefully designed practice and an outlook on the nature of persons and their interconnects to the cosmos. When someone takes a class, and begins in the practices, they receive more than just a technique; they are, *in some sense*, bought into newer sensibilities. Yet none are asked to leave his or her "Religion"—as the presence of Euro-Americas, still claiming their Christian identity, attests. In a study of such movements in the US, Lola Williamson argues: "Taken together they have enough family resemblances and enough differences from other religions to be considered a new category" (14). Naming this category has proven difficult. In his study of the United Kingdom, Paul Heelas speaks of "Spiritualities of Life"; Williamson, working in the United States, writes of "Hindu-inspired meditation movements." But here the issue of religion, spirituality, and these new guru-centered movements need to be contextualized *within Asia*, where many of these organizations originate.

Recall Guruji's ad hoc definition of *Religion*: "Religion is about your name, your marriage, your death." Within a very Indian and Southeast Asian framework, birth determines identities and is closely linked with both religion and ethnicity (i.e., culture), what Robert Hefner calls "ethnoreligion" (2001, 37–42). To convert to a *religion* in a formal sense often means taking another name and accepting new limits in marriage partners. In a world of arranged marriages, this denies parents a crucial part role in their children's lives—a very serious change of social and even national identity. The government of Singapore presumes discrete, religious "Traditions" and bounded ethnic identities closely connected to religious affiliation—especially in the case of the minority communities of Malays, who must remain Muslim, and Indians, who are presumed Hindu with a small minority of Muslims. In Singapore, I was shocked to find a line asking for my religion on my application for a visiting research position at the National University. The expected answer was my natal religion, which indeed was obvious in my seldom-used full birth name, Joanne Mary. In both Singapore and South India, *religion* is about bounded identities. When Sadhguru promises "boundlessness" and Guruji moves his *kriya* into the realm of culinary choice—Indians eating Chinese food in the mix and match world of urban Asia—both gurus are acutely sensitive to the world of markers, borders, and emerging new spaces in between.

In the last chapters of *Selling Spirituality*, Carrette and King acknowledge the existence of "new forms of spirituality grounded in an awareness of our mutual interdependence, the need for social justice and economically sustainable lifestyles may yet prove our best hope for resisting the capitalistic excesses of neoliberalism and developing a sense of solidarity and global citizenship in an increasingly precarious world" (182). This description fits Isha Yoga and Art of Living. Sadhguru's offered his Mahashivaratri as a universal hope for wellbeing and spiritual growth to the world at large. Guruji's lecture in Singapore sounded his concern for the environment and for universal peace and understanding. Both organizations work for welfare of the poor, in health services, in planting trees, and in advocacy for education. Currently Jaggi Vasudev continues his *Project GreenHands* to replant deforested areas, especially in South India, and has launched a major environmental project *Rally for Rivers*, now "Hosting Multiple Classical Dance And Music Events Across United States" in support of "reviving the dying rivers of India." This ultra technosavvy website features an inset video with Sadhguru's stunning voice singing, chanting, and proclaiming with beating drums as a crowd forms a map of India holding river-blue cardboard squares.[45]

Nonetheless, Carrette and King miss a crucial point: at the same time that Isha and Art of Living may affirm the value of social uplift and economic justice, *neither* equates their work with "resisting the capitalistic excesses of neoliberalism." They are not Gandhian in their critique of industrialization or contemporary consumer capitalism. Certainly, like many contemporary new gurus, they speak out against the evils of extreme materialism. But in the context of Singapore and South India, Isha Yoga and Art of Living are at home with capitalism and with its world of advertizing, business styles, and conscious manipulation of the new media. I go ever further here: they use the very spaces created by the *newly* successful Asian capitalism as their workplace and workshop.

To put this another way: in South India and in Singapore, the place of religion in the public sphere has moved only recently into what Charles Taylor calls "the post-Durkheimian age" which occurred for Europe and the United States in the postwar era. For Taylor—who interestingly framed his theory via William James, *Variety of Religious Experience*—the "postwar slide" into this period in the West meant "either gradually releasing people to be reconstructed into the fractured culture or, in the case where the new consumer society has quite dislocated the earlier outlook, of explosively expelling people into this fractured world" (2002, 106), earlier asserting, "The spiritual, as such, is no longer intrinsically related to society" (102–6). Taylor, like Carrette and King, missed two key elements. In urban areas of South India and in ultraurban Singapore, when people slide into the consumer world—joyfully, after long watching the "West" with once seemingly limitless resources—the gurus are standing there offering another kind of connectedness that is at the same time "boundless." And for many in this newer world, the tight old family bonds, the demands of rituals, or the strictures of caste rules are too recent to be romantic.

Looking again these events that span a decade—Sadhguru at "Mix, Mingle, and Meditate" at the Expo center in 2017, Guruji in Suntec City, and Sadhguru at Mahashivaratri in 2008—all assume a "fractured world." Sri Sri Ravi Shankar's videographer even played with a fracturing technique, erasing backgrounds, highlighting Guruji's head—at once both conflating yet splitting the "live" from the video. Again, at the Mahashivaratri, the same splitting allowed some to watch Jaggi in the flesh, but many—like those in the back rows of the Suntec City auditorium—saw him onscreen, as did many others on TV or televideo. Both gurus carefully played with their screen image, in dressing and in staging. Onstage at the ashram, on the dais at Suntec City, and on a platform in the Expo center, both took their seats on the gaddi of the traditional guru right with the eye of the video camera fixed on them and projecting their image to the audience at the rear or out into the yard or out to the world. They both played in a world that Philip Goodchild might call, "excessive meditation" in lieu of "real piety" (2002, 242). But before condemning this as mere consumer hype, note how the ease of movement from the living body of the guru to his technological reconstruction onscreen fitted the juxtaposition of rich traditional materials with very new but equally familiar technological equipment—*both* of which Asia now excels in making and exporting. These very forms, this very technological savvy, is modern South India's pride conjoined with a consciousness of the brilliant technology that once built the still-standing Bṛihádīśvara Temple in Tanjore in 1010. When savants like Carrette and King or Taylor or Ward condemn raging capitalism, they ignore the important reality that middle-class urbanites in Singapore or India, joined by Chinese and Koreans, are eating our capitalistic lunch and enjoying it.

The new gurus provide their own kind of "conversion" into a new world, as Amanda Lucia has recently shown for many yoga movements (2018). They see no need to convert their meditators into another bounded space, another religion, rather they seek to bring a variety of people already on the edge into something old, something new, and even something borrowed—and in Guruji's case literally something blue. Gauri Viswanathan, in her passionate preface to *Outside the Fold*, takes issue with the influential Subaltern theorists who do not take "belief" seriously, and asks, "what possibilities for alternate politics of identities might be offered by conversion as a gesture that crosses fixed boundaries between communities and identities?"(1998, xviii). Perhaps the gurus, for all their showmanship and spectacles, are performing the very slow conversion that Carrette and King seem to fear: the parting of borders, for just a moment, just a crack to re-form that *space-between* into a space for what they call "transformation" or "boundlessness." This space is not for everyone, but it's there. And they do reach out; they send out, they get out their messages on the air, in posters on corners all over Singapore, and the world.

Within the Indian nation, however, the *space-between* occupied by gurus has recently moved into the public sphere—which resembles civil society in a very Indian sense. In the *Daily O*,[46] a commentator and longtime Art of Living member, M. Rajaque Rahman, (2016)[47] openly hailed this new "third space"—his term—created under the regime of Prime Minister Modi for "unofficial players" to interject moral heft, not between government and established religion as in Europe, but between a divisive politics coupled with deeply divided religious identities. Hence "politically neutral leaders can help reduce the trust deficit and act as the balancing force between the Left and Right of the Indian polity. The Modi government's efforts to engage spiritual leaders in matters of governance is a welcome sign." This Muslim-born follower of Guruji provides a genealogy back to ancient times for such government-guru interactions: "Spirituality used to be a vital aspect of governance in ancient India with pious kings regularly turning to their raja gurus (spiritual guides) to seek guidance on matters of administration." He then excitedly goes on to declare:

> In the short span of his prime ministership, Modi has shown enough indications that he intends to leverage India's spiritual wealth as a powerful diplomatic tool. He has already won a battle for India by getting the United Nations to declare June 21 as International Yoga Day. India's long tradition of spirituality and its impeccable track record of uniting people is a ray of hope for the beleaguered world today. However, this hasn't been effectively purveyed so far. On the strength of her spiritual prowess, India can shape a new world order.

The intense nationalism here seems to bely the internationalism of both Sadhguru and Guruji but strongly reflects the prime minister's speech before the United Nations calling yoga "an invaluable gift of ancient Indian tradition" as he rose to urge the adoption of June 21 as "International Day of Yoga"—interestingly on the summer solstice.

Spaces-between are not always easy to occupy neutrally: the landscape is tricky here. That same multilayered modality that Sadhguru displayed in Singapore and in Coimbatore still holds: the inner world is beyond borders, but the land of India, especially Coimbatore and the ashram, retains a special status. However, under Modi's regime, the status of the *spiritual* as differentiated from *religion*, I would argue, materializes as a nationalist banner hoisted by "spiritual prowess," as Rahman puts it, and on the power of star gurus. Especially conspicuous here are both Sri Sri Ravi Shankar and Jaggi Vasudev. The *Hindustan Times*, while reporting on Sri Sri's controversial 2016 World Cultural Festival[48] held on the banks of the Yamuna River near New Delhi, bemoaned the special status of "rockstar gurus," who have "made meditation popular among India's emerging middle class, which ... seems to be discovering the basics of spirituality." Then the reporter astutely comments, "corporatisation of spirituality has a non-controversial and yet powerful pull that few can ignore. Social work, charity, healthy living and respect for heritage come together in a potent mix to create a new soft power of gurus" (Mahadevan 2016).

Prime Minister Modi, posthumously honoring his own guru,[49] appears to have attempted to maintain his party's religio-nationalism by shifting from the highly charged espousal of the *Hindu* religion towards a glorification of *Indian* spirituality. Over and over again, the prime minister couples the spiritual with the ancient power of

India while decoupling religion and spirituality: "Hailing spirituality as India's strength, Prime Minister Narendra Modi on Tuesday lamented that some people tend to link it to religion and asserted that the two are very different."[50] The *Common Yoga Protocol* published for the first International Day of Yoga by AYUSH (the new Ministry of Ayurveda, Yoga & Naturopathy, Unani, Siddha and Homeopathy) affirms with official panache: "The science of Yoga has its origin thousands of years ago, long before the first religion or belief systems were born" (2). In the Indian context, then, spirituality, gurus, provide the "soft power" for the state—they are not boundless but very much framed by a remade guru-government axis under the banner of spiritual-but-not-religious.

However, very recently the Babri Masjid-Ram Janmabhoomi controversy, centered very much on a disputed *place* and two *religions*, has reached final arguments before the Supreme Court of India with Sri Sri Ravi Shankar publicly attempting to use his soft power to effect the compromise between Hindu and Muslim claimants as earlier suggested by the court—at this point unsuccessfully.[51] While not directly involved, Jaggi Vasudev has defended his fellow guru, as acting properly in his role as a concerned citizen of the nation, exercising his "rights and responsibilities."[52]

Modi's International Day of Yoga captured a day on the United Nations calendar, but his presentation of yoga moved between nationalism and globalism as a cultural claim on a broadly popular movement, which his ministry presented as prior to the formation of any religions. The Babri Masjid-Ram Janmabhoomi controversy returns to *Religion* and *bhoomi* (from Sanskrit *bhūmi*) —land, soil, earth, place, extent, limit[53]— once again constructing hard borders within the Indian state. On their home turf, gurus or prime ministers find riding the lines between religion and spirituality precarious in the Indian context. Compare two images of the prime minister just a few years apart. The first International Day of Yoga, Narendra Modi dressed in white *kurta* and *pajamas* (long shirt with loose cotton pants) with a long *dupatta* (scarf) in the Indian tricolors as he sits in lotus position to lead yoga practices on the mall in Delhi.[54] In another photo, taken as he campaigned in the Gujarati state elections in December 2017, Modi posed with his BJP party leaders in a *kurta* but now with a gold embroidered bright saffron shawl, bold saffron turban, and holding a gilded sword.[55] *Place* is not so easily displaced here, and the soft power of new-style guru Sri Sri Ravi Shankar so far has failed to broker a compromise. Rather, other kinds of gurus, the saffron-clad heads of traditional maths, are elected to public office with promises of a temple in Ayodhya in Uttar Pradesh—i.e., Shri Yogi Adityanath Mahant (head) of a major monastery and chief minister of the state. Soft power at the moment appears countermanded by hard power, and traditional religious authorities are not a dead thing of the past in contemporary India, as Sadhguru's hasty requiem in the Expo hall in Singapore supposed.

But what of Singapore, where religion in the form of temple, masjid, and church continue to mark the landscape. These institutions are thoroughly under state power and move in the public space only for approved social services or heavily controlled religious processions. Ironically, in Singapore, the macrocosms of the gurus do not collide or collude with the state, but rather occupy either the unbounded inner space of the self or commercial or domestic places transformed temporarily into consecrated space, which in Singapore must remain temporary. But also remember that the macrocosm of Singapore, the very landscape, takes on its own kind of consecration, its own mythic presence and cosmogony, as a nation without ancient history reconstructed out of thin air but built in concrete and steel. The high-rise HDB flats remain a stage for the production of life, so the events held within are layered and already bounded by other kinds of near sacrality.

4

Yoga on the Move

All over the island from glitzy malls to mixed-use industrial buildings, community centers to elegant multipurpose halls adjacent to temples, many Singaporeans eagerly practiced yoga on the first International Day of Yoga on June 21, 2015. Conceived and executed by Prime Minister Narendra Modi, the celebration marked an official claim on globally popular yoga by the government of India. With the repositioning of ANUSH (Ayurveda, Yoga, and Naturopathy, Unani, Siddha and Homeopathy) as a cabinet-level department in 2014,[1] Modi moved yoga into a high-priority government concern and at the same time created an alternate narrative of India's glory—this time using what many consider the heart of transnational spirituality. In Singapore, the subsequent fourth-year celebration stretched from June 16 to June 24, 2018 with High Commission of India Facebook page proclaiming: "#Singapore embraces #Yoga like no other city in the world. 100 Centers, 170 Sessions and more than 30 partner organisations. Choose your center and session."[2] High Commission (fellow Commonwealth nations do not have an embassy) meticulously planned and executed these events for International Day of Yoga—in good bureaucratic nomenclature termed IDY—with cooperation from multiple yoga-centered organizations, corporate sponsors, and interestingly in conjunction with *ActiveSG*, an offshoot of Singapore's Ministry of Community Development. The High Commission maintained a presence at most events, with an official offering greetings or words of thanks. Present at both the first and the fourth IDY, I chose to attend large public practices under bridges in a park, in malls, or literally on the streets, as well as more intimate settings in industrial buildings and community halls.

To my spatially-focused eye, these International Days of Yoga events made unspoken claims on the *space* of this state not through discourse—but in keeping with yoga via bodily occupancy—such subtle assertions seemed unnoticed and uncontested, or simply overlooked by the many diverse participants themselves. As *the* technique to invoke the ultimate nexus between the smallest *microplace* (inner consciousness) with the grandest *macrospace* (the cosmos), yoga nonetheless remains embedded in alternating claims over the its geography and genealogy—its *place* in the power dynamics of the Indian state as well as its relationship to *religion*, *spirituality*, and *secularity*. In Singapore the issue of yoga and the state becomes more complex. Sharing a common British colonial heritage, India, as a near neighbor across the old trading route of the Bay of Bengal and the Straits of Malacca, has Indian nationals working at all levels in Singapore with a portion of the state's citizens of Indian origin, primarily

Tamil heritage (Tamil being one of the four official languages). *And*, as the previous chapters have argued, Singapore has its own multilayered spatial regimes—officially a secular state with intense regulations but much more. These celebrations of the IDY in Singapore once again reconfigured the relationships between secularism, religion, spirituality, and the space of the state—in yet another complex mode.

Moreover, the very definition of *yoga* remains indeterminate (Singleton 2010; De Michelis 2004), and this takes on special complexity in this context of the official religious pluralism of the city-state as so many Chinese-heritage Singaporean and some Muslim denizens adopt the practices but within their own cultural sensibilities. In multiethnic Singapore various modalities of yogic practices flourish, such as Yin Yoga with a decidedly Chinese stance, and more recently an Islamic Sufi meditation from the lineage of the Mujaddidi Order by a small group of Tamil-heritage family and friends. This Sufi group explained that their silent meditation without chanting or prayers "starts with the 'intension' fixing on the most important of the subtle centers of consciousness (Lata'if), Heart (Qalb) is the first subtle center"—reflecting, although not copying, the current ethos of yogic practices[3] (Ernst 2016), which often view postural yoga as preliminary to meditation.[4] Yet at the same time, amid the ubiquity and multiplicity of yoga practice in Singapore, *yoga* has turned into an icon of urbanity and cosmopolitan consciousness—widely argued to be above ethnic or religious identities, and even a necessity of life here—amid the complex aggrandizing moves by the Indian state to assert claims on the practice.

Walking along streets in Little India—with a nod to Michael de Certeau (1984)—I have passed numerous yoga studios or meditation centers with diverse genealogies. The particular shops and centers change from year to year as do their locations but such spiritual enterprises remain a visible presence on the streets. For example, most recently on Serangoon Road, walking toward Shirdi Sai Baba Center—a mix between a spiritual organization and temple with its own connections to Sufi practices,[5] which I will introduce in a later chapter—I spotted the new Singapore Bodhi Meditation Center, which like many yoga organizations offers to "impart practical, effective meditation techniques as a way of strengthening the energy of the physical body, and to inspire the spiritual mind so as to bring greater health and joy to the world at large."[6] In a typically ironic Little Indian streetscape, both venues neighbor a row of nightclubs with flashing enticements for liquor and entertainment (Fig. 4.1), but nevertheless with one displaying a small shrine to a very popular Thai Buddhist group. Earlier walks down the ever-evolving Kerbau Road once included The Yoga Shop run by the Brahmakumaris (2006, Fig. 4.2) and later a sadly unsuccessful shop proffering images of Shirdi Sai Baba in a meditative Sufi-style pose from tabletop dimensions to near life-size (2013, Fig. 4.3). Layers of posters for various guru-centered or yoga or mediation events always embellish the pillars on this old shop-house street. Such a poster, actually a banner, near Kerbau street, introduced me to Isha Yoga.

Manoj Thakur, a key coordinator for the International Day of Yoga and the director of VYASA Yoga in Singapore, confirmed my impressions: "I do not have the figures but I feel that Singapore may be number one or two for the maximum people who are practicing yoga, every street you will find a yoga studio. So many people are coming and practicing yoga because they cannot live without yoga." We were discussing the

Figure 4.1 Serangoon Road houses bars with flashing neon signs along with several spiritual centers.

Figure 4.2 The Yoga Shop of the Brahma Kumaris in 2006 on lively Kerbau Street.

Figure 4.3 Nearly life-size, an image of Shirdi Sai Baba sits in the window of an erstwhile shop dedicated to the saint.

hectic life of Singaporeans in the ubiquitous high-rise flats, which Manoj depicted as a tense existence without ever seeing the horizon or eating really fresh foods. Yoga, he felt, provided both the mental and physical buttress to cope with this environment. But, perhaps because of this shared fraught as well as fruitious world, participation in yoga overflows boundaries. As Manoj calculates, based on participants in the many yoga classes offered at VYASA Yoga: "As far as yoga is concerned I think the foreigners and Chinese are more numerous compared to Indians." This certainly is *not* the case with most of the guru-centered organizations that I know in Singapore.

So an irony surfaces in Singapore: guru-lead spiritual organizations like Isha Yoga and Art of Living proudly proclaim their place above ethnicity, religion, and even nationality, but nonetheless derive their members predominantly from those of Indian heritage and often of Indian citizenship while including, welcoming, and actively encouraging other ethnicities.[7] However, the *yoga* so fervently claimed by Prime Minister Modi as India's gift to the world and over which he fully intends to maintain control—as will be obvious below—appears to involve far more people with more diverse backgrounds than the guru-centered spiritual movements—at least in the Singaporean context. During the last decade, I have noticed an increase in yoga activity since the inception of IDY—the master of ceremonies at the VYASA celebration on June 21, 2018 beamed that since 2015, IDY just "grew and grew." While almost all of the guru-centered movements now offer some form of *yoga*, as meditation, physical postures, or both, not all yoga organizations embrace a *guru*, although they may acknowledge a revered founder. At this point the distinction is debatable, but it does capture some ironies. With the ever-expanding venues and multiple yoga events, the International Day of Yoga covers more ground—literally—than any single yoga organization or any guru-led group within this island. The chief architect, the prime mover, behind all of this is Prime Minister Narendra Modi, who, unlike Mohandas K. Gandhi, is neither a confessed *karma yogi* (van der Veer 2014, *kl* 3191), nor an acknowledged Mahatma, nor a *guru* (although closely allied with several popular guru figures). However, his star power seems at points to come close, with political power shading into celebrity power, in turn hedging divinity for some. Newspapers featured photos of the prime minister leading yoga *asanas* on the mall in New Delhi and the website for ANUSH flashed images of the prime minister leading groups of young people all sporting the ubiquitous yoga T-shirt.[8] The *New York Times* described a moment at the Delhi event in 2015 when Modi moved into the crowd of children "who touched his feet reverently"; when he then called them, "they rushed to him, touching the scarf he had used to wipe his brow. 'When he touched my hand, it was like nothing I've ever felt before,'" a young student exclaimed afterward "amid a gaggle of students."[9] Modi remains an effective political leader, and perhaps more, with unusual territorial ambitions claiming another kind of macrospace; but whether he rules this macrocosm—the Y-Cloud?—as progenitor, protector, and prolonger remains a question.

Tied into this IDY phenomenon, the *interlocking* issues of the state, secularism, religion/spirituality emerge, Samta Pandya—in her analysis of what she calls HIFM (Hindu Inspired Faith Movements) in India—uses another suggestive term, "a coagulum of . . . nationalism, secularization, and syncretism" (2017, 187). The list of "supporting organizations" at the bottom of the huge banners hung at all of the IDY 2018 events (Fig. 4.4)—all working under the umbrella of the High Commission—illustrate this murky coagulum. Some are clearly guru-centered such as Isha Foundation, Art of Living, Sahaja Yoga, Ramakrishna Mission, Brahma Kumaris, and Heartfulness. Others are official or semiofficial offshoots of the government of Singapore, i.e., ActiveSG, NUS (National University of Singapore), LISHA, Narpani Pearavai, Yoga Sports Association, while others are private internationally connected schools with roots in India, such as Yuvabharathi International School, DPS International School, or businesses with strong connections in India, such as Biztech.[10] Jal Yoga, Trust Yoga, and True Yoga, on the other hand, acknowledge no guru. Some of these forms of yoga borrow heavily from traditional yoga terminology but all feature multiethnic instructors, and several offer club rooms, steam baths, and wellness in a very New Age vein. By 2018, the Indian High Commission had squeezed all thirty-five of these logos under its own insignia, and stretched and hung this standard banner at each event all over Singapore,[11] along with providing free International Day of Yoga T-shirts—at some events adding a good-quality yoga mat with carrier! Such banners usually formed

Figure 4.4 The official IDY banner here displayed in front of the Indian Cultural Center just before an outdoor yoga session.

the backdrop of raised stages where carefully trained yoga teachers directed the order of *asanas* taken from the full-color printed *Common Yoga Protocol* issued by ANUSH, "prepared in consultation with leading Yoga experts and heads of eminent Yoga Institutions of India," as the copyright page declares.

Covering Singapore

For one of the first events on the initial IDY on June 21, 2015, Isha Yoga offered a version of its Upa Yoga at the fashionable mall, ION Station, in the Public Events Hall—an open space on the ground floor of a three-storied egg-shaped atrium. The event was in full view of all the levels with people wandering by looking and watching as they rode up the escalators or glanced from railings on the third floor (Fig. 4.5). The extreme publicness of the event paralleled Prime Minister Modi leading thousands of bureaucrats and schoolchildren—all out from offices and schools—on the majestic mall leading to the Raj Bhavan in New Delhi. If yoga had any esoteric roots, these were severed on this day. The Isha leader (of Chinese heritage) was careful to distinguish these *asanas* from the full-blown yoga, as was Sadhguru in his video calling these Upa yoga practices preparatory and forms that could be done by anyone: these were primarily exercises not meant as a way to enlightenment but only wellbeing—a first step toward other goals or an end in themselves. Registration was required although people did register on-site. The participants were more diverse than I have seen at Isha Sathsangs with Chinese-heritage participants nearly equaling the Indian. The gift bags—a Isha organizer called these "goodie bags"—included a printed program outlining the Upa Yoga for the day. We did not complete everything as the session was short and included a screening of messages from Sadhguru. Only the official Isha volunteers wore matching T-shirts in bright orange with a stylized lotus blossom with the message "Blossoming of a Being." Only later did I realize that Isha had not followed the *Common Yoga Protocol* and did not project any message from the prime minister. This would change in 2018. However, earlier, Jaggi Vasudev addressed a distinguished audience at the Embassy of India in Washington DC, on "The Relevance of Yoga for Modern Life," introduced as "a curtain riser" for the International Day of Yoga.[12] Later an Isha volunteer confirmed that Sadhguru had joined the prime minister and others for the planning sessions in India.

The *Straits Times*, the next day, headlined "5,000 strike their poses in 50 venues," and featured a photo of a VYASA Yoga session in a terminal at Changi Airport (June 22, 2015). The Isha event at Ion Station went unmentioned. Later Manoj Thakur of VYASA confirmed that VYASA (Vivekananda Yoga Anusandhana Samsthana) had supplied the instructors for thirty out of fifty of the venues: "We had a training program for instructors to teach the same practice everywhere. You should not teach whatever you want. It's a protocol the whole world is practicing a particular program which comes from the National Affairs Ministry of India … from Modi. You should not teach whatever you want. If everyone is talking something different, people get confused … there must be the same message." At this point he kindly gave me a copy of the *Common Yoga Protocol*, and explained:

Figure 4.5 Isha yoga session in ION Station mall on Orchard Street—the major upscale shopping area of the city.

This was the Bible for us on that particular day. . . . It was so well organized, that's why Modi is such a fantastic person. Can you believe . . . the whole world should follow this that day, and why follow this, because there is a message: Yoga for Everyone. These are the practices everyone can do. Whether you have disabilities, whether you are lady or gent, everybody can do these.

Manoj clarified that the High Commission had initiated the organizational process. They called all of the yoga organizations to ask for help in supplying instructors. Because "that is what VYASA does," offering training programs and, with 1,100 already graduated yoga instructors, VYASA was in the best position to provide instructors. VYASA completely organized six of the programs; for others they served in conjunction with other sponsoring groups.

Two weeks later, a major organizer for Isha's events for IDY took time to speak with me at length. Summarizing the information that Manoj kindly provided me, I asked for his assessment of the day. He did not know Manoj, but confirmed that VYASA covered many venues, while Isha functioned in only three. With the organizations working with the High Commission: "It happened differently with different organizations, for sure. For example, with Isha, we already had experience in doing yoga in bigger places, so all we did with the High Commissions was keeping them in the loop of what was happening." For all the other centers, the practices were confined to the mornings; but Isha planned for the entire day until 8:00 p.m. and ultimately served 2,000 people in all three venues. When I asked about the practices that I had experienced at ION Station, called "Upa Yoga," he clarified that "we generally teach hatha yoga, which Sadhguru designed, "which is very intense" and "requires commitment and attention to detail." The official *hatha yoga* teachers train intensively at the ashram for twenty-one weeks— his wife completed this training—to impart this "with almost surgical precision." In India, Sadhguru, who was on the panel with the prime minister to organize the event, had proposed that the instructors have at least two weeks of training for that IDY in India. But in Singapore, ANUSH was not present and the responsibility fell solely to the High Commission. Although Isha was very much involved in the planning in Singapore as well, "we were very conscious as to where to execute it and concerned about the level of commitment by the participants and the scale in which they were doing it." So, considering that the session was limited to only ninety minutes, Ishas decided that if they could not confirm that the participant would have properly prepared (i.e., the required fasting), then "we would stick to a simple set of practices which would cause no damage if they made any errors."

I expressed my surprise that Isha had chosen a noisy commercial space like ION Station, and asked, "Did you do that purposely?" The answer was yes: "for a long time we wanted to do something like this but the nature of the programs we do generally demands certain kind of an ambiance . . . demands absolute stillness in a place, no disturbance, no distractions.[13] So, this was particularly crafted by Sadhguru so that we could take it to mass; so if a little distraction happens people can still come back on without losing much. So, because we had a package to deliver like this, we were able to do it." Was there any subtle message with this? "What we wanted to show was that what we refer to as yoga is not so esoteric, so academic, so traditional that people refuse to look into it. There was a message but we tried to keep it very subtle." He explained that because Sadhguru dresses and looks like a very traditional Indian guru, people sometime hesitate to even listen to him, so Ishas wanted to counter that public perception. I then asked whether these practices were considered only preparatory. "Preparatory but toward something that is more profound and subtle in nature so if you are looking forward to that dimension, yes, that is preparatory; but if you are looking for wellbeing, then this is good enough for you, so it is no longer preparatory." So, like Manoj at this point, the IDY event for Ishas was about wellbeing.

More important than the details of VYASA and Isha's level of participation was the organizational style of each, which revealed key differences between guru-led yoga groups and an organization like VYASA. Both are extremely effective, as I have experienced them, and they both deliver powerful programs and retain deeply committed members. But the presence and the power of a guru, or the absence, *does* change the dynamics of each organization. Manoj speaks with deep respect for Dr. H. R. Nagendra, the founder of VYASA (Vivekananda Yoga Anusandhana Samsthana) Yoga,[14] and with esteem for his own yoga "guru"—here in the sense of *teacher*—in his home city of Gwalior, Anil Sarode. But (here the difference is subtle but I think crucial) Manoj does not appear to reverence either. Their power remains an aspect of the quality of their teaching, their commitment, and their training. Joachim Wach's observations in the 1920s—as one of the first European scholars to consider gurus—still holds true: while the *student* reveres the teacher for "a certain faculty, a skill, knowledge, or capacity", for the *disciple* the significance "rests in the master's personality" ([1925] 1988, 1–2). Today, Ishas would soundly reject the nomenclature of *disciple,* and certainly Sadhguru offers well-designed yoga programs. However, when I asked a key Isha about the organization for this IDY or any other event, his answer revealed more than mechanics at work.

He began by affirming that Isha's style was *not bureaucratic* but based on volunteers and their own passions—the kind of skills that they can bring to an event, photography, ability to communicate well, effectively monitor sound systems. Only the financial accounting was professional because of Singapore government oversight on these matters, but "every other thing is done in a more fluid style, not really writing it down and holding someone accountable." There are people who usually do certain things like decoration so everyone knows who to ask, but "it's not a day-job experience . . . mostly it's a passion; we don't have a trained photographer running around; they have their day jobs but in their free time they do this as a passion." While there are the trained Isha Teachers who can be consulted, at events "more or less it happens very autonomously." He continued: "The beauty of volunteers . . . they are all doing it as their own thing, not because someone is asking them to do it." In the Singapore, "no one is elected to any office, there is no president." "Frankly," he offered, "there is a beauty in that; when things don't happen in the way you want them to happen, if you are in the right state—you are doing your practices well, you're keeping up with what you have been taught—it's alive for you and you automatically understand that you have little control over so many things in life anyhow, so you just move on."

Then, knowing from experience that, in Isha, volunteers function as the de facto strength of the organization, I asked, "How does someone become a volunteer?" My kind interlocutor explained that sometimes people ask to serve and then are usually directed to regularly attend the monthly Sathsangs and to begin by coming early to help with these. Or, the volunteers usually observe those who come often and may approach them about volunteering. The prerequisite, of course, is completing the Inner Engineering Program and subsequently learning the Shambhavi Mahamudra Kriya which serves as an initiation. Then aspiring volunteers are usually asked to do Bhava Spandana Program, which, unlike Inner Engineering or even the Shambhavi Kriya, is usually offered at the ashram in Coimbatore or at the Isha center in Tennessee by Sadhguru *in person*: "The firing fuel to any kind of volunteering is how strongly you feel toward Sadhguru." He continued his explanation, linking the force of this relationship with Sadhguru—as I heard this—with the reasons why the fluid organization works: "Unless a person has a very clear head, when the activity is more than what you can take on, people generally ... become too overwhelmed. So, *either* they are very clear, they know what they are doing and, if it's too much for them to do, they come out and say they are not able to do this *or* they should feel so strongly for Sadhguru that they don't care." In this very honest and articulate recounting of the Isha style, the working "fuel" is the guru, and notice that the *kriya*, the practices (which are after all the "outcome" of Sadhguru's "profound experience of the Self," as the Inner Engineers website puts it)[15] are key to making this connection. Sadhguru belongs to no lineage and hands down no set teachings, but his *presence*, his pervading *being*, becomes the catalyst for another kind of chemistry, one concerned with meticulousness in the execution of *asanas* and *kriyas*, an intense strictness that I experienced in my own Inner Engineering Program—but *not* for exactness in workings of the organization, which depends on the strength of a deeply personal relationship with him.

Under the Bridge and on the Street

The website for the new Marina Bay East Garden describes the scene of my first IDY event of 2018: "Set amidst beautiful pavilions, wide open lawns, and amazing views of the iconic Conservatories and Supertrees against the Marina skyline, Bay East Garden welcomes you to immerse yourself in picturesque serenity."[16] Here under a highway bridge redesigned as an "open hardscape,"[17] VYASA Yoga-led yoga session began at 7:30 a.m. I had the taxi drop me off at the Welcome Center and I walked the short distance to an area under the bridge which indeed provided a panorama of the bay area with new condos in one direction and a view of the downtown from another. As I arrived at the venue, a yoga instructor using a cordless microphone intoned instructions for hand and wrist exercises to a very ethnically diverse group (Fig. 4.6). I spotted a bus, and indeed Manoj later told me that some participants who had attended other VYASA Yoga sessions were bussed in. I counted over seventy people under the bridge. The MC followed much of the same protocol that I would experience at the other venues. These were not always identical but used much of the same format from the *Common Yoga Protocol*. Neck and then hand stretches began the *asanas*. I noticed great seriousness. Participants moved through the positions well. Even without Manoj telling me, these participants did not look to be raw beginners.

Figure 4.6 The session begins with hand and wrist exercises on the first day of IDY 2018.

About equal mix of men and women stood there on this pavement on an early Saturday morning. No yoga mats were supplied today—everyone had brought their own—but at later events, mats were given free. I also noted a common pattern: people came in casual clothes and then changed into their special Yoga Day T-shirts on-site, often pulling these over their tops so that soon almost everyone wore the same T-shirt. I would see this same changing at all IDY events with a constant and seemingly limitless supply of the special shirts. I have my prized collection of five. Although I observed the order of the *asanas*, which generally adhered to the *Common Yoga Protocol*, the juxtaposition of the positions and the location provided far more interest. Why were we under this bridge in a garden? Why right at a crossroad and under a major thoroughfare? At one point, the giant vine-covered pillars of the highway—concrete now alive with climbing vines—seemed to be mimicked by the *asana* pose with legs looking like pillar and pillars seeming like giant legs holding up a precarious ceiling of cement (Fig. 4.7). All of this remained located within a classic Singapore skyscape of well-designed high-rise offices on the one side and the red tiled roofs of new condominiums on the other. At the final *asana*, the *śavāsana* (Dead Body Posture), as all lay very flat and deadly still on the surface of this Singaporean soil, two women leaders used Chinese-style singing bowls to intone a mystical soundscape—very emotive and affective (Fig. 4.8).When the main practice ended as the MC announced a special program to follow, some did leave but many stayed for yoga-dance performance, and then a brief, very Indian-style, function with bouquets of flowers to honor performers and guests, and a short speech by an officer from the Indian High Commission.

The next two events in which I participated were entirely open to the public, requiring only registration on the official IDY website (connected to the High Commission site); but their location was less visible to the general populace. The Brahma Kumaris offered a program in the heart of Little India at their Raja Yoga Center on Hindoo Street in the newer Peace Building that contrasted with abutting shop house buildings (Fig. 4.9). I arrived in time to find a group of white sari-clad ladies whom I immediately recognized as Brahma Kumaris. They kindly led me to the venue upstairs hall. This time there were lots of chairs in the rear for older people and those not comfortable sitting without back support; mats were also arranged on the open floor in the front. A short stage for the demonstrations was up front along with the now familiar IDY banner. The MC introduced the head of the Brahma Kumaris Singapore who lauded "the bold move of Mr. Modi" to share the wealth of yoga "that has been in India from time immemorial" with the whole world. She continued: "When someone does something with the energy of their own conviction, there is an extra power in it"—here speaking of the prime minister's personal conviction and his own globally publicized practice as a major for reason for International Yoga Day's wide appeal and continued expansion. Again, an official of the High Commission was present as we began to move through the *asanas* in the protocol including the popular *ṛkṣāsana* (The Tree Posture) and ending with the *bhrāmarī pranāyāma* (black-bee breathing). As the lights turned dramatically red, we all blocked our ears to produce the buzzing sound of bees (Fig. 4.10)—a form of breath control. At the end of the practice, a longtime Brahma Kumari gentleman, who worked in high tech, gave a presentation on a blackboard, outlining, in very scientific style, this global organization's understanding of yoga. A sophisticated video on the movement followed.

Such added introductions to the sponsoring organization's perception and practice of yoga was repeated at the Sahaja Yoga program three days later located in the new AZ Building, advertised as centrally located with "a classy lobby" and "air-conditioned corridors" in a rapidly developing part of Singapore.[18] An openly commercial venue, the cool white corridors were almost blinding and I had to carefully mark my way to avoid getting lost. Fortunately, I met an older gentleman in the elevator who was on his way to set up the venue and who guided me. Entering the room, the oriental rugs on the floor and the small crystal chandelier with a series of hanging Chinese-style lights gave the room an orientalized ambiance—not strictly Indian (Fig. 4.11). A wall hanging with the stylized tree—an emblem of the group—divided the entrance table and watercooler from the main room. As I entered, Ricky,[19] our leader for the night, was setting up the projector. Below him, the small framed photo of the founder-guru, Shri Mataji Nirmala Devi, sat on a simple cloth-covered table between a single candle and a vase of flowers. The room included charts of the cakras, so important to the guru-founder's mode of yoga, which Ricky later explained involves "the awakening of a subtle spiritual energy known as Kundalini which lies dormant in the sacrum bone at

Figure 4.7 Here a practitioner's legs appear to mimic the massive columns under the expressway bridge.

Figure 4.8 Two leaders of the yoga session sound singing bowls and bells to end this yoga session under the bridge.

Figure 4.9 The Brahma Kumari yoga center located in this modern building abutting the more typical shop house of Little India.

Figure 4.10 The lighting in the yoga studio of the Raja Yoga Center turned red as we hummed like bees in this exciting breathing practice.

the base of the spine" and added that "Sahaja yoga mediation is meant for everyone who desires to find his or her true self, which is full of peace, joy of life, and love for others." Ricky began by introducing yoga as "union with Mother Nature." We could feel such energy in our hands so we began with a practice—not part of the protocol—to awaken that energy in our hands as a means to balance the channels of such energy. We invoked "Mother" as we asked for this equilibrium. Then Ricky led us through a selection of the poses in the protocol including the ever-popular tree posture (Fig. 4.12) among others. The participants again were ethically eclectic, many with ties of Sahaja Yoga. All took the practices seriously. I left braving that long white hall still not sure now if I could find my way out, but others were following (Fig. 4.13).

The second very public event that I attended occurred at the end of this long week early on Saturday morning at 8:00 a.m. Sponsored by LISHA and the new Indian Cultural Center, the venue was a now pedestrian street—recently closed to traffic—at the side of the Little India Arcade shopping complex on land owned by the Hindu Endowment Board. LISHA, Little India Shopkeepers & Heritage Association, is a government-encouraged community organization established almost twenty years

Figure 4.11 Sahaja yoga studio with an oriental ambiance in a very contemporary building.

Figure 4.12 Ricky demonstrates the Tree pose. With the kind permission of Ricky Anupom Saikia.

ago, "with the strong support from government bodies such as the Singapore Tourism Board (STB) and Hindu Endowments Board (HEB)."[20] The new Indian Heritage Center with an impressive four-storied steel and glass fascia, described as "translucent shimmering façade to create an impression of the Centre as a 'shining jewel' in the day,"[21] appears to provide local residents with a welcome place to sit, but somehow still felt disconnected to the neighboring community in spite of its shining light and excellent display of local history. Here in the street fronting the Cultural Center, VYASA led another yoga session. We all spread out gifted yoga mats on the paved walkway and waited, still a bit sleepy on a Saturday morning. The yoga teacher, again with a microphone, lead the *asanas* as she moved onto the street, with assistants demonstrating the poses seated on a raised plinth in front of the center—the High Commission banner hung behind them (Fig. 4.14). Again the *Common Yoga Protocol* reigned with modifications. However, the spatial configuration engaged my primary attention with the determined aspiring yogis resolutely continuing their *asanas* as shops doors opened onto the street and early shoppers, tourists, and shop attendants

Figure 4.13 We all file out into the long white hallway after the session.

shifted around the seated or prone bodies, sometimes ignoring them while others looked on with curious or bemused expressions (Fig. 4.15).

These two bookends to the now extended International Day of Yoga occupied very public spaces—one in the new Marina Bay Gardens East and the other in an old preserved section of Little India that was spared the wrecking ball, as I heard the story, because the government realized that tourism—a keen source of income—demanded something more romantic/exotic than steel and glass skyscrapers. However, recently a campaign to clean up Little India produced the typically colorful ominous billboard announcing fines for littering in a local high-fenced playground with charming clay animals seemingly too nice for comfortable use (Fig. 4.16). The new Indian Cultural Center continued this trend. The VYASA Yoga practice happened between the old arcade and this very new addition of steel and glass—between old Singapore and the very new. The same could be said of the contrast between the venues for the Brahma Kumari event on Hindoo Road but in a new steel and glass building, on the one hand, and Sahaja Yoga set in an ultramodern commercial building near an under-construction Circle Line metro station, on the other.

Figure 4.14 Early morning, yoga session begins in front of the ultramodern Indian Cultural Center.

Figure 4.15 Shop attendant ignores the prone yogi in front of this shop for tourists.

Figure 4.16 Large sign shows exact fines for each type of offense artfully illustrated.

But why were we under a bridge and on a street doing yoga so very publicly? The last time yogis took to the streets hawking their skills, early visitors to India were scandalized, as Mark Singleton describes this early public display of postural yoga:

> Perceived as dissolute, licentious, and profane, these groups were greeted with puzzlement and hostility by early European observers [late 1600s]. The performance of yogic postural austerities was the most visible and vaunted emblem of Indian religious folly, and as yogins increasingly took to exhibitionism as a means of livelihood, this association became consolidated in the popular imagination.
>
> 2010, 39

And later at the turn of the Victorian century, the famous Sanskritist F. Max Müller, in a rare foray into contemporary Hindu practice, continued to equate postural yoga and street performers. Writing on Vivekananda's master *Râmakrisha: His Life and Sayings* in 1899, Max Müller takes care to distinguish the Bengali saint from those "who hardly deserve to be called Samyânsins [*saṃnyāsi*], for they are not much more than jugglers or Ha*th*yogins" unlike true Samyânsins who "devote their thoughts and meditations to philosophical and religious problems" (1899, vi). More than a century later, the organization VYASA Yoga, which developed out of the Vivekananda Kendra named for the great swami, became the most active organization in the International Day of Yoga. Contemporary aspiring yogis, clearly middle class and relatively prosperous, were nonetheless *in some sense* "taking to exhibitionism" in the streets with the blessing of the government of India, and apparently the government of Singapore as well.

Open performance also marked the exciting and excited celebration of yoga held at the Civil Service Club on the edge of Little India on IDY in 2018. While not public—people did have to register—over 300 participants filled a large hall making this a far from intimate setting, although many were yoga instructors trained by VYASA so participants seemed familiar with many others in the room. As I took my seat expecting a yoga session—I had met a man also armed with his mat anticipating the same—we were both surprised and, as I later openly admitted to Manoj, a bit taken aback. Again sponsored by VYASA Yoga and Ayurveda Singapore, rather than a bare room with yoga mats, participants began to occupy the now familiar golden chairs with red cushions—much like those at the Expo center for the event with Sadhguru—which filled the hall. Meeting old friends and chatting as children ran down the central aisle, the MC had difficulty quietening the excited mass as we awaited the arrival of the dignitaries, which included the Deputy Indian High Commissioner of India and the chairman of Hindu Endowment Board, to begin the formal program. The audience finally settled down, but the MC's message to silence cell phones did not stop many from remaining glued to their screens (Fig. 4.17). The fine-voiced MC asked why an International Day of Yoga, what is it that the whole world is looking for: peace, "so much so that Trump and Kim had to come to Singapore to look for peace." That summit had just occurred days before the event. She reminded the audience that yoga was really "off the mat," about living life fully; then she declared excitedly that, this event, "for me it's like Deepavali, coming back and meeting all my favorite people, my friends, my teachers and then having a nice dinner." She then invited the dignitaries to begin by lighting the lamp in front of an altarlike display with a garlanded photo of Swami Vivekananda fronted by a large brass *viḷakku*, a South Indian oil lamp usually used at functions (Fig. 4.18)—what followed was indeed a "function" in the full Indian sense with speeches and recognitions and awards. After the awards and recognitions, children presented a yoga-dance followed by the same fine professional group that performed at the event under the bridge. Then we did yoga, modified for chairs (Fig. 4.19)—quite fun—and heard a talk on yoga and science, and finally, as 9:00 p.m. approached, a vivacious young woman with a baby strapped to her chest led us in "Laughing Yoga," first telling us: "We laugh when we are happy, but we can become happy when we laugh." We were asked to hold hands, and at this point I actually tried to escape, but was stopped near the door and asked to take time to experience this. Everyone else, except another bewildered woman in my row, seemed really excited as everybody laughed—except this grumpy academic—and then yelled, "Very Good, Very Good, Yeh!" Nothing could shake my inexplicable annoyance as this continued: I burst the bounds of good observation and manners, and eventually did escape without having dinner.

The next day, my own surprisingly discourteous behavior prompted me to contact Manoj again, and finally we found a minute to debrief the event. I talked to the two women who staffed the VYASA office, and they, too, did not really find the laughing yoga their "cup of tea" but they did tell me that in one case her mother in India had

Figure 4.17 A panorama of the VYASA event at the Civil Service Club with participants bonded to their cell phones.

Figure 4.18 Swami Vivekananda has the place of honor in the room.

Figure 4.19 A session of chair yoga helped after a long night.

found this very therapeutic, and I later discovered that this innovative yoga had become popular. We did it again on that street in Little India. When I frankly—and almost rudely—told Manoj that the event did not seem serious and that people seemed to be there primarily for social reasons—just like the more typical critique of the spiritually-inclined when speaking of temples—he reminded me that this was a *celebration* of yoga with some practice, some speeches. So, if some came primarily for celebration, then maybe they did hear "something good, this is what society needs today." Manoj then attempted to rewire my attitude by asking me, "What has the world gained by logic?" Suggesting that we must become like children and leave logic behind, he reminded me that yoga says our nature is bliss; but to develop this at a basic level, we can use laughing yoga to induce a childlike innocence to reset our fundamental attitude.

Later, I reflected on the issue of publicness with Manoj's insights in mind. On the streets and in commercial buildings, had we turned Singapore into a playground modeling the unselfconsciousness of children at play? However, seeing this all as good fun was somehow belied by the distinguished guests—the events happening in the presence of the Deputy High Commissioner of India and the chairman of the Hindu

Endowment Board—who acted as an intense reminder that behind this International Day of Yoga stood the powerful, charismatic prime minister of India, and that a social-political ethos hung, like the High Commission's banner, as the backdrop to all of these events. Yoga had become a truly *public* event.

On that same morning of June 21, I had risen early to attend a yoga session offered by Isha held at the new function hall at the Shri Perumal Temple on Serangoon Road next to the offices of the Hindu Endowment Board (Fig. 4.20). The fully air-conditioned room in this impressive renovated building provided a quiet environment in stark contrast to the event that would occur later in the evening. Here the feel and the sensitivities exuded Isha-ness. We quietly took to our mats which had been carefully unfolded and placed evenly on the floor (Fig. 4.21). Soon after the video of Sadhguru's welcome appeared onscreen came the vibrant face and the charismatic voice of Narendra Modi. Dressed in a pale orange *kurta* with flags of India arrayed like desktop wallpaper behind him, he began in comfortable, fluent English: "Greeting to all Yoga lovers. Yoga is one of the most precious gifts given by the ancient Indian sages to

Figure 4.20 I stand at the entrance hall in the newly renovated hall facing the grand Sri Perumal Temple.

Figure 4.21 Isha volunteers carefully laid out yoga mats for this early morning session.

humankind."[22] The prime minister went on to stress that the practical value of yoga is not just as an exercise but "doing our day-to-day activities with diligence and complete awareness is yoga as well." Modi kept the utter inclusiveness of yoga to the fore in what was to become his most quoted statement: "When we understand ourselves, we become ready to form a constructive bond with the society at large, a bond of oneness with our families, with the society we live in, with fellow humans, with all the birds, animals, trees with whom we share this beautiful planet. Thus, yoga is the journey from me to we." Then he ended his greeting with his goal for the future: "Our next challenge is to produce institutionally trained yoga teachers, standard yoga system, who can ignite this flame further especially among the youth." Enter the *Common Yoga Protocol* and the work of the government of India to ensure standards for this emerging global phenomenon—now also an economic powerhouse.

Interestingly and perhaps ironically, commentators on this and other such pronouncements by the prime minister particularly note (as they see it) his careful, clear avoidance, with global audiences, of any connections between yoga and Hinduism as a religion. Peter van der Veer traces this move toward a *secularized spirituality* as key in "historical and political phenomena that are intimately related to the construction of modernity," (2014, *kl* 2896–8) especially in the Asian context. Vivekananda—solely honored that evening in the Civil Service Club—pioneered this move: "A lack of religious specificity together with the claim to be scientific is crucial for both the nationalist and the transnational appeal of Vivekananda's message. I would suggest that Vivekananda has developed a translation of Hindu traditions in terms that derive from the global production of 'spirituality'" (van der Veer 2014, *kl* 3055–60; also, Waghorne 2009). A *New York Times* commentator at the time of the first IDY put it more cynically:

> What's striking about Mr. Modi's grand project, given his formative years in Rashtriya Swayamsevak Sangh, a right-wing Hindu organization, is the presentation of yoga as a secular activity. His government takes great pains to point out that 47 Muslim nations supported his United Nations resolution. In his United Nations address, he characterized yoga as "an invaluable gift of ancient Indian tradition," rather than Hindu tradition.
>
> Mr. Modi's careful scripting shows him to be a consummate businessman. By presenting yoga as one of the monumental achievements of Indian thought, he is increasing the country's visibility, promoting its brand on the world market. He will not allow the distraction of religion to interfere with the return on his investment.
>
> Suri 2015

Meanwhile, after the prime minister's greetings, our Isha yoga session closely followed the *Common Yoga Protocol*, unlike the 2015 event at Ion Station. After the session, the CEO of the Hindu Endowment Board, Mr. Segar, walked over to greet us and showed some of us the very impressive new theater in the function hall. I then followed the volunteers for a group photo in front of the traditional *gopura* (gate) of the Shri Perumal Temple (Fig. 4.22). The lines between Hinduism, spirituality, religion, secularity, public events, and private venues were not so easily ignored, given the context in this beautiful heart of Hinduism in Singapore.

There are questions that the grand celebrations of IDY left lying on the roads and floors here in Singapore. Given the intensity which the government of Singapore usually regulates the use of public space, the broad ethnically diverse participants, the unambiguous umbrella of the Indian High Commission, the continued diversity and interpretation of the practice along with the hovering presence of the *Common Yoga Protocol*, what happened here? Keeping in mind the loose distinction between bureaucratic procedures and the charisma of gurus and political stars, and leaving behind our logic—as Manoj suggested—may suggest *not* searching for a clear, overall, rationality at work. Samta Pandya adopts the language of "flavours" and "shades" in her discussion of spiritual movement and Hindu nationalism (2017, 184), while others write of "nontotalizing and multidirectional structures of relationality" (quoted in Lucia 2018, 41). As obvious at the end of the last chapter, with Prime Minister Modi's Gemini actions in India, welding the Hindutva sword at the same time as sitting on the yoga mat with a massive following wearing the IDY T-shirt slogan "Yoga for Harmony & Peace" across their chests—in both cases he stands accused of overtly and subtly marginalizing India's many Muslims. Here in Singapore, the hovering presence of a

Figure 4.22 I stand with others for a group photo of the volunteers and their families. Someone kindly took this with my cell phone so I could be in the photo.

Hindu ambiance remained unacknowledged, or carefully renamed as "spiritual" both in the protocol and in the actual practices, yet the CEO of the Hindu Endowment Board was present at the Isha event near the Shri Perumal Temple, and the chairman of the Hindu Endowment Board lit the votive lamp at VYASA's celebration. Interestingly, the Government of Singapore apparently chose to file yoga as a "sport" with ActiveSG (Singapore Sports Council) as a major sponsor hosting nine venues at various sports centers, *or* as an Indian community matter with both LISHA and Narpani Pearavai (the Indian community wing of ActiveSG)[23] as sponsors. But whether yoga morphs as a *sport* or an Indian community enterprise, the space of Singapore was *intentionally* occupied by a practice with Indian religious/spiritual roots, which even ActiveSG acknowledged in its "mass workout" in 2016, "held to increase public awareness about yoga, which is a physical, mental and spiritual practice originating in India."[24] That web page sported visuals of rigorous yoga but also lotus-seated participants with prayerlike folded hands.

The photos of the event posted on the High Commission Facebook page made the intentionality of *some kind* of territorial claims deeply visible. Pictured with hands raised in a seeming victory shout, over twenty-five yoga practitioners stretch on a stone patio in front of the now iconic Super Trees with the ship-shaped Marina Bay Sands Hotel in the background (entry dated July 14, 2018). Even more visibly proprietary, a finely produced photo essay from 2016 whose creator "was invited by Manoj Thakur to document this particular day," includes multiple images of multiethnic practitioners in front the major icons of Singapore, the Merlion and the Marina Bay Sands (Choo 2016). All participants wear the IDY T-shirt. Also captured is the culminating event at the Civil Service Club in what appears to be the same room as the celebration in 2018—but in 2016 yoga mats reign with no chairs visible. The *viḷakku* burns in front of Swami Vivekananda and honors awarded—but with the focus remained on mass participation in yoga by a diverse community of Singaporeans in the presence of "the Guest of Honor," the then High Commissioner of India, Mrs. Vijay Thakur Singh.

What was the *nature* of the spatiality and the *form* of occupation in the events at Ion Station in 2015, in the photos from 2016, on the streets of Little India, under the bridge in Marina Bay East, or in those commercial buildings in 2018? Listening again to Manoj Thakur, and recalling long conversations with Vijay Rai of Art of Living and Thulasidhar of Isha, and many others, I began to question my own surprise at this seemingly new publicness of yoga. Certain Hindu temples in Singapore had long been part of Thaipusam (Tamil, *Taippūcam*), an iconic Tamil festival now also billed as a tourist attraction which "often brings traffic in Singapore to a standstill"[25] with a daylong procession winding through major streets. Like yoga, Thaipusam participants use their bodies, often piercing lips or chests or backs as they carry or pull elaborate platforms with icons of Lord Murugan (called "carrying kavadi," Tamil *kāvaṭi), and* I have witnessed the very public Ratha Yatra festival of the Krishna Mandir[26] at the Toa Payoh sports stadium: these are openly deity-centered and god-conscious. Certainly, in India in the past, yoga was public in the less savory sense of a sideshow, but also with yoga as a key element in displays of masculine prowess including gymnastics and sports as Joseph Alter's work so clearly reveals (2011, 154–62). Until recently yoga has worn a less public face as the practice moved from the margins of the social worlds to its rising center—the middle classes—behind walls into studios or commercial buildings, but maintaining some of its esoteric/secret quality.

With organizations like Isha Yoga and the Amriteswari Society of Singapore,[27] just a decade ago, I had to sign confidentiality agreements (usually used in the corporate context) not to reveal the practices *at all*, not even to family members. While the Amriteswari Society in Singapore did not participate in IDY, Isha recently reported proudly, "Isha Singapore volunteers made 21 Yoga sessions possible in 12 different venues touching 823 lives, introducing powerful tools for transformation."[28] Here in Singapore, yoga went *public* not as a sideshow but with middle-class, modern, and economically secure participants willing to take to the streets and bridges and shopping malls. This had not happened on this scale *in Singapore* before Modi's International Day of Yoga. However, this trend of yoga-in-mass with matching yoga outfits happened in the US—as Amanda Lucia reminded me—pointing to an account on a yoga blog, interestingly from September of 2015: "10,000 Yogis Wear White For Heavily-Sponsored Yoga Event In Central Park," which described the event with a touch of snide: "On September 2nd, 10,000 yogis dressed in their uniform white, marched to Central Park's Great Lawn, took their designated spots on their regimented yellow mats, sipped their sponsored Fiji water, and saluted the sun for the cameras."[29] The description, with some changes, could fit the events in Singapore: the water was free, the shirts and mats alike, cameras abounded but with a decidedly different tone—the presence of government officials provided a certain gravity and sanction. These were not acts of mass consumerism, or of defiance, or even simply of display, but something else.

Bringing Yoga into Public Space—in Singapore

A very insightful volume, *Public Hinduisms*, considers "the dynamics involved in conceptualizing the encounter between Hinduism and public space," using cases from India, the United Kingdom, and the United States—the usual suspects in studies of transnational Hinduism (Waghorne 2004). Arguing that discussion of *changes* within both "religion" and "Hinduism" are usually set in the colonial and early postcolonial period, the volume shifts the focus "by mapping the multiple ways in which the idea of Hinduism has presented itself in the modern and late modern, as the complexity of public space has proliferated." While the discussions of *public space* in the late modern period here remain very relevant, this once very up-to-date discussion of "what creative tensions and power plays inform the presentation of symbols, performances, buildings, and communities as Hindu?" (Zavos 2012, 4–5) now becomes incongruously outmoded by the actions of the prime minister of India on June 21, 2015. In the Indian context, Narendra Modi has made yoga very public again and arguably tied to ruling power with all of its tensions. But recall that, even in India, spiritual movements closely associated with yoga are actually working to distinguish themselves from a *Hindu/ religious* identity *especially in public*. Expressly in context to Singapore, yoga-based groups *redefine* their symbols, performances, communities, and venues but deliberately as *not* Hinduism and *not* Religion. In the highly conscious and controlled state of Singapore, Modi's IDY has another face, with wrinkles.

Untangling the complexities of secularity and spirituality in what she terms HIFM (Hindu Inspired Faith Movements), Samta Pandya, professor at the innovative Tata Institute of Social Sciences in Mumbai, offers key insights from years of close observation of seven global spiritual movements[30] in the Indian context, four of which participated in International Day of Yoga in Singapore. The Art of Living and the Brahma Kumaris were both very active; the Ramakrishna Mission[31] offered one session; VYASA Yoga developed from and remains closely associated with the Vivekananda Kendra (another of her major cases). In a section provocatively titled "Camouflage: Secularization flavours and syncretic components," Pandya reveals the "package" offered to middle-class seekers with modern sensibilities and education. Her emphasis is on the possibilities or hindrances for social transformation:

> The peculiarity that emerges for the HIFMs is that there is a clear faith assertion alongside the modes of knowledge and sensibilities of modernity.... This means that in a secular scheme of things and modernity frame, religious decline creates insecurities, a situation in which HIMFs intervene with their faith package. This package is such that it contains faith capital and monopoly of the cultural goods of salvation and its management. The dimensions are so determined that they fit

seamlessly into the secular-modernity canon.... From their mystical fund, the sacred is regained and communicated differently".

2017, 184

Note her important implications: a desire for security hence hegemony/order, her assumptions that "faith" wants security and a package but an equal desire for modern cultural goods—a sense of scientific validity, continued economic wellbeing and progress for themselves and the nation, and a continuity with certain aspects of India's past greatness. All of her terminology seems carefully taken from the world of commerce—package, capital, monopoly, goods—as per the more usual sense of spirituality as enterprise, part of the material flows of capitalism. However, the terminology of "faith package" and "clear faith assertion" and "faith discourse" (184) carries many more connotations from its use in US policy work on nonprofit organizations in civil society, where the term has become an almost standard cypher for religion and religious. The term "faith"—because of its old association with Protestant "faith" over "works"—unintentionally weights the discussion toward *discourse* and away from space and bodies. Interestingly, the movements Pandya studies all offer forms of yoga or *kriya*, which she analyzes.

Her emphasis on a "package" within a secular modernist regime also shifts the center of analysis back to the image of Modi & Co. as consummate businessmen, but may leave aspects of spirituality behind. Discussion of the intertwining of yoga-state-economy are refined with van de Veer's analysis of an intense relationship between spirituality, the body, and the very construction of an Indian modernity: "religious movements, dealing with spiritual matters and body exercises—in short, with spiritual transcendence attained through the body—are a central part of modern political and economic history" (2014, *kl* 2904–6). The value of van der Veer here is his connection of breathing techniques with power and hence the political:

It is precisely the importance of these techniques in religious traditions that makes them central in social and political history. The operative term here is "power," since these traditions claim that these techniques provide the practitioner with knowledge, but also with power to act on the world, both in terms of visible and invisible forces.

kl 2900–2902

Missing in both, however, is another "package" that my conversations and observations also revealed: a *theological* element, a sense of "God" and "guru" directly related to spacemaking, placemaking, *and* power.

Manoj Thakur arranged a meeting with his guru, Anil Sarode, from his hometown of Gwalior. Sarode had retired back to an ashramlike community, the Vivekananda Nidam, vividly described by Daniel Gold (2015, 171–83), after years serving at the headquarters of the Vivekananda Kendra in Kanyakumari at the southern tip of India where Vivekananda, while meditating at this conjunction of three oceans, was "transformed into a reformer, a nation-builder and a world-architect" (Atmashraddhananda 2010, 12). A recent blog lauded Sarode as an "unsung hero" for

Figure 4.23 Anil Saroda kindly posed for a photo before we talked. Used with the permission of Manoj Thakur.

his "selfless work" inspired by Swami Vivekananda, and goes on to say Sarode "follows his ideals with a pure heart" (Chaturvedi 2018). Seated facing each other in a yoga studio near a window, I asked Anil why the prime minister worked so hard to initiate the International Day of Yoga (fig 4.23). His answer at first had seemed very indirect, beginning from his sense of yoga, and then ending: "So this is the beauty with this motivation Mr. Narendra Modi is working to spread yoga." However, I began to understand that, for Anil, yoga was an "inward journey" marked by a refocusing from the external to the internal. Yoga "is the tool" for this journey inward, "because by practicing yoga you have to be with yourself":

> You do not need any external thing such as the mats or even the equipment and all other facilities or even the control of diet or a particular pattern that you do not need because you have taken bath or not, that doesn't matter. If you have AC or do not have, if you have a mirror or do not have, that doesn't matter. So externally you do not need anything. The whole laboratory is you and your inner reality so this

laboratory you are working with so you do not need anything externally outwardly
and that is the beauty of yoga. This is the only system which elaborates and which
gives this technique that you can go within.

Careful listening reveals coded language: the references to bath and control of diet
releases the practice of yoga from core restrictions of caste differences usually defined
in term of diet and bodily cleanliness. Included also are the key elements of middle-
class status: affording the expense of an AC and "mirrors" which assume a concern
with appearance. But also yoga becomes a matter of daily life— "it should be useful to
everyone wherever he is because the person has many things to do in the life"—a point
the prime minister emphasized in his IDY 2018 video address: "Yoga is not only what
we practice in the morning, doing our day-to-day activities with diligence and complete
awareness is yoga as well."[32] And finally the language of science enters Sarode's
discussion, with echoes of Gandhi's "experiments with truth": "The whole laboratory is
you and your inner reality so this laboratory you are working with so you do not need
anything externally outwardly and that is the beauty of yoga."

Then answering my question on yoga's relationship to its Indian roots, Anil returned
to Modi's agenda for IDY in India arguing that, in the Indian context, people are likely
to assume that God will take care of things so they do not act for themselves. Connecting
Modi's program for general public cleanliness with his promotion of yoga, Anil
explained that the prime minister needed to change *attitudes* at a root level:

> so someone who could hammer the point was needed and the prime minister has
> done that—it's not exactly a new thing that cleanliness is next to godliness even
> Mahatma Gandhi was decisive on that ... but basically yoga is a combination of
> physical activity and mental activity so that mental activity—or psychological
> adjustments you can say—is a more important thing in India, the emphasis is
> given on that particular thing *not* on the bodily things *not* the outward things ...
> so that makes a difference to the Indian attitude for yoga that it should change the
> nature of the person: moreover moral, moreover mental, psychological adjustments
> so that way yoga has got a very powerful thing which can change the person totally
> not only external thing not only physically.

So here yoga becomes a tool in India to change the very nature of the person—to
participate in public life consciously and fully? But the place of this transformation is
between person and space where all of this occurs—the inner remakes the outer.

However, Anil's answer to "What is the place of God in Yoga?" proved the most
revealing. I asked the question because "God" is both external *and* internal and most
difficult to deflect from terms like Religion and religious. For many modern yoga
movements matters of debate usually turn to Patanjali's *Yoga Sutra*, "required reading"
(White 2012, 1) and usually the authoritative text. Indeed, this is where Anil Saroda began:

> The concept of God is *not* there, basically it is not there. But then he has used
> one word *Ishvara-pranidhan* [Īśvara + praṇidhāna] nothing can be created without
> a creator if some form is there then it means that some creator was definitely

there so he says you should be always in a mood, always be thinking that you are surrendering to that almighty *not exactly* God but that *almighty* he says, *almighty* is the conjuring power, the whole world in the sense of not only this earth but the cosmos. . . . I am also part of this which is created like out of mud, different shapes are there humans are there lions are there tigers are there dogs are there cats are there so these are the different forms but then somebody is the creator who has created these forms so that creator if he is there why am I worried, so stressed, because you have been created by him I am also created by him so we are brothers, we are sisters, so why are we quarreling? To that we bow down to that we surrender ourselves we will do our duties properly but we have shifted our burden to him, we are free now in that sense so in that stress conditions, I will perform my duties.

Here Anil is echoing parts of the Bhagavad-Gita as well as Vivekananda's collected writing on the philosophy of "Ishvara" as befitting a well-educated member of the Vivekananda Kendra, but with much of his own reflections. Sarode moves between and around two sides in a significant debate on the meaning of this conjoined term, *Īśvara praṇidhāna*: is this "Lord," a deity to which a yogi surrenders, or is this a primordial "master" of sorts, to whom a yogi remains "committed." This is no mere counting angels-on-a-pin debate—and one that surprisingly moves from the nature of God into the nature of space—but the trajectory of those steps will take time to reveal.

One of the most debated issues within yoga circles both past and contemporary are (1) the nature of "lord" as either deity with personal form or more simply "master" *and* (2) the meaning of *praṇidhāna* as either "surrender" or "commitment." The differences on the presence of God in yoga practices are deeply implicated in theological concerns over the need for divine grace *or* self-reliance—or, as Heelas and Woodhead put it, "subordinating subjective-life to the 'higher authority.'" But neither position on *Īśvara* or *praṇidhāna* is easily subsumed under "faith commitments." As Gordon White shows in his "biography" of the compound *Īśvara praṇidhāna* in Patañjali, the debate began early and involved the famous Sanskritist F. Max Müller, credited as the founder of comparative religions/history of religions, as well as Swami Vivekananda, again credited as the initiator of modern yoga.[33] White sides in the debate with *master* and *commitment*: "Commitment to such a Master would in no way have implied devotion to a deity of any sort. Indeed, in the centuries prior to the Yoga Sutra's time, the word "ishvara" had never denoted a god, but was rather applied to a human lord or king" (2014, 178). White buttressed his point, quoting Müller in 1899:

> The Isvara, with the Yogins, was originally no more than one of the many souls, or rather Selves or Purusas, but one that has never been associated or implicated in metempsychosis [using the Greek rather than Sanskrit term for transmigration of souls, rebirth], supreme in every sense, yet of the same kind as all other Purusas.[34]
>
> 2014, 179

White then quotes Barbara Stoler Miller: "the Lord [Master of Yoga] is not a creator god who grants grace; rather, he is a representation of the omniscient spirit as the archetypal yogi."[35] Here note the stark contrast with Edwin Bryant's spectacular translation of Patañjali's *Yoga Sutra* along with major commentaries, in which he declares unequivocally: "Yoga has always been theistic" (2009, *kl* 2774).

But why the century-long, passionate debate on the nature of *Īśvara*? What is the difference, or indeed the commonality, between *commitment* and *devotion, lord* or *deity*? *Both* commitment *and* devotion remain internal experiences, felt responses—but to what? For Prime Minister Modi, Sadhguru, Guruji, and those defending spirituality in the US or UK (Woodhead and Heelas), all of whom at one point in their lives shifted their seeking—Lucia would say "converted"[36] to yoga (2018)—*Īśvara* cannot be and must not be equated with God in a "Western" sense. India must have distinct roots, a unique gift to give the world or, as Jaggi Vasudev puts it, "Nowhere else on the planet.... Nowhere else has it been looked at with the profoundness."[37] And yet Anil Sarode, who firmly holds that "inner reality ... this laboratory you are working with so you do not need anything externally," calls *Īśvara* the creator. Interestingly when Swami Vivekananda famously addressed the World's Parliament of Religion in 1893, or when early teachers of yoga like Paramahansa Yogananda needed to bridge terms like *Īśvara* to anglophone ears, they used God.[38] Such bridging can still be heard in Sri Sri Ravi Shankar's 1990s talks outside India. But, in the current religious/spiritual ethos, the task is the opposite: the differentiation of *Īśvara* or any such Indic terms from the common-sense "God." Ironic because there also may be Nowhere Else where deities are so concrete, so visible, so present, as in India. And indeed in the *other* hand of Modi is the Ram Janmabhoomi, the powerful movement to build a grand temple at the (disputed) birthplace of an incarnation/*avatāra* of God. This insistence *on difference* of *Spirituality* and *Religion*, even in the face of seemingly contradictory actions, is striking in very recent works like *Adiyogi* by Sadhguru Jaggi Vasudev and Arundhathi Subramaniam (2017), as well as his website discussions, "Who is Shiva?" (2014) and "The Presence of Shiva" (2015), *and* that "Bible" for IDY, the *Common Yoga Protocol* (2015).

Adiyogi, Sadhguru's latest statement on Shiva, begins with Jaggi Vasudev's collaborator in conversation with her guru who has asked her now to do a book on "Adiyogi, Shiva." When she calls Shiva a god, "'He isn't a god,' Sadhguru says crisply" and later, "He's my breath" and still later, "I don't know any teachings, any scriptures. All I know is myself. I know this piece of life absolutely," then, adding a statement to aggravate any postmodern/postcolonial theorist, "knowing this piece of life, one knows, by inference, every other piece of life" (Vasudev and Subramanian 2017, 1–3). Arundhathi Subramaniam superbly summarizes multiple contradictions: "Whether formless or embodied, celestial or terrestrial, mythic or historic, Shiva for him is *real*. Urgent, immediate, throbbingly present" (2017, 21). Then as the "eavesdropper" for this storyteller par excellence, she begins by relating what I would again call a *cosmology*, a creation story, of sorts—the same that also appears in the *Common Yoga Protocol*, but in a governmental idiom.

"The Beginning" unfolds with a date and a place, "over fifteen thousand years ago" in the Himalayas (Vasudev and Subramanian 2017). In his earlier website article, Sadhguru gives an exact place, "on the banks of Kanti Sarovar," including his photo at the glacial lake (Vasudev 2014). This is not as a once-upon-a-time tale. Here a "being" appears nine feet tall, sometimes sitting still, other times dancing "wild and ecstatic." The story progresses with the clear sense that both humans and the earth are preexistent, yet, as he danced, "planets and stars, rivers and forests, mountains and oceans exploded into life around him. He seemed to become life itself" (2017, 25). People gathered to see him, waited for some special miracle and, when nothing happened as he sat still and motionless, they left. Only seven continued in his presence and waited, even after initially dismissed. Finally, the "Adiyogi—or the first yogi" relented and began to teach "the nature of life" to "these seven thirsty seekers." This day on the first full moon after the summer solstice, when this Being consented to act as Adi Guru, the first guru, continues to be celebrated as Guru Poornima (*guru*, "teacher" + *pūrṇimā*, "full moon"). Then narrator (Sadhguru via Subramaniam) asserts:

> It was on this day that it was declared for the first time in human history that biology is not destiny, that it is possible for a human being to evolve consciously. The finite can turn infinite. The particular can turn universal . . . a piece of creation can become one with the source of creation. The human creature can become a divine entity.
>
>   26

The last sentence declares a sharp difference with religion. These teachings did not engender "faith" but rather a "science" to make "humans the rulers of their own fate." Guru Poornima "predates religion" occurring "before the idea of religion even entered the human mind." The aim of these "insights" was "not God" but "liberation," "roaring unfettered life. Ecstatic boundless, infinite life" that is "within the reach of every human being" (27).

Untroubled (he *does* know and is very well read) by over two centuries of academic work on the *history* of religions—these are not the kind of teachers or knowledge that really matter—he is disclosing the *deeper meaning* "revealed only to those who seek" (Vasudev 2014). Sadhguru can declare that for the "first time in human history," a great teacher, indeed the first guru, expounded *not* creeds requiring "faith" but a method for humanity to rise above the physical fetter of their biology. What was offered was *not* religion, and the one who offered was *not* a miracle-welding god but a *guru* with a science. And in the next chapter of *Adi Yogi*, and in more concise form in his earlier website posts, he reveals Shiva as *not-god*, "non-being, not as a being," but that the "nothingness can hold everything." He seamlessly melds this very Shiva, this Adi Yogi, to the newly proven scientific knowledge that the "basis of existence and the fundamental quality of the cosmos is vast nothingness." But so fundamentally inherent in the land of India is this "dialectical culture" that its people can shift "from this to that and that to this effortlessly." Yet scientists around the world stand "amazed" at these ideas, which the people of India have known for millennia: "Almost every peasant in India knows about it unconsciously. He talks about it without even knowing the science behind it" (Vasudev 2014). So, Shiva is neither myth nor "a construct of collective imagination," but that *nothingness* at the heart of cosmic reality.

Ironically to this Historian of Religions, the narrative in *Adi Yoga*, and the prior web articles, displays all the marks of a *myth*—a story centered in the explanation of the major rite of a community (*guru pūrṇimā*), the coming of its founder (Adi Yogi), a clear revelation of the nature of the cosmos, and the good news of salvation (boundless, infinite life). But my very words here would be anathema to Ishas. The narrative pointedly denies the primacy of religion *or* of God, *or* myth. In the beginning was a great being, a master, a guru called Adi Guru or Shiva empowering human beings "to blossom to their ultimate potential." Here is *science, history,* the secrets of *transformation,* and an intense *reality* birthed in India but offered to all.

The *Common Yoga Protocol* offers a strikingly similar narrative but in a *bureaucratic dialect* under the heading, "Brief history and development of Yoga" (2015, 2–3):

> The science of Yoga has its origins thousands of years ago, long before the first religion or belief systems were born. According to Yogic lore, Shiva has [been] seen as the first *yogi* or *ādiyogi* and the first *guru* or *ādiguru.* Several thousand years ago on the banks of lake Kantisarovar in the Himalayas, *ādiyogi* poured forth his profound knowledge into the legendary *saptarishis* or "seven sages." These sages carried powerful Yogic science to different parts of the world including Asia, the Middle East, North Africa and South America. Interestingly, modern scholars have noted and marveled at the close parallels found between cultures across the globe.

Sadhguru in *Adi Yoga* claims his narrative as *true* history not myth or legend, but primarily as *deeper meaning* at the level of insight. In that sense the book remains a narrative, or as his collaborator puts it, "the form is prose but the logic poetry . . . like all mythic stories, this is meant to be approached intuitively" (6). The *Protocol,* while using terms like "lore" and "legendary," presents itself unambiguously as a *history* derived from legends. Clearly indebted to Jaggi Vasudev—pointing to the same locale in the Himalayas for Ādiyogi's revelation—their text adds the intriguing claim that the seven sages initially spread yogic knowledge worldwide naming the locations of all of the ancient civilizations,[39] a new diffusionism with the origin in India not the Caucasus[40] or Egypt or elsewhere. The unnamed authors of the *Common Yoga Protocol,* consulting with "leading experts and heads of the eminent Yoga Institution of India," termed the document not a *manual* or a *guide,* but chose *protocol*—a term from diplomacy but also medicine and the newer digital world. In the old colonial British sense, *protocol* often meant the correct order of precedent in diplomatic situations. Currently, in diplomacy, in medicine, or in digital coding, it means following a proper order of procedures,[41] the right code of conduct. The term carries a sense of formal propriety: correct actions with a bureaucratic-cum-scientific flavor. As Manoj Thakkar told me multiple times, *yoga* for VYASA Yoga remains a tool for good health, wellbeing, peace—which remained the theme for Prime Minister Modi and for Anil Sarode, but with the added hope that personal transformation leads to community, a national and global sense of oneness.

But what of God? What of the theological issues? And what of that takeover of public space in Singapore? Sri Sri Ravi Shankar begins to answer these questions in his own commentary on the Yoga Sutras with a section, "Who is God?" Here he asks the same questions debated a century ago, over "Eshwara pranidhana [*Īśvara praṇidhāna*]" (2012, *kl* 23187–9). "Where is God? Who is Lord? Who is Lord of this creation? What is lordship?" (*kl* 8390–401). His answer to his Swiss audience invokes Jesus: "Love is in-built in creation. That's how the whole of creation functions. And that—'in-built'—is the core of consciousness. That's why Jesus said, 'Love is God. God is love.' Synonymous!"

(*kl* 8518–44). Later, he muses on where this special Being resides: "Not hanging somewhere in the sky, but in your heart" (kl 9289–95). These are the almost expected tropes—God is love, God is within you—but then his imagery turns to the spatial:

> All worship is always the mind to its Being. It's like the circumference collapsing into the center. A boundary, a circumference that is outside, collapses to the center. What happens when a boundary collapses into the center? It becomes infinite and limitless. When our little chattering mind prays, it prays to the infinite Being that you are. That is prayer. Do you get it?
>
> *kl* 9367–407

And finally to an equation of God, guru, and self:

> That's why there is no difference between God, Guru and your Self. Eshwaro guroratmeti murti bheda vibhagine.[42] It is a matter of words. Whatever the master is, it is nothing but the core of your being, and it is the same as the Divine that rules this entire creation.
>
> *kl* 9519–56

But then in a question and answer session on the Art of Living website, Guruji turns even more emphatically to *space*:

> Space is God. That in which everything "is" today; in which everything has "come from" and into which everything "will dissolve," that is the Divine. That is the centre core of everyone's existence.[43]

In his message for Guru Purnima, Sri Sri Ravi Shankar affirms:

> You are not the body, you are the soul, and the form of the soul is like that of Space. The same is true for the Guru as well. Don't think of the Guru as the limited physical body. The Guru is the field, the energy which is all permeating; so is the Self. And honoring the Guru is honoring your own Self.[44]

Here Sri Sri Ravi Shankar is on the same page as Sadhguru Jaggi Vasudev (although my own Isha Teacher Tina disagrees, arguing strongly that these two gurus are like apples and oranges, not comparable), at least in a basic common sense that God and Self and Guru are best understood in *spatial* rather than *metaphysical* terms. A Heideggerian reading may be the best parallel.[45] As Sri Sri says, the guru is the all-permeating field, or, as Sadhguru puts it, Shiva as *not-god*, the nothingness can *hold* everything.

All of these seemingly abstract sensibilities gained ground in a long interview with my articulate Isha interlocutor. Sitting in Albert Court at an outdoor restaurant, I asked him about the secular venues of the International Day of Yoga events that I was witnessing and wondered about the importance that Sadhguru stresses on residing in a consecrated space, but places like the streets and industrial buildings did not appear to be such spaces. He affirmed the importance of a *space*, a *place*, for practice, arguing that, before initiating a yoga practice, "you need to provide proper support first then you initiate them into something so when they want to make it stay alive in themselves that consecrated-space-support works for them." Confused at this point, I could not understand how an area like the one we occupied—very public with tables, chairs, and potted palms shared by multiple restaurants—could become consecrated. His answer: "If I know how to access Sadhguru—when I say *guru* we are not talking about a person or a being we are talking about a space and an energy, which is there, which is accessible—if you know how to access it, there are certain methods and processes to access it—*guru pūjā* for example." He continued:

> Suppose you want to do a yoga class here, the first thing you do is guru puja. For example, if you are setting this place up, before even lifting a chair, first thing we would do is light a lamp and do guru puja. We need to get a connection to that dimension before we get into that activity so that we do the best that we can do, that is the space/energy that we call *guru*—it is very difficult to put in words. I do not even know what I am saying is correct but this is how I would do it.

I asked if a picture of the guru was necessary: *good* if possible, but "the bare minimum is a lamp which has a certain energy so you do guru puja to that energy in an attempt to connect." He turned to the nature of gurus, which for him was Sadhguru as a person, but "when you hear him talking about it, he will say guru is not a person, it's a certain space and energy. Now there could be a *being* that embodies that space and energy so you call that person *guru*." He continued with a common understanding I have heard to explain the embodiment of divinity in an image: humans need some sensory, material connection. But then I asked about those who see God as an external as a well as a spatial or internal reality—a Being of great power, a lord to whom we submit. He argued in return that all experience of God or guru ultimately comes from within each body within the human system: "So what other space is there, in terms of working, the human system is the only thing you can work with … Can only speak from within."

Space/God in a New Key

Light a wick soaked in ghee, do a simple puja to the *guru*, and access a *space* that is at once within/without "the field, the energy which is all permeating"—in Sri Sri's terms— at once the Self and Guru and "God," (an old equation of oneness in South India).[46] But here with the added definition of all *as spatial field* at once "infinite and limitless," yet also a center collapsing on itself, as Sri Sri explained for a Guru Purnima celebration. That *place* in a physical sense can be a courtyard, a cement slab under a bridge, a pedestrian roadway in Little India, a room in an industrial building, or a temple annex. More important *spatially* are those carefully distributed "ubiquitous" yoga mats, as Susan Newcome describes them in an American context, a "portable sacred space" but also the "'personal space' of each individual" (2018, 566). Here the "human system" becomes the "the only thing you can work with," but it stretches out to infinity.

That *place* where the practice will take place is now consecrated but also concentrated; but only for the time of the practice. Then it once again is a courtyard of a popular tourist hotel just outside of Little India or a free yoga mat to sling over a shoulder on the way home or back to work. I know that VYASA yoga did not do guru puja in that street in front of the Little India Arcade, but they did intone those vibrant notes from the Chinese singing-bowls under the Marina Bay East bridge, and at the grand celebration the dignitaries did light a *viḷakku,* a multitiered oil lamp, to invoke Vivekananda—as a memory or a presence or both? For Isha and VYASA and Art of Living in some sense, *the space* of yoga practice was consecrated, celebrated, invoked, made present—as a little bit of the infinite in a very finite setting.

Is this really a matter of a constructed faith package to further a political agenda? *Yes and no.* There are theological issues—actually the *logical* here may not fit, perhaps *theotopoical.* As Anil Sarode put it, "you are surrendering to that almighty *not exactly God … almighty* is the conjuring power." Why is this "*not exactly God*"? Again, with Jaggi Vasudev, in the beginning is a great being, who is his very life breath but definitively not-god. So, the same theme: the space of the yoga mat is *internal*—the deep locus of all with an equation of god-guru-self. But what about the differences with those yoga groups with and those without a guru? Interestingly, the language seems the same. I think Isha and Art of Living are better at discourse. But even for VYASA, GOD is there—yet *not* god *but a creator*? How can anyone separate God and creator? Usually the more typical reaction is to affirm God but not as creator, yet here the not-exactly-God exists as creator. But notice, there is a distinction; this begins to feel like Deism: the creator sets this in motion and exits. But not this creator, he did something different, he provided a method, a technique for continued personal evolution, ultimately to transcend common "biological destiny" to "blossom" into fullness. But again, is this pure rhetoric for the sake of constructing a phony secularity? Here sacred-secular makes little sense. There is no God outside the world; there are natural laws and yogic techniques to overcome that system but these are no miracles. No *deus ex machina* will come to the rescue—nor is any promised. But there are techniques to enter guru-space—for some the divine and the living teacher offer means for access.

But when the Prime Minister of India Modi goes to the mats, something *is* afoot. In the context of India, the goal is to re-form those bodies and spirits into a working whole, to move in unity from me to we; but what would be the political undercurrent in Singapore? For the government of Singapore with their twin foci of community identity and general wellness, on the one hand, and building the inner and outer strength of its citizens, on the other, their embrace of yoga does make sense, but not completely. Again, unlike the more official satsangs of the many spiritual organizations involved, Chinese-heritage practitioners equaled or outnumbered those with Indian roots at most events that I attended, and were equally if not *more* enthusiastic. They embraced this new macrocosm, this Y-Cloud—if Manoj Thakur is correct, as a way to cope with the overly developed, ordered high-rise environment of Singapore. But then this would not be a transformation into a "we"—the inner and outer landscape already carefully molded into a unity—but a route to something else? I cannot say here or begin to know. Complex layers of motives and desire still sit on those mats. The space of the state was very publicly claimed by *another macrocosm* related to, possibly coterminous with but not the same as, the macrospace of the gurus. Here the pioneering work on space by Yi-Fu Tuan in *Topophilia* affords a sense of how *new* this macrocosm is. He brilliantly outlines all of the types of spatial worlds but does *not* anticipate the self on the mat:

> Human beings have persistently searched for the ideal environment. How it looks varies from one culture to another but in essence it seems to draw on two antipodal images: the garden of innocence and the cosmos. The fruits of the earth provide security as also does the harmony of the stars which offers, in addition, grandeur. So, we move from one to the other: from the shade under the baobab to the magic circle under heaven; from home to public square, from suburb to city; from a seaside holiday to the enjoyment of the sophisticated arts, seeking for a point of equilibrium that is not of this world.
>
> [1974] 1990, *kl* 3340–4

But the yogic point of equilibrium is of this world, yet at the same time not.

5

Reading Walden Pond at
Marina Bay Sands, Singapore[1]

Young lotuses are just getting their start in the new pond surrounding the base of the world's first ArtScience Museum, the *pièce de résistance* of the newly opened Marina Bay Sands complex in Singapore.[2] Shaped like a lotus, the giant petals extend from the raised base with steel stems and painted-pipe roots (Fig. 5.1). Another bit of nature, microscopic but now remolded giant-sized in steel, stretches across the bay: the double-helix bridge, the new DNA of a commercial life, is claimed as the first of its kind. Actually, all of the shapes of this complex are organic (Fig. 5.2). The steel and glass roof of the shopping mall forms a large tunnel on the inside but here jutting buttresses form a sunscreen making the tunnel look like a caterpillar body with protruding wings—not yet a butterfly but no longer a worm. At the corner of the pond, a dead lotus clings to the side—the only sign of death within this steel and glass permanency. Across Marina Bay the new financial center of Singapore rises, shifting the center of gravity from the old downtown toward an area that once held go-downs and gritty barges. The grit is still here but not the dirt, as this center of banking visualizes its determination in the height of its skyscrapers.

Inside this giant lotus, an elevator rises to the gallery levels. At the time of my first visit in 2012, the museum had only recently opened and the architecture was stunning. Connecting the third and fourth floors, an undulating staircase floated seamlessly into the blond wood forming the stairs, while very neutral walls curving outward obscured the stair treads from the walls. A twisting silver stripe painted along the wall only added to the disorientation. Messages appeared on the walls almost magically from an invisible source, asking in successive flashes in English with Chinese subscript, "What wisdom does nature hold?"; "Can we see the unseen?"; "Can technology heal our planet?"; "Where do life and technology meet?" And, finally, the most unexpected question appeared: "Can a building have a soul?"—a query no scholar of religion could resist (Fig. 5.3).

These floating questions suggested an eerie continuity with another piece of digital magic: my own simultaneous reading of *Walden* on a Nook. Outside, the ArtScience Museum seemed afloat in the clear water as if some giant carnivalesque magnifying mirror had altered a tiny lotus into a colossal form, conjuring Thoreau's own aggrandizement of Walden Pond. Thoreau's much quoted description of his beloved

Figure 5.1 ArtScience Museum and Marina Bay Sands. Photo by Dick Waghorne.

Figure 5.2 Moving through the double-helix bridge as the sun glows on the panels. Photo by Dick Waghorne.

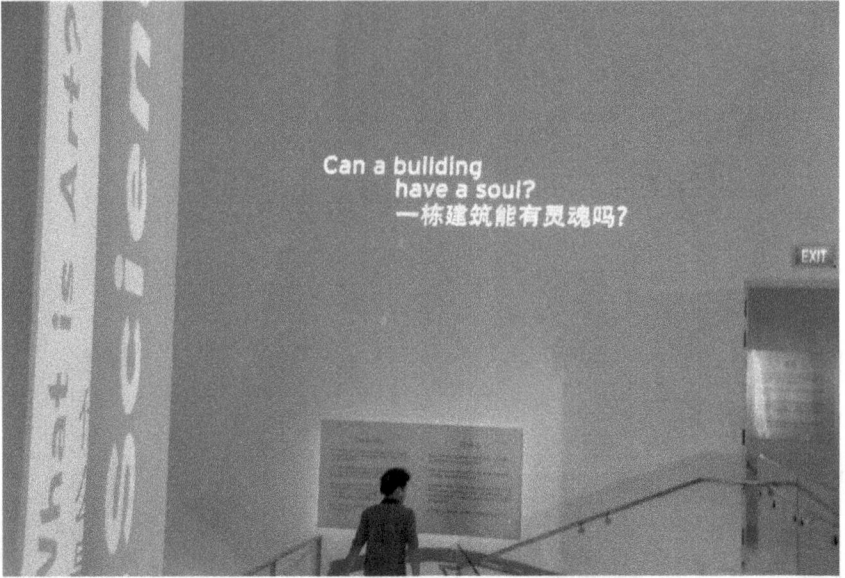

Figure 5.3 Floating stairway with appearing and vanishing questions. Photo by Dick Waghorne.

little lake seems refracted in time and space in an Asian city many miles from his nearby Boston:

> A lake is the landscape's most beautiful and expressive feature. It is earth's eye; looking into which the beholder measures the depth of his own nature. The fluviatile trees next the shore are the slender eyelashes which fringe it, and the wooded hills and cliffs around are its overhanging brows.
>
> 355–356

Here the lotus pond appeared fringed not with tall trees but with skyscrapers, which nonetheless took on magical form as the sky darkened for a storm (Fig. 5.4). Something of the ethereal—or perhaps the surreal—continued here: the intense invocation of nature, the vague spirituality, and the open play with size and with imagination kept conjuring Thoreau in spite of all of the seeming contradictions in scale and in purpose.

So, I take the plunge and ask that flashing question on the walls of the ArtScience Museum, "Can a building have a soul?" Seconds before this, another question central to Thoreau at Walden Pond appeared on the same wall: "What wisdom does nature hold?" This conjoining of "nature" and the built environment, as we will see, well fits the ArtScience Museum, but still startles the viewer. Especially in the American context, the sense that "Nature" has a consciousness and wisdom weaves in and out of daily life, predating Thoreau and continuing to current-day New-Age sensibilities (Albanese 1991). But to say that a building has a "soul" is to say that something of steel, glass, and fiberglass-reinforced polymer can have a presence, a living quality that effects a change in those who

Figure 5.4 Reflections of a forest of steel and glass.

live, work, or pass through its walls. To put the question in another way, can such an overscale building—and the even more wildly overscale complex within an ardently commercial setting—bring about a transforming experience for the urban dweller in any way likened to the effect[3] of the little Walden Pond on "America's first Yogi" (De Michelis 2004, 2–3; Syman 2010, 26–36)? To ask this question means taking the current "spatial turn" (see Warf and Arias 2008) to seriously consider "the setting in which we live," and to acknowledge "vis-à-vis the lived experience, space is neither a 'frame,' after the fashion of frame of a painting, nor a form or container of a virtually neutral kind, designed simply to receive whatever is poured into it" (Lefebvre [1974] 1991, 92–4). *Walden* and the development at Marina Bay Sands, whatever their differences, are neither inert objects nor whims of imagination, but something far more complex.

Conversations in the Middle

Returning to the ArtScience Museum in 2012, I spoke with the then new director, Nick Dixon,[4] who confirmed, and yet complicated, some of my initial impressions of the museum. Calling the museum "an architecturally stunning building," he also pointed to its rich ambiguity. Widely interpreted as either the "welcoming hand of Singapore or the lotus," the museum was designed by a Western architect as part of an American commercial enterprise but built in Singapore where older Chinese spatial concepts, Feng Shui, remain important interpretive tools. But all of this mixing was appropriate for Singapore, which exists "at the crossroads of culture": "It's a complex building."

As I listened, the crossroads quality of my conversation partner and me, along with the unusual population mix of the city, came into focus. We were not speaking in, or even from, a place of cultural purity, but rather of "cosmopolitan contamination"—the term for a "counter-ideal" to notions of authenticity suggested by Anthony Appiah (2006, 111). We both shared a "contaminated" identity among those "global souls" (Iyer 2000) with multiple experiences of many homes. Nick Dixon became the director of the museum after serving as International Culture Curator at the King Abdulaziz Center for World Culture in Dhahran Saudi Arabia[5]—he left the ArtScience Museum and is now back in his native New Zealand as New Dunedin City Council arts and culture manager.[6] I have traveled to and lived in India and Singapore intermittently for the last forty years. Moreover, with 70 percent of the population of Singapore sharing a Chinese heritage, and others with roots in South India, few here can claim to be "children of the soil," *bumiputera*, as in nearby Malaysia (Hefner 2001, 19). We were indeed sitting at a crossroad.

As our conversation continued, the complexity of ArtScience Museum as a concept, as an institution, and as a work of architecture emerged. Invoking the name of the museum, Nick Dixon cautioned, "The word ArtScience is not about bringing art and science together and seeing what happens, it is about understanding that there is something there in the middle which is a thing in its own right. What underlies all of this stuff is human creativity." He prefaced this with his own sense of a post-Enlightenment moment when "art got taken away from us and put into art galleries, natural philosophy got taken away from us and put into labs . . . religion got very complicated so that now we are in a world where art and science and religion are supposed to be mutually antithetical." In line with these sensibilities, the ArtScience Museum, unlike the standard dictionary meanings, is not "an institution devoted to the procurement, care, study, and display of objects of lasting interest or value" (merriam-webster.com). With no permanent collection, this museum, like the Latin root of the term, seems to honor the Muses (Fig. 5.5)—that is, in Dixon's terms, focuses on the creative process "not the product": "Bring together Art and Science and one of the things you have at that intersection is architecture." Dixon explained that, in fully developing the mission of the museum, "the building is going to be an extremely powerful asset because the building is an embodiment of ArtScience." As an embodiment of that something in the middle, the ArtScience Museum seems at once a thing and an event.

Aware of the many discussions of museums as instruments of "perpetual self reflectiveness," (Bennett 2006, *kl* 884), my focus remained on processes evoked within persons as they take the walkway over the pond into the glass atrium and move up the glass lifts into the upper galleries and come under and into its polymer petals. I found that the director and I shared sensitivity to the experiential—indeed moving—quality of the architecture. Earlier in our conversation, Dixon noted, "This building itself is about process," as I added my own sense of the powerful effect of the almost transparent

Figure 5.5 Words in water at the ArtScience Museum.

winding staircases when I moved through the building. But for Dixon that process cannot be separated from the exhibitions displayed within the museum. As the conversation turned to the then current exhibit on Andy Warhol, organized in conjunction with the Andy Warhol Museum in Pittsburgh, Dixon added that an architect had planned the exhibit, rather than an exhibition designer, because "by using an architect we are resonating with the building in a really effective way." In the foreword to the stunningly designed catalogue, "Andy Warhol: 15 Minutes Eternal," Dixon sounds the theme of creative contradictions as the sources of that effective energy: "His radical approach—a celebration of the production technique, elevating mass production to an art form—was a game-changer.... We, too, aspire to find new ways to bring together seemingly contradictory ways of working and thinking to identify an exciting and innovative strand of human creativity" (Macdonald 2012, 9). In the final addendum to the catalogue, once again the emphasis on processes reemerged: "In an encounter that is both immersive and experiential, Andy Warhol: 15 Minutes Eternal will walk visitors along a path of the iconic Pop Artist's life, with the Museum's unique spaces forming an imaginative backdrop to Warhol's broad creations" (135).

The processes that the museum space enables—or perhaps instigates—move the museumgoer through an "immersive" "encounter" with a radical creator who used everyday commercial products as his working material. The wording here echoes Nick Dixon's comment that, in a very pragmatic city-state like Singapore, "we cannot be drawn into an arcane philosophical discussion of the nature of human creativity, it's got to very immediate, visceral, it's got to be experiential." Indeed, the exhibit's designers, the International Singapore- and Paris-based architectural firm WY-TO, defines its design process, on their website, thus: "to combine functionality and dream, to create spaces for everyday life as well as exceptional occasions." This immersion, into the real and imaginary, ended at the museum store in the basement. A photographer standing in front of a replica of the iconic Campbell Soup Can, printed on cut-out canvas with ArtScience Museum in black-trimmed white lettering mimicking the familiar logo, offered a final shot at the experiential. My husband and I dived into the commercial can and, as we pushed our head and hands out of the flaps, the camera clicked. I love the photo (Fig. 5.6).

Within the space of this giant lotus, multiple dualities seem to be in the soup together, none dissolved and none resolved. The real and the imagined, the commercial and the creative mingle. Of the four exhibits I experienced in this museum, the artist/art was never presented à la romantique sans the commercial or the social context; nonetheless something almost magical persisted. Andy Warhol showed with Harry Potter: The Exhibition in the galleries in the basement floor. Here Harry's glasses, Hermione's ball gown, and all of the wands lay displayed within the original sets for the movies. Ironically, these items were the real thing, the actual prompts to a world of

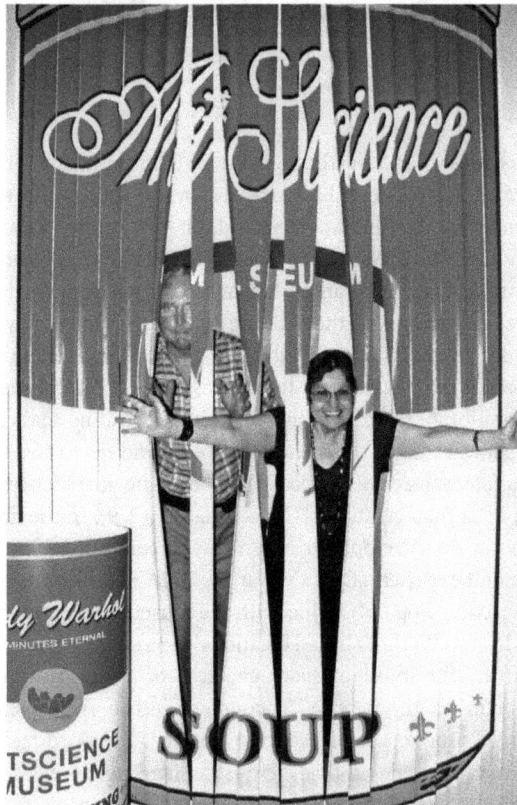

Figure 5.6 In the Soup. Photo used with permission of the Marketing Department of the ArtScience Museum.

fantasy that has now made over 7 billion dollars for the movies alone. An earlier exhibit, "Dali—Mind of a Genius," featured the surrealist, who like Warhol enjoyed wealth during his lifetime, yet his melting clocks and elongated animals make the ordinary extraordinary. For "Vincent Van Gogh Alive," the Australian curators decided to forego exhibiting the actual parlor-sized painting. In keeping with the megascale of the building, they presented a thousand images of Van Gogh—his paintings and photos of his Paris. Feeling like I had taken too much out of the bottle marked "Drink me," I walked through the gallery rooms as 30-foot images faded and newly appeared in brilliant succession. In all of these exhibits the commercial, the creative, and the charmed lived together.

This mix mirrors the ArtScience Museum, fully a part of a huge commercial complex owned and operated by the Las Vegas Sands Corporation and ultimately housing a wildly successful casino. Considering the close historical connection with the birth of the museum and the department stores as "display and collecting institutions," including fairs and theme parks, the ArtScience Museum as an openly for-profit institution may actually return the museum to its roots[7] (Karp and Kratz 2006, e77; also, Bennett 1995). Moreover, the government of Singapore constructed the entire Marina Bay promontory from landfill, fully intending to set aside a portion of this for a distinctive landmark public attraction.[8] An early color brochure shows the then empty landmass with an invitation to "Explore . . . Make Asia's new lifestyle epicenter home to your heart, mind, and soul"; "Entertain, picnic on the promenade, indulge in retail therapy" (Singapore 2005).[9] Already the language of commerce mixed with souls and therapies. Now to add to the real-fantasy-commercial nexus, the government gave over the land just behind

Figure 5.7 Supertree, Skyway, and truck. Photo by Dick Waghorne.

the Marina Bay Sands to "Gardens by the Bay," designed by UK-based firms.[10] The "garden" has a Supertree Grove of twelve giant metal trees connected by a Skyway—seven stories above the garden (Fig.5.7). The website invites visitors to "Chill out at the 50-metre Supertree-top bistro and be captivated by the panoramic views of the Gardens." An environmental blog describes this as "almost like stumbling into a scene from Alice in Wonderland—a wonderland turned entirely green" (Preuss 2012). Widely reported as a green project, the Gardens are nonetheless a commercial enterprise mixing constructed fantasy trees with real plants.

The ArtScience Museum, then, remains embedded in Singapore's life processes. Not a nonprofit organization above the fray, underneath its steel stems and polymer petals is land "reclaimed" from the sea by the will of the government of Singapore, behind is a shopping mall with a grand casino, and behind that a new garden of green nonnatural wonders. But keep in mind my musings with the ArtScience (and indeed the Marina Bay complex): like Thoreau's Walden Pond, this building has "soul."

Moving East and Moving Up: Surprising Connections

Las Vegas-based Sands Corporation hired the celebrated but often controversial Israeli-born Canadian architect Moshe Safdie[11] to design the entire Marina Bay Sands complex—an equally amazing high-rise hotel, convention center, shopping mall, and, of course, casino. Deeply embedded in modern consumer culture with what some consider its worst edge, the love of gambling, how could such a complex resonate with *Walden*? In a newspaper interview with Safdie just before the museum opened, waves from *Walden* reached Marina Bay: "Safdie's office of 60 people is housed in a century-old, former wicker factory in Somerville, just north of Boston. During our late-summer interview, he sported a blue collarless shirt of his own design by 'a shirt maker in Montreal who's been making my shirts for years.' He appeared fit from daily swims in Thoreau's Walden Pond" (Cook 2010).[12]

On his 194th birthday, Henry Thoreau was "remembered best today for . . . his most famous exploit—leaving civilization to live in solitude on the banks of nearby Walden Pond" (Center for American Progress 2011). Moshe Safdie may swim in Walden Pond but he works and writes within the urban terrain, most recently in the rapidly expanding cities of Asia where solitude is rarely more than an emotional state. But tantalizing similarities do exist between these swimmers in Walden Pond separated by a century and a half. As we will see, both play with scale and with issues of the effects of space and place on human transformation. Both "write" in the built environment as well as with words. And both literally and imaginatively constructed an icon of the East from bases near Boston.

Even though Thoreau found some seclusion in the woods, reading him now without the retinue of articles, books, and activist essays that accompany him becomes daunting.[13] But like Safdie, I will plummet into *Walden* directly and, as need arises, seek company as I proceed. Such musings on Thoreau do not conjure an exhaustive comparison between the American Yogi's philosophy/activism and Safdie's architecture, but rather a visual meditation on urban scale and urban sensibilities with the presence of the forest-dweller from Concord on the horizon, often considered a harbinger of an increasingly powerful mode of religiosity, or "spirituality." Keep in mind that the Marina Bay Sands complex stands at the heart of a major Asian cosmopolis where the entire country is a city. Singapore has no outlands; all of the old forests have mutated into copses of often-glittering high-rise residential towers (Fig. 5.8). This sign of changing economic power might also forecast another shift—the transfer of the venue of the spiritual from the sylvan to the urban, a move that would parallel other facts of life in Asia—once considered rich in spirituality and rooted deeply within their traditions while the West remained lost and impoverished in its profuse materialism. Now economic success in Asia rapidly creates the world's tallest buildings and the newest megalopolises, and here global architects like Safdie find their major assignments.

During the opening ceremonies for the new Waterfront Promenade surrounding Marina Bay, Prime Minister Lee reflected on the massive project:

> With waterfront promenade completed, we can now walk around the whole Marina Bay, and take in the magnificent views . . . Nothing but sea was here in the

Figure 5.8 View of Marina Bay and the high-rise city. Photo by Dick Waghorne.

1970s but even then we had a vision of building an extension to our city centre. Hence we reclaimed land, planned ahead and invested in development year-after-year. Eventually we built up a new downtown with a signature skyline. Marina Bay is a key platform and catalyst for our future growth. It hosts our new financial district, boosting Singapore's position as a leading financial and business centre in Asia ... We hope it will develop to define Singapore, in the same way that the Bund defines the city of Shanghai.

Lee 2010

For all of its pragmatism, this speech has—as also in the portion quoted in Chapter 1—a mythic quality of new land arising from the sea. Marina Bay is a freshly constructed world, and, to signal this, the prime minister has his eye on the new China and not old New York City or London. Government and capital enterprise now write the defining signature of Singapore in the new skyline, with skyscrapers subtly erasing earlier concern for continuity with Asian Confucian social principles in this city-state (Chua 1995, 167). The Israeli-Canadian American-based architect Moshe Safdie invoked Asia in his giant lotus design for the ArtScience Museum; but not by government fiat, commenting in an interview: "Everyone was speaking from day one about icon, icon, icon ... Someone said it should be the Sydney Opera House for Singapore" (Cheong 2006).

Anthony King, an architectural historian, highlights this turn to the novel, the iconic, and the gargantuan in Asia. He begins his discussion "of spectacular architecture, and especially high rise towers" (2004, 3) by pointing to an increasingly obvious fact. By the 1990s, just as the éclat of the skyscraper was losing its gloss in the United States, the "contest for the tallest, most architecturally unorthodox postmodern 'signature buildings' was well underway" in the rising global cities of East and Southeast Asia (14). "I take the production of architecture," says King, "as the most important material and visual realm in which this competition takes place" (1).[14]

King also points to the irony of China symbolizing its identity and progress "through the language and architectural codes of American capitalism" and then hiring American firms for the designs (see also Langdon 1995). Adding an historical perspective, King notes that China abjured its own architectural principles that "emphasized harmony with landscape, 'building with nature' and the spiritual ecology of feng shui." The contemporary move up represents the abandonment of long low-rise buildings, such as huge Forbidden City, as the traditional representation of power of authority framed "horizontally rather than vertically" (18). Size alone is not the issue here, but harmony with nature giving way to the new international signs of success in capitalistic enterprises—the ultimate irony for a once "Marxist-inspired utopian society (see Chi 1997, 3).

This same move from low horizontal to verticality epitomized Singaporean development with blocks of once iconic shop houses designed by city father Sir Stamford Raffles leveled to make way for a high-rise "integrated modern city"—even old high-rises are now meeting the wrecking crane to make way for more highways. The demolition only stopped when the Tourism Task Force opted to preserve "our Oriental mystique" (Kwek 2004, 116). In a complex discussion of the "vertical order" in

Singapore, Ryan Bishop posits this overarching verticality as an even darker image of "the integration of a certain type of militaristic strategy in architecture: specifically the desire to overcome horizontal limits, gain the high ground" (2004, 65). What Bishop adds to King—no, this is not about chess—is a more specific accusation of both the denaturalizing and dehumanizing process inherent in gargantuan verticality. This issue will continue in the next chapter.

Surprisingly, Moshe Safdie, the designer of several large apartment complexes in addition to the Marina Bay Sands in Singapore, also railed against what he calls "mega-scale" and its attendant loss of identity: "A more subtle issue of building scale has to do with a sense of personal identity: what is the psychological mind-set as we compare our bodies to the size of the structures around us" (1997, 87–8). Writing in 1997 in *The City after the Automobile: An Architect's Vision*, Safdie invites architects "to intervene, in search of a more humane, spiritually uplifting, and unoppressive environment" (92). In this early book and in his most recent ethical manifestos, Safdie sees Ren Koolhaas, who has designed signature skyscrapers in China, as caring neither for context nor preserving cultural identity nor ameliorating megascale (2009, 9–10). So, while Koolhaas represses human scale, Safdie calls for "humanising the big." He openly calls for buildings to be "spiritually uplifting" (1997, 92).

With all of this language—some may say mere rhetoric—of human scale and concern for cultural roots, Safdie's most recent projects "are larger in scale than projects of the previous phases" (Albrecht 2010, 41). The Marina Bay Sands includes the fifty-seven-story hotel advertised on the website as the "most spectacular hotel in Singapore." The original plan for the hotel with the world's largest cantilevered structure, a "skypark" covering three towers with deeply sloping sides, "has got some geomancers here in a tizzy. They say the towers are like ancestral tablets; the skypark is like a broken flyover, suggesting imperfection; and the towers' flat roof is like a blade, suggesting restricted growth. Some Singaporeans have also griped about how the three towers resemble joss sticks and glorified factories" Cheong 2006).[15] Indeed, Albrecht in the catalog to a major retrospective of Safdie's work, summarizes the critiques by architects as well: "For his proponents, Safdie's aesthetic language of transcendent light, powerful geometric forms, and metaphoric imagery produces buildings that are ceremonial and uplifting, without being intimidating. His detractors see a different side.... Safdie's grand forms seem bombastic" (28). Although Safdie stressed that "he had consulted a Singaporean geomancer," his attempts at cultural continuity can seem disingenuous despite claims that his roots in Haifa, Israel and his early transplantation to Canada, make him "a bridge between East and West" (*Straits Times*, 13 June, 2006). However, with all of his critique of inhumane verticality, Safdie never abjures creating an "uplifting" verticality or constructing cultural continuity with a vague Eastern flavor. He continues to play wildly with scale.

With all of these conundrums, and with Thoreau's *Walden* on my Nook in a shoulder bag, I returned to Marina Bay Sands. Recall that contradiction tends to chase constructors of the transcendental. Thoreau—the defender of forests—when forced to earn his bread after his sylvan sojourn, resumed production in his father's wooden pencil factory, delaying the publication of *Walden* for a decade (Syman 2011, 34).

Human scale/Megascale

The true iconic piece at the Marina Bay Sands is a fifty-seven-story hotel[16] with its three convex split-based towers topped by the one of world's largest cantilevers: the boat-shaped SkyPark, "stretching longer than the Eiffel tower," according to the official website. Media photos show a private guest swimming pool—interestingly named the Infinity Pool—running right out to the edge of the deck with no visible protective walls.[17] A special elevator in the lobby provides access to the smaller public area of the SkyPark. Sublimating my acrophobia, I decided to take the long elevator ride up to the SkyPark Observation Deck to experience Safdie's megascale within my own human scale (Fig. 5.9).

As I entered the lobby, ethereal light characteristic of Safdie's designs caught a web of vaguely visible geometric forms, the light emanating from a wall of glass. Rows of large celadon-colored urns bending inward mirrored the shape of the atrium as they added another touch of *nature d'Asie*. After enduring the long elevator ride up skyward, I bought a costly ticket, passed up the opportunity to purchase a commemorative photo with my picture embedded at the edge of the panoramic view, and walked out to the deck. I felt simultaneously floating and falling as I moved toward the glass railing to look down at the giant Singapore Flyer reduced to a toy, and the clusters of high-rise apartments now the size of a clump of mushrooms (Fig. 5.10). With such a seemingly thin glass protective membrane, my sense of my body and my size again altered much like the experience of the ArtScience Museum—this time as if I had swallowed the cake marked "Eat me."

Figure 5.9 ArtScience Museum looks like a small flower opening in this SkyPark view. Photo by Dick Waghorne.

Figure 5.10 The overwhelming grand atrium becomes a prelude to the SkyPark above.

Was this mind-altering quality intended, this play with perceptions? In a video tour of his famous National Gallery of Canada, Safdie turns to his controversial decision to add portholes in the walls allowing museum patrons to view the normally hidden spaces, to see "the source of light that's feeding the floor below," the Mylar plastic sheets tacked to the rafters. Safdie recalls the controversy among the curators: "Will they distract people? Will they mystify them? So I said, 'Oh mystify them, that's good. Distract them, that's not bad either.'"[18] Moments of spontaneous creation that mystify and distract the viewer—skyparks that awe, portholes that open to reveal the source of light, nature on a roof, culture in an urn, infinity in a pool—ah, that's good.

Exemplified by Thoreau and so well expressed by his mentor, Ralph Waldo Emerson, the infinity of nature works to lessen the ego and yet aggrandize the self: "Standing on the bare ground,—my head bathed by the blithe air, and uplifted into infinite space,— all mean egotism vanishes. I become a transparent eye-ball; I am nothing; I see all; the currents of the Universal Being circulate through me; I am part or particle of God" (1836, chapter 1). In his description of Safdie's Skirball Cultural Center outside Los

Angeles, Albrecht writes of "an intimate sense of urbanism within the largely undifferentiated expanse of greater Los Angeles" (2010, 40). An intimate urbanism, megascale yoked to human scale seems like a set of oxymorons but recall the primary question here: Can a megascale building play with the human consciousness of self and universe in any ways similar to the awesome experience of Nature on human nature?[19]

The Real-and-Imagined within Urban Space

When I have publicly shown many of these images of Marina Bay Sands, some see red, angered by art put in the mode of production, the commodification of nature, and the constant incursions of a powerful hegemonic state bent on unrelenting economic development in open collusion with global capitalism—especially given that 90 percent of the profits of the Las Vegas Sands Corporation came from the resorts in Singapore and Macau and its billionaire CEO provides massive donations to conservative causes.[20] And indeed, at this point in my argument, readers may critique this mystification of a capitalist process into an iconic delusion, the seeming naiveté of naming such a process spiritual, and then comparing this reification of nature to the revered work of Thoreau. Nevertheless, understanding such contradictions as potentially creative, as Nick Dixon suggests, and as somehow soul-full, as I suggest, actually requires taking a left turn into spatial theory. Left, because the discussions of such creative contradictions in an urban setting point to a very au courant circle of Marx-à-la-Lefebvre inspired interlocutors on urban space. Neither pure dialectics nor alterity, this discussion of an unresolved lived space between the imaginary and the concrete may begin to enhance and complicate that affective something in the ArtScience Museum and the Marina Bay complex and the possibility of revelatory moments within an otherwise quotidian urban world.

Urban geographer Edward Soja put Henri Lefebvre (1901–91) on the map in the anglophone world in his *Thirdspace: Journey to Los Angeles and Other Real-and-Imagined Places* (1996). Lefebvre's now influential *Production of Space* had just been translated in 1991, almost two decades after its initial publication in France.[21] Soja provides a reading of this complex work that shifts the geographical context from the small and great urban centers of France to Los Angeles amid the intense urban upheavals of the 1990s. A newer "third wave" of Lefebvre evaluations calls now for a radically different reading. And yet what both Soja and this newer wave have in common is the tantalizing sense of "Lefebvre's anti-structuralist romantic-revolutionary claim for a new subjectivity" arising out of an urban landscape (Goonewardena et al. 2008, 10). In addition, for their purposes and mine, Lefebvre's radical erasure of fixed lines between the real and the imaginary, the mental and the material, makes this mid-1970s work made-in-France not only useful for Los Angeles in 1991, but also for "globalizing Lefebvre" (Goonewardena et al. 2008, 297–9) in Singapore in the second decade of the twenty-first century.

Lefebvre remained a committed Marxist who devoted several major works to a "materialist critique of 'Everydayness' (*quotidienneté*, Altäglishkeit, or 'banality') as a soul-destroying feature of modernity culture, social interaction and the material environment."[22] And yet, he is also described as a "Neo-Marxist and Existentialist Philosopher" who was influenced by an interesting mix of Schopenhauer, Surrealism, Hegel, and Marx "to develop a romantic humanism, which glorified 'adventure', spontaneity and self-expression" (Shields 2011, 279–83). The roots of some of his theories "come back to the traditions of German idealism" (Stanek 2011, 140). Interestingly, he shares these roots with Thoreau who was a contemporary of Schopenhauer (see De Armond 1932) and acquainted with German Idealism.[23]

Thus, even with his often-stinging Marxian critique of the capitalist-dominated urban world, I remain intrigued by an ever-growing discussion of his open-ended proposal of spaces of and for liberation within the urban world at the level of the person. These tantalizing elicitations remain with Marxian materialism but move toward a sense of emancipation beyond mundane economic or political adjustments— hovering on the edge of transcendence. The new wave of his ardent readers turns now to Lefebvre's mention of "the self-fulfilled person (*l'homme totale*)" (Shields 2011, 283), revelatory "Moments" (Merrifield 2008, 181), and, most recently, "jouissance" (Stanek 2011, 249–51). These moments of revelation, even bliss, exist in a dialectic relationship— Soja would say trialectic—within the contemporary urban world, paralleling the seemingly contradictory and precarious position of the ArtScience Museum and the Marina Bay within consumer capitalism.

To a recovering liberal such as myself—sometimes quite unrepentant—a Marxian circle of spatial theorists initially seemed an unlikely source to redescribe the intricate nexus between production, imagination, and the fulfillment of the self. However, Łukasz Stanek recently provides an innovative reading of Lefebvre in the context of architectural theory/practice, teasing out the subtle connotations for Lefebvre of key Marxian terms, product and production. Stanek explains that production in a narrower sense remains "fabrication of commodities by labor executed by repetitive gestures" as opposed to work (oeuvre) that produces something unique and not liable to exact reproduction. However, "In the wider sense, production refers to the concept of social practice defined as the material and 'spiritual production' simultaneously.... In this perspective, production is a creative activity" (2011, 140). For Stanek, this creative process

> understood in a materialist way is conceived as a multiplicity of social activities that transform both nature and human 'nature', ... that produce means of existence and subjectivities. In that sense the concept "transcends the philosophical opposition between the 'object' and the 'subject'" [quoted from Lefebvre 1991, 71] and defines humanity as transindividual ... produced by multiple interactions among individuals who cannot be conceived in isolation from these interactions.
>
> 141

In other words, symbols-bodies-nature are transformed/produced within the circle of construction of selves-symbols-stuffs. I read this in the double sense of the English term manufacturing—both "to invent fictitiously; fabricate" and "to make or produce by hand or machinery, especially on a large scale" (dictionary.com). In this sense of a materialist analysis, neither Mind nor Consciousness nor Spirit acts as a *deus ex machina*, but minds, consciousnesses, spirits, bodies, and matter are not denied, but made concrete in their interactions rendered once real and imagined. But for Lefebvre amid these necessities and signs are moments of "revelation, emotional clarity and self-presence as the basis of becoming more self-fulfilled" (Shields 2011, 283).

Now the locale, where all these creative encounters occur for Lefebvre, is in the last of his complex multileveled understandings of the urban space, the "perceived-conceived-lived triad" ([1974] 1991, 40).[24] Edward Soja redescribes this lived space as his now famous Third Space, which, some say, left him "lost looking for Lefebvre in the prison-house of spatial ontology" (Goonewardena et al. 2008, 9). However, Soja's seemingly problematic terminology makes his redescription all the more interesting in the context of the ArtScience Museum and Marina Bay. His Third Space, that space between, emphasizes almost unlimited possibilities and wild mixtures as if a Marxian mystification morphs into magic:

> Thirdspace: the space where all places are, capable of being seen from every angle, each standing clear; but also a secret and conjectured object, filled with illusions and allusions, a space that is common to all of us yet never able to be completely seen and understood as an "unimaginable universe," or as Lefebvre would put it, "the most general of all products".
>
> 1996, 56

Thus Soja openly emphasizes the creative power of these enigmatic ambiguities in the underground side of social life and, importantly, in art, "which Lefebvre describes as a coding not of space more generally, but specifically the space of representation. Clearly an attempt is being made here to retain, if not emphasize, the partial unknowablity, the mystery and secretiveness, the non-verbal sublimity, of spaces of representation" (Soja 1996, 67). All of this language of the intermingling of illusion and allusion, of secret and conjectured, and nonverbal sublimity lives within a breath of becoming a mystical Marxism.

To summarize, production as a process extrudes not only stuffs but also bundles of perceptions that make and are made by the self in the context of society. At the heart of Marxism, capitalism covers its tracks with mystification and commodification—a world of imaginary/meaning naturalized in everyday life. But Lefebvre opened the Marxian process of mystification to the possibility of another open-ended, even mysterious, process—a moment, an insight, that liberates persons, not as neoliberal individuals, but nonetheless toward a singular human fulfillment. Unlike the overwhelming homogenization of spaces created under the aegis of capitalistic regimes that Lefebvre associates with a fantasia of image/sign/abstractions so closely associated with art-media, a transgressive art can nonetheless return persons to insight, to truth:

> Wherever there is illusion, the optical and visual worlds play an integral and integrative, active and passive, part in it. It fetishizes abstraction and imposes the norm. It detaches the pure from its impure content—from lived time, everyday time, and from bodies with their opacity and solidity, their warmth, their life and their death. After its fashion, the image kills. . . . Occasionally, however, an artist's

tenderness or cruelty transgresses the limits of the image. Something else altogether may then emerge, a truth and a reality answering to criteria quite different from those of exactitude, clarity, readability and plasticity.

[1974] 1991, 97

In my interpolation, commodity production is at play in the same field as a work (oeuvre) of art; they occupy the same soup. They are in a dialectic relationship bound by a common process if not a common purpose. Commodity production lives in the world of mystification; an oeuvre is at once both a thing and a sign that liberates the human consciousness. The difference is at once both slight and vast. But within Lefebvre's "original heterodox Marxism" (Goonewardena et al. 2008, 3), within this process of image production lays a space for liberation, an "irreducible and singular lived experience" (Stanek 2011, xiii), without loss of the social context/wholeness.

But for the circle of Marx-à-la-Lefebvre-inspired interlocutors, the venue for this process and its fragile possibility for liberation is not a sylvan world of nature but, as Stanek concludes:

The city covers the double sense of the term "produce." A work [oeuvre] itself, it is the place of production of various works, including that which decides about the sense of production: needs and bliss [jouissances]. It is also a place where goods are produced and exchanged and where they are consumed. It gathers these realities, these modalities of "production," some of them immediate, others mediated (indirect).

2011, 140–1

As the place of production, the city can also be the site of liberation. The question then becomes, can the ArtScience and the Marina Bay Sands—with its vast moneymaking casino and its endless designer-brand shopping—ever incubate *l'homme totale* in the Asian cosmopolis of Singapore?

Keep in mind that the processes that I have identified at the ArtScience Museum and the Marina Bay complex centers on the manipulation of scale—perhaps now better understood as the production of powerful sets of dialectics for those who pass through: the disorienting inner feeling of aggrandizement and diminution playing with oversized proportions of the human body and elements of nature—giant metal lotus, six-story metal trees, a SkyPark on top of three high-rise hotels, and a bridge formed like human DNA. Inside the ArtScience Museum the exhibits also play not only with wild scale as in the Dali, Van Gogh, and Warhol exhibitions, but also with a confluence of commercialism and creativity—a playground interestingly opened by Lefebvre and company. Nick Dixon spoke of the museum in terms of "finding new ways to bring together seemingly contradictory ways of working and thinking." Like Soja's Thirdspace, he looked for "something there in the middle which is a thing in its own right" that sparked insight. I doubt he or anyone at the ArtScience Museum had Marx/Soja/Lefebvre in mind with their emphasis on creative spaces in the middle, amid contradictions, or by fostering encounters "immersive and experiential" as a recreation of lived space. Yet these phrases do resonate with that circle of new

Marx-inspired interpreters of space, especially in their mutual understanding of the potential transforming power of spaces in the middle—places of contradictions between commerce and creativity, between the body and nature mirrored in steel and glass, between human scale and megascale poured into concrete and imaged as buildings that rise on the banks of Marina Bay.

The context here is ultimately Asia in general and Singapore in particular. Taking language from Lefebvre-inspired spatial theory, the urban complex of Singapore is constructed out of contradictions. The People's Action Party that has directed Singapore from its independence in 1965 combines a state socialism with an ardent capitalism, democratic processes with autocratic style, a totally planned state with constant search for innovation and creativity as CNN reported in an article with the telling title, "Can Singapore engineer creativity?" (Ryder 2011). Not only has the government restructured education to foster innovation (Jackson 2011) but constructed two new colleges for the arts. The Marina Bay complex fully participates in these contradictions, seemingly a place of unredeemed consumerism that nonetheless features at its most prominent point in the bay, the ArtScience Museum.

Intimate Immensity/Intimate Urbanism

Meanwhile, amid these meditations on space and creativity and commerce, Thoreau still sits on banks of his Walden Pond; his words live in my Nook as Moshe Safdie plays with megascale and human scale near those woods in suburban Boston. Thoreau's meditations still define a powerful trope of nature and human nature, of the evils of the growing capitalism in mid-nineteenth-century America, and of a deep rift between the spiritual and the urban. Turning to works on space outside the Marxist orbit that both predates and postdate Lefebvre, most tether human creative and spiritual potential to encounters with nature but retain interplay among the inner space of the mind, the imagination, and the scale of the natural world in the context of the human body. Gaston Bachelard in his elegant *Poetic of Space* termed this conflation of imagination with diminutive enormity within the human as "The Intimate Immensity" (*L'Immensité Intime*)[25] (Bachelard [1958] 1969, 183). Gaston Bachelard has less currency now than Soja or Lefebvre but his phenomenology allowed him to embrace the language of infinity, immensity, vastness.[26] Uncannily resonant with the homilies I have heard from Hindu gurus on the powers of meditative stillness, this French savant declares, "Immensity is within ourselves ... Indeed immensity is the movement of motionless man. It is one of the dynamic characteristics of quiet daydreaming" (184). Then, after delicate passages laced with *rêverie phénoménologique*, Bachelard quotes Thoreau:

> In *Walden*, Thoreau followed this enlargement of images quite naturally. 'A lake is the landscape's most beautiful and expressive feature. It is earth's eye; looking into which the beholder measures the depth of his own nature.' ... And once more, the dialectics of immensity and depth is revived. ... But any doctrine of the imaginary is necessarily a philosophy of excess, and all images are destined to be enlarged.
> 210

But the question of whether the image of contemporary urban enlargement, the excesses of the vertical city, leads to the same kind of reverie and imagination is not answered in Bachelard's poetic-scholarly masterpiece.

When critics discuss the megascale in the contemporary urban environment, they warn of diminishing the human—a feeling not of inner vastness but of agoraphobia, as I will show in the coming chapter. Thoreau revels in solitude at the edge of a small lake, when alone in a city we speak of the ennui and loss of a sense of personhood. The sense of becoming lost in the density of the forest leads to intimate immensity, while the density of the city creates claustrophobia. Why is the urban immensity a nightmare while the dense forest, the fertile field, or the night sky are the stuff of daydreams leading to intimate wholeness? The muck of the casino, the crass commercialism of the mall, the expensive tickets and shining logos within—could the sensibilities of *Walden* take life at the Marina Bay Sands?

Safdie, the designer of urban megabuildings asked, "What is the psychological mind-set as we compare our bodies to the size of the structures around us?" (1997, 87). Two decades later in Marina Bay Sands resort, Safdie begins to answer his own question—not in words—but in fiberglass, glass, and steel. The installation of an Infinity Pool, the souvenir shop selling photographs of "you" floating above Singapore, all play into this dynamic power of the awesome and the surreal to destabilize, to "mystify," "to distract." The cluster of terms used to describe the Safdie affect in architecture (sometimes by Safdie himself): "intimate sense of urbanism," "spiritually uplifting," "ceremonial and uplifting" hover between matter and imagination, between soul and building—the writing is, literally, on the wall. Safdie's buildings come alive in Third Space, representational space, that locale of creative contradictions that reframes the old conflict between subject and object in the context of the human person and the imagination. This is what can render the urban experience "intimate" in the much the same way that Edward Mooney describes Thoreau's work as "intimate" (Mooney 2009).

Such effects between bodily perceptions and environment have long been inherent in theories on place-making and spatial sensibilities from Bachelard (1958) to Edward Casey (1993). Although Bachelard remains close to nature, Casey comes to bat with a long discussion of "Built Places" (2009, 109–81). He opens doors to "ever-new possibilities of building and dwelling ... Everywhere we turn when we build and dwell—and we always turn with and upon our lived bodies" (180–1).[27] I have suggested that something more radical may be at work as an "ever-new possibility" in bodily modes of engagement with the built environment—something within Asia's rapid megascale vertical urbanization.

Here I take my biggest leap, eating perhaps more "cake" than I should. During the time that I watched the construction of the Marina Bay Sands, my major project was yoga-based spiritual movements in Singapore. Moving thorough a Safdie building can be a meditative act, paralleling the process of yogic practices, which disrupt normal perceptions, disengaging the normal mind and inviting the viewer into Vastness or a totality that remains social. I do not claim that this is Safdie's deliberate intension but rather the way his architecture, intentional or not, can act on a perceiving body. And this may also be his closest affinity with the Yankee yogi of Walden Pond. Here in Safdie is an orientalist like Thoreau—an affinity, either conscious or by common cultural consensus, toward the meditative, toward the world of "the subtle body", as Stefanie Syman terms it, "a strange ontological status—not physical and yet not wholly imagined" (2010, 7)—a space that Soja and Lefebvre could name. In her history of modern yoga in America, Syman begins with Thoreau affirming and complicating the long-held thesis that Thoreau practiced yoga or some form of meditation making his Walden Pond experience "liberating." She quotes a longer passage at the conclusion of *Walden*, where Thoreau predicts "new universal and more liberating laws will establish themselves around and within," but adds another closely following phrase: "If you have built castles in the air, your work need not be lost; that is where they should be. Now put foundations under them" (608–9). I am left wondering if Safdie's Marina Bay Sands is not just such a castle in the air—with a foundation.

Now that yoga is out of the bag, there are other players in this conversation about scale, the human body, the urban self, and the forest self. Changes in scale have long been the stuff of meditation, with the self both diminished and aggrandized in the process; but in Singapore such dramatic telescoping sets its sight within the commercial world. And while I spent days in wonder at the Marina Bay Sands, I also attended a Sathsang for Isha Yoga in the meeting room within a large commercial complex in which a visual meditation played with the size and space of our inner imagination, asking us to imagine ourselves within both a limitless vastness as well as an intimate hut opening into "the Ultimate." Call it crass commercialism, call it "selling spirituality" (Carrette and King 2004), or condemn it as a sad detour in the "opposition of God and money" (Goodchild 2009, 6), but many of Singapore's gurus play in that same space as the Marina Bay Sands. But then I am ending at a beginning. I, too, play with scale seeing the "little red dot"—as Singaporeans often term their nation—as a grand real-and-imagined place with a lot to say about urban Asia: "To know Singapore is to know where the urbanized world is heading."[28]

How Is a Guru Like a High-rise?

With a quote from Lewis Carroll's tale of a topsy-turvy world, Jeremy Carrette and Richard King colored their trenchant critique of contemporary commercialized spirituality and the prime hawkers of this global phenomenon, the various Hindu gurus like Osho (Rajneesh) and (yes) Dr. Deepak Copra with their "feel-good spirituality of consumerism":

> ... Behind the sugary veneer of spirituality lies a subtle form of privitisation, now increasingly linked to the marketisation of all dimensions of human life. Like Alice in Wonderland who falls down the rabbit hole into another world, spirituality deflects criticism and obscures meaning.
>
> 2005, 49

Their critique, as outlined in a previous chapter, appeared to center on the social effect of the spirituality movement, but here their concern shifts to the havoc wreaked on the inner person.[1] Along with others in religious studies, they sounded dire warnings: spirituality, abetted by gurus, dealt out glittering but obscuring "vagueness and ambiguity" that turned adherents inward toward an ephemeral self and away from commitment to community. An influential essay by the respected theologian Graham Ward presented concerns of those faithful to the traditional religions:

> To establish the authenticity and value (social and personal) of their religious convictions, believers of whatever school within a major faith grouping will have to define themselves over against those who consume religion as a special effect. This will cause divisions among the liberal camps themselves. Some may become increasingly eclectic and disappear beneath the rising tides of a vague but phosphorescent spirituality. Others will define their practices and belief systems more tightly (while still wishing to avoid the literalisms and coercions of fundamentalism). These groups will increasingly be forced to denounce "religion as special effect" as the soft and undisciplined option; the road that leads to shops selling scented candles, yoga-focused fitness centers, and dot-com companies trading in Lord of the Rings and Harry Potter memorabilia.
>
> 2006, 186

The commercialized Alice joins Harry Potter and Frodo as icons of an emerging personality without a clear sense of place, of belonging, of time, of orientation, and now, worst of all, *fallen* into the phantasm of the consumerist self.

An early subtle critique of these critiques suggests, with a touch of irony, a disease to describe the supposed malady of the postmodern urbanite, *psychoasthenia*:

> Incapable of demarcating the limits of its own body, lost in the immense area that circumscribes it, the psychoasthenic organism proceeds to abandon its own identity to embrace the space beyond. It does so by camouflaging itself into the milieu. This simulation effects a double usurpation: while the organism successfully reproduces those elements it could not otherwise apprehend, in the process it is swallowed by them, vanishing as a differentiated entity.
>
> Olalquiaga 1992, 2

Celeste Olalquiaga also turns to Wonderland, prefiguring Carrette and King's intense concern but with a wily undertone: "Alice goes through a series of adventures that confuse her sense of physical identity, in an experience similar to postmodern culture: she floats among domestic objects that fail to give her any hold—gravity, like referentiality, has been suspended—and is later completely lost in Wonderland" (3). However, rather than despairing at the "loss of spatial boundaries," Olalquiaga sees potential subversion of hierarchy in this "shattering of perceptual referentiality" (5).

Perhaps not coincidentally, an assault within architectural circles began at the same time on the growth of the high-rise as an iconic edifice but especially as an increasingly common residential structure. Again, practicing architects and theorists depicted visions of glittering tall buildings rising in the midst of isolated parking lots constructed by, and constructing, a disorienting and disconnected spatial world in the megapolis with an attendant loss of place, of personhood, and even of humanity for their inhabitants. Again "market forces" are to blame (Gehl 2010, *kl* 86). Declaring, "Low buildings are in keeping with the human horizontal sensory apparatus but high buildings are not," Danish architect and professor, Jan Gehl, continued his decades-old critique of unlivable cities (see also Gehl [1971] 1986):

> Communication from tall buildings to their surroundings is correspondingly excellent from the two lower stories and feasible from the third fourth and fifth floors. From there we can watch and follow the life of the city; talking, shouting and arm movement can be perceived. We are actually taking part in the life of the city. Above five floors the situation changes drastically. Above the fifth floor, offices and houses should logically be the province of the air-traffic authorities. At any rate, they no longer belong to the city.
>
> 2010, *kl* 674

Over three decades ago, just as the new economic policies in India took effect and buildings began to rise, the Indira Gandhi Center for the Arts, as if in defiance of the coming changes, published a massive volume on architecture, *Concepts of Space: Ancient and Modern,* which included chapters on the Hindu temple plus contemporary buildings. Writing on the modern "technopoles" in the context of Indian traditional sensibilities, the famous Ramon Panikkar lamented its dehumanizing environment:

> Landscape not only forms but also informs the human being. A person without a proper landscape becomes dehumanized. This is one the causes of the erosion of humanness in agglomerated and over-congested apartments and slums of so many big cities. Dehumanization occurs when humans lack the vital Space which constitutes their lives. It has to do with the 'inscape' of each individual which links to landscape. This is also the case with modern urbanism. Modern technopoles force people into strait jackets which change their very constitution.
>
> 1991, 21

As in Gehl, the same tropes appear throughout *Concepts of Space*: scales unnatural to the human body, disoriented and dis-placed persons *and* buildings that are losing their groundedness in vast undifferentiated space. And the firm conviction continues from the 1990s to well into the new millennium: architecture has the capacity to transform the human consciousness and constitution. Again, this spate of criticisms did not go uncontested but remained mainstream (see Davies 2012, Cooke 2010).

Reading Gehl, high-rise buildings appear to take on a sinister, or perhaps tragic, life of their own. Note the ambiguous referents[2] here:

> Market forces and architectural trends have gradually shifted focus from interrelations and common spaces of the city to individual buildings, which in the process have become increasingly more isolated, introverted and dismissive.
>
> Gehl 2010, *kl* 86

I thought this might be a slip of referents inadvertently mixing people with cities and buildings, but later Gehl speaks of "introverted high-rise buildings" (*kl* 122). My suspicions of a strange animism—to which I will return—here matches descriptions of similar perceptions in a recent volume on high-rise living. Stephen Appold begins his evaluation of community life in high-rise residences in Singapore by harkening back to riots in Paris which erupted in government-built high-rise public housing: "Curiously, the 2005 outbreak led to architectural, not national soul-searching. Before they petered out, the 2005 riots were blamed on high-rise housing. Architects quickly accepted responsibility for creating living environments that created environments so alienating that the riots were a near inevitability and sheepishly promised to do better in the future" (Yuen and Yeh 2011, *kl* 4657). In a careful and complex analysis—see below— Appold abjures easy assumptions about supposed social isolation of high-rises, arguing provocatively, "In the debates on tall residential buildings, the utopia, not the reality, has often been on trial. Tall residential buildings are fodder for societal culture wars" (*kl* 5051). I will modify this and later argue that the wars may actually be *theological*; the notion of an "ineffable" quality of a building continues with sacrality at stake (Britton 2010), or more importantly the *domain* of sacrality. Nevertheless, some architects appear to attribute seemingly secular tall residential buildings with the power to transform, or rather deaden, their inhabitants, like some sinister cocoon.

Spirituality and high-rises appear to have drunk from the same bottles, producing unholy economic yields, unnatural scale, ambiguous identities, bodily and mental distortion, and appearing and disappearing presences. As such, they invite a return to Alice and another question from Wonderland. The Mad Hatter asks Alice, "How is a raven like a writing desk?" And now I will ask the seemingly absurd question, "How is a guru like a high-rise?" Wonderland here will not be the world but the wonder of Singapore, where relentless planning has transformed a once two-storied shop house environment into a landscape of stunning skyscrapers, soaring corporate offices, and increasingly tall residential towers, most constructed by the Housing and Development Board (HDB flats for short) where the vast majority of denizens live and work. Recall that the gurus in question, often called *global gurus*, likewise are not the traditional learned teachers bearing the authority of recognized lineages but self-made masters emerging in the 1960s[3] but mainstreaming in the 1980s (Urban 2015, *kl* 317–92). They are as newly constructed as the high-rise residences of their adherents.

More detailed examples will follow, but while the issue of how a guru is like a high-rise remains on the table, visiting gurus and members of guru-centered spiritual groups, as I have already shown, continue to meet together in such high-rise flats all over the island-nation, but seldom choose the many Hindu temples here with their adjoining community rooms as venues, although these rooms are "increasingly focal points for visiting gurus," but as traditional teachers offering spiritual discourses (Sinha 2011, 246). For larger events such as the periodic *satsang* (meeting, Sanskrit, *sat+ saṅga*, "association with the good," or in the company of the true), these *spiritual* groups—who abjure the term religious—gather in public multipurpose rooms or auditoriums in schools or businesses, often also embedded into large high-rise complexes. Very little has stayed low in Singapore. Recently, the Ministry of National Development (MND) approved, the *Straits Times* reported, "multi-user places of worship" for the first time. This means that multiple groups of the same religion can be housed in the same multistory building. Both Taoist, Christian, and Buddhist groups with small congregations and often charismatic leaders welcomed the opportunity to move up with a permanent place in such multistoried buildings.[4] However, whether by design or pragmatics, gurus and high-rise buildings are spatially interlinked in Singapore unlike the more established Hindu or Buddhist temple, or church, or gurdwara (*gurdwārā*), or masjid (preferred to mosque), all of which wear a clear religious identity, and continue to occupy their coveted low-rise locations.

Buildings Fixed and Floating

Singapore, along with Hong Kong, has set the trends in high-rise residential buildings. The greater majority of the HDB residential blocks are high-rise and getting even higher, yet ironically the majority Chinese-heritage population shares with those of Indian heritage a long tradition of religiously based spatial practices close to the ground—both horizontal and earth-centered (Fisher 2016, 112–13). The old well-defined practices of Feng Shui (Chinese, *fĕng shui*) and Vastu Shastra (Sanskrit, *vāstu śāstra*) now have an international following, especially among many of the spiritually inclined,[5] and continue in Singapore. The US-based architect of the now iconic Marina Bay Sands Hotel in Singapore, Moshe Safdie, for example, claimed to have "consulted a Singaporean geomancer" in his design.[6] Spatiality remains intertwined with religiosity here.

Although used in house construction and decor in India, the Vastu Shastra developed in the context of Hindu temples; even now in the global Hindu diaspora, most temples claim to be built according to these spatial principles that align the temple to the cosmos—the ordered world—to the human body, and to divine form (Sanskrit, *murti*, "body") (Waghorne 2004). Most famously Stella Kramrisch writing in *Concepts of Space* explained:

> Thematically the cosmic pillar and the small space of the heart within the heart coincide in the *garbha gṛha* of the Hindu temple in stone from the eighth century onward. The *garbha gṛha*, the "womb-chamber," is the symbolic equivalent of the small space within the heart. Anthropomorphic terms refer to *puruṣa*, man, the "dweller in the city," the human being, in the *Upaniṣads* and to *Puruṣa*, cosmic man, with regard to the temple.
>
> 1991, 103

The Hindu temple embodies both the inner and the outer cosmos—the macrocosm and the microcosm—and cosmos is always the ordered world firmly embedded in place. In the context of Singapore, by the 1920s, temples were often marked by ethnic identity: they are Hindu and Indian, often not in general but in particular, with administrative boards dominated by certain communities (Rai 2014, 167–9; Sinha 2011, 245). Hindu temples *feel* fixed, as ancient consecration rituals bind their divine inhabitants to the soil—even if, in fact, they are not. In Singapore, the government can pull, and has literally pulled, the rug out from under certain temples or refused permits for any new construction. The grounds on which temples stand are held on lease from the state and, in some cases, have been resumed, forcing demolition and relocation to accommodate the relentless planned development (Sinha 2005, 108). Taoist temples have suffered even more radical relocations and demolitions (DeBernardi 2016, 100).

But high-rise building, those massive megaliths, must be equally as embedded in the soil as any temple. However, the sheer physicality of the building—its actual tonnage and depth of its footer—somehow does not determine fixity or belonging to the soil, to the locale. Something more appears to hold a "traditional" building to its location, while these giant structures are assumed to float outside the real human world. Again, a caption from Gehl under a Singapore skyscraper captures this sensibility:

> Scale shift at the Singapore River. The old four and five story buildings meet the new skyscrapers. It is easy to fantasize that the different buildings were envisioned for two different species.
>
> Gehl 2010, *kl* 823

Our photo taken of the same location with remaining shop houses with red-tiled roofs appear like little mushrooms amid the towering office buildings (Fig. 6.1). This photo was taken atop another skyscraper and illustrates the argument about extreme difference

Figure 6.1 View from the Marina Bay Sands SkyPark showing the mix of skyscrapers overwhelming an old shop house enclave now a tourist area.

between old Singapore and the new. However, the fact remains that Singapore is now *by design* a nation of skyscrapers and high-rise residences. Along with its spectacular move up from *Third World to First* (Lee Kwan Yew, 2000), Singapore citizens live, work, meditate, practice yoga, and meet their fellow devotees in the heights.

I am suggesting that more than spatial/temporal linking, and a simultaneous de-linking from the religious or architectural pasts, conjoin the rising gurus to the high-rises in a place like Singapore. As the Mad Hatter might say, not only have we fallen down a rabbit hole but also gone through the looking glass with things upside-down and inside-out, which implies a radical shift of perspectives both for the residents of Singapore *and* for the academic analyst. In current theoretical perspectives, what might have been absurd or wildly conjectural less than a decade ago has serious adherents: buildings have agency. The animism apparent in Gehl has mainstreamed. And statements like Gehl's, that high-rise buildings and old shop houses "were envisioned for two different species," would have some saying yes, they are envisioned for different genera: the human and the posthuman. Serious anthropologists and religious studies scholars have countered those who were shocked at the confluences of economic trade with the sacred by recovering old theories associated with animism/sacrifice/gift, and uncovering the religious economy in everyday transactions that nonetheless transcend the ordinary (Lofton 2017; Appadurai 2016). And all of these changes in perception live under the sign of the new digital world. But first we need to get back on the ground in Singapore.

High-rise Homes for the People

A pamphlet from the early days of intense urban redevelopment, *The Residents' Handbook* from the Housing and Redevelopment Board, touted the remarkable achievement: "one Housing Board flat built every 20 minutes and one new town ... a year—that is the rate at which new flats are being provided for the people" (1975, 3). A drawing shows happy kids of all races high up on interlinking ladders in a playground with blocks of interlocking high-rise flats in the backdrop—smiling and waving, the children show no sign of vertigo. An earlier handbook explains "in a nutshell" that the origins of the project, which began in early 1960, "arose from an urgent need to provide families in the lower- and middle-income group with decent and comfortable housing at rents they could afford" (1973, 2). However, within a decade, the HDB flats covered the island and became ubiquitous owner-occupied dwellings that now house all but the richest classes of people in the nation. These high-rise flats were featured on commemorative plates for the celebration of the fiftieth anniversary of Singapore as one of four iconic emblems of the nation. Singapore, success, progress, and the high-rise flat inextricably intertwine.

Like those of Singapore, government-sponsored high-rise residences were a worldwide phenomenon in the 1960s—marks of modernity in Europe and a vibrant postcolonial sign of new beginnings in Asia. In much of Europe and North America, high-rises eventually imploded, metaphorically and literally, as failed housing for the poor, but remained increasingly viable and inevitable in the land-scarce cities of Asia. In contrast to the early bureaucratic "nutshell" publicizing abundant and affordable housing in Singapore, recent retelling of the story of the global high-rise phenomenon portrays a deliberate melding of modernity, technology, and domestic life in these finally feasible tall buildings. For example, urban geographers Jacobs, Cairns, and Strebel tell "A Tall Storey" about the rise and fall of Red Road, a housing project in Scotland. They trace an initial excitement for these ultimate heights of modernity now made possible by the use of structural steel: "The high-rise ... was intended to be a pragmatic, technically driven housing solution that would radically restructure the patterns and quality of domestic life" (2007, 610). The drawings, if not the text, hint at such social reshuffling in *The Residents' Handbook*. But to *see* these building as effecting changes requires a newer mode of analysis as these geographers attest: high-rises were not simple attempts at social engineering with "an assumption about the building technology and the occupant as distinct entities" (611), but rather a "socio-technical co-evolution of the world" (613).[7] Beginning, with an emerging perspective adopted from Bruno Latour: "The analytical approach of actor-network theory attends more vigilantly to the 'seamlessness' of the socio-technical field" (613). Concluding: "This perspective solicits a more heterogeneous range of actors and forces (human and non-human) which is especially useful when considering the socio-technical assemblage produced by the high-rise" (626). High-rises, it seems, initiated a blurring between building/person/technology, or rather, *assemblages*, co-evolved from buildings, persons, and technologies with beingness, an *ontology*, held somewhere in between.

The *agency* of buildings appears recently less "bracketed as metaphorical" hedging texts and discourse analysis, but rather engaged within the metaphysical (Wharton 2015, *kl* 282). Recent works by architectural historians join anthropologists and urban geographers in affirming what Bruno Latour announced a decade ago:

> There might exist many metaphysical shades between full causality and sheer inexistence. In addition to 'determining' and serving as a 'backdrop for human action', things might authorize, allow, afford, encourage, permit, suggest, influence, block, render possible, forbid, and so on. ANT [Actor-Network Theory] is not the empty claim that objects do things 'instead' of human actors: it simply says that no science of the social can even begin if the question of who and what participates in the action is not first of all thoroughly explored, even though it might mean letting elements in which, for lack of a better term, we would call non-humans.
>
> 2005, 72

Such ideas are not new, and Arjun Appadurai and others trace their insistence on the agency of *things* back to ambiguities in Marx and discussions of the *gift* in Marcel Mauss (Appadurai 1986, 4–16). But *now* seems the moment for *things*, especially buildings, to reemerge with *agency* edging toward *beingness*—challenging the supposed line between human and object possibly because such notions coemerge with affect theory and the blurred line between human and animal (see Schaefer 2015) and the increasing interest in material culture.

The line between human and building becomes quite thin when Annabel Wharton proposes "a biographical treatment of a building" and "makes the case that buildings exert a force on the world independent of human intention or even human consciousness" (2015, *kl* 209–305). Or even earlier, when Anthony Vidler confessed his desire—perhaps more playfully—to psychoanalyze monumental architecture in Vienna and Paris at the turn of the nineteenth century as a coconspirator in the near epidemic of neurosis:

> I have from time to time imagined that a psychoanalysis of architecture might be possible—as if architecture were on the couch so to speak—that would reveal, by implication, and reflection, its relationship with its 'subjects.' Thus personified as the 'other,' architecture and its relationship to space ... figured as the mirror, and hence the frame of anxiety and shape of desire ... a way of stressing the active role of objects and spaces in anxieties and phobias.
>
> 2001, 13

More recently, in an analysis of the controversy over the demolition of the American Folk Art Museum to expand the Museum of Modern Art in New York City, architectural historian Robert Beauregard highlighted a public meeting where an architect from the famous firm hired for the expansion defended the demolition because "the building is obdurate." He then takes her animism seriously, but chides her deflection of shared responsibility:

> This relationship is not one of human mastery over built (and ostensibly inert) forms but more dynamic and recursive, with non-human things behaving as actors in two senses: first, by causing humans to respond to them and, secondly, by sharing responsibility (via delegation) for collective action and its consequences.
>
> 2014, 534

But note a building's beingness is *relational,* existing between all the actors—in Latour's terms, *actants* (2007, 71)—making a term like *agency*, with its connotations of interaction, perhaps more than accurate for this new sense of *assemblages* than ontology or metaphysics. Nonetheless, within this Actor-Network-inspired theory, humans and buildings coevolve in the urban space—a step closer to conjoining a raven and a writing desk, or a guru and a high-rise.

The call to take buildings in general, and tall buildings in particular, seriously as actants emerges at a moment when high-rises once again surge as prime residential dwellings both in Asia and in the United States, but moving well beyond pragmatics to the spectacular. No longer dwellings for the poor or affordable housing "for the people," new exclusive addresses like 432 Park Avenue—advertised as the "tallest residential tower in the Western Hemisphere"[8]—and World Towers by Lodha in Mumbai stand tall as "reserved for the privileged few of the city" (Jhaveri 2016). Moreover, they are "designed to maintain physical, emotional, spiritual, and mental balance,"[9] or promise "an oasis of beauty and tranquility."[10] Again, the confluence of even newer technology has conjoined the rerise of the high-rise with a new "vertical urbanism," a re-visioned social-spatial-commercial terrain—now openly conjoined with the spiritual as well as the spectacular.

In an eye-opening and widely quoted article, Stephen Graham and Lucy Hewitt—both working interdisciplinarily in architecture, technology, and urban geography—declare, "the majority of critical urban writing emerging over recent decades has neglected the vertical qualities of contemporary processes of urbanization" (2013, 72–3). Such "horizontalism" runs the risk of ignoring "vertical qualities of contemporary processes of urbanization" and its attendant connections to "social secession and ascension" (75)—the deliberate withdrawal of the rich (I think of everyday spatial terms like highbrows and upper crusts) from the streets and daily life of the city in a new vertical stratification with all the richness of that imagery. However, I still hear echoes of those older equivalences of vertical/inhuman and horizontal/humane.

Their title, "Getting off the ground," neatly summarizes Graham's and Hewitt's double-edged analysis. Arguing for a renewed concern for verticality, they also keep the ground firmly afoot in a trenchant and brilliantly argued warning of the ingredients mixed into the new vertical urbanism replete with new technologies. A major component is Google Earth's space-eyed view of the world looking upside down not horizontally across the landscape—or is it spacescape now? This "unprecedented mass accessibility of the top-down visualities of computerized remote sensing and actual routine physical access to aerial and vertical spaces" (Graham and Hewitt 2013, 75) has encouraged corporations and nations alike to brand the earth—'brandscapes'—with spectacular vertical and virtual scenes for these new top-down "megastructural urban landscapes" (78). Here the virtual and the real play together in Google Earth. Their examples from Mumbai, and Dubai's famous mixed-use skyscraper Burj Khalifa, nail their analysis. They ask a heartfelt but revealing question:

> Does the proliferation of secessionary vertical landscapes, in turn, necessarily work to exacerbate the polarization of spatial practices that Michel de Certeau (1984: 82) famously identified in Manhattan between urban 'voyeurs', lifted up 'out of the city's grasp' to God-like positions from which they could 'see the whole' of the 'concept' city far below, and those less privileged walking subjects down below forced to continue inhabiting the street level?
>
> 2013, 80

Certeau's much-quoted walk in Manhattan asks for a regrounding of our sensibilities, to awaken to the dangers of those who would escape the streets and fly to the safety of the upper stories—to a "God-like" world—or perhaps go both up and down into a new kind of rabbit hole turned inside out by aerial surveillance? Undeniably, examples of the sheer hubris of those would-be inhabitants of high-rises are literally written on signboards and into the website of these chic addresses. Openly declaring its exclusivity, World Tower in Mumbai entices new überrich residents to "A place only the chosen few will call home."[11] Graham and Hewitt include a stunning sign on a mega high-rise construction site in Mumbai, in bold capital lettering, "SHARE THE SAME ADDRESS AS GOD," with the prior "Consider it a blessing to" in much less obvious type (81). Burj Khalifa in a Muslim state cannot invite this kind of near *shirk* (*širk*); however, the website credits the inspiration of Dubai's ruling Sheik "who inspires us to reach for the stars."[12] In Singapore, I spotted a huge hoarding at the construction site for a massive shopping complex, ION Orchard, "Where it all Comes Together." The boards invite those stony-faced walkers in the streets to connect with the stars, revel in charisma, and join these aggrandized fair-faced sparkling people in an open affirmation of fantasy, invoking the primal element of sky, stars, and grand spaces of pleasure. References to the earth are conspicuously missing (Fig. 6.2).

Walking with Certeau

My purpose here is not to deny either the political or ethical issues surrounding these gargantuan high-rises, or even the more modest HDB blocks that cover—some would say, cover over—the terrain of Singapore. But as Beauregard explained in his discussion of the MOMA-Folk Art Museum controversy, "My objective is to engage in moral inquiry and not to pass judgment" (2015, 534). By moral inquiry, I intend to take a closer look at the accompanying and often-sweeping value judgments within the analyses of the high-rise whose origins, much like those of the hyped advertisement for tall towers and massive malls (if I may use a problematic metaphor), are rooted, I suspect, in other modalities akin to "myth." Look *closely* at that much-used city stroll of

Figure 6.2 Giant billboard advertising the ION mall as the construction began in 2008.

Certeau with its now darkly poignant recollection of the World Trade Center that now has others "writing in the shadow of its absence, seeking new practices for this reconfigured space" (Carlson 2006, 396):

> To be lifted to the summit of the World Trade Center is to be lifted out of the city's grasp. One's body is no longer clasped by the streets that turn and return it according to an anonymous law; nor is it possessed, whether as player or played, by the rumble of so many differences and by the nervousness of New York traffic. When one goes up there, he leaves behind the mass that carries off and mixes up in itself any identity of authors or spectators. An Icarus flying above these waters, he can ignore the devices of Daedalus in mobile and endless labyrinths far below. His elevation transfigures him into a voyeur. It puts him at a distance. It transforms the bewitching world by which one was "possessed" into a text that lies before one's eyes. It allows one to read it, to be a solar Eye, looking down like a god. The exaltation of a scopic and gnostic drive: the fiction of knowledge is related to this lust to be a viewpoint and nothing more.
>
> Certeau, 1984, 92

The passion here, to my ear with its early training in biblical studies, evokes a prophetic voice: warnings of *lust* coupled with *idolatry*—these harlots of Babylon chase after false god-like power. They deny their embeddedness in the streets—that "turn and return it according to an anonymous law". What law? Is this a denial of their embeddedness in the earth from which they were made, and to which they must return? Such a theological reading should not be surprising: Certeau was an ordained Jesuit, and yet his "unwavering religiosity … has been quietly dropped from view altogether," (Buchanan 2001, *kl* 110) as is obvious for those invoking him in architectural and urban studies circles above.

Significantly, a *New York Times* video on the history of the high-rise[13] begins with the story of the Tower of Babel and the sin of humans to dare to build something as a species that challenged the heavens. That strange vignette in Genesis 11:1–9 NIV says:

4 Then they said, "Come, let us build ourselves a city, and a tower with its top in the heavens, and let us make a name for ourselves, lest we be scattered abroad upon the face of the whole earth."

5 And the Lord came down to see the city and the tower, which the sons of men had built.

6 And the Lord said, "Behold, they are one people, and they have all one language; and this is only the beginning of what they will do; and nothing that they propose to do will now be impossible for them.

7 Come, let us go down and confuse their language so they will not understand each other."

8 So the Lord scattered them from there over all the earth, and they stopped building the city.

9 That is why it was called Babel—because there the Lord confused the language of the whole world. From there the Lord scattered them over the face of the whole earth.

Of course, God confounds the construction of this tower, this human denial of godly power, by confusing their language, "that they may not understand one another's speech" (verse 7). Recent interpretations of this passage, which "has become famous as a political symbol of metropolitan ambitions as well as metropolitan megalomania," offer radically different readings instead of warnings against hubris, and rather "focus on the divine predilection for diversity, which confronts the human inclination to remain the same" (Korte 2012, 128–9). By either interpretation of the Babel story, and by Certeau's famous vignette, those inhabiting and building towers appear to have sinned, if not against God, then against "an anonymous law." Persistent assumptions that people are happier and more humane, more engaged with society on the ground, seem less an ethnographic than theoretical, and I would say *theological*, perspective.

In considering Certeau's theology within his famous walk, I have good company with Christian theologians, although they are unlikely to follow me in all my turnings. Graham Ward wants to "emphasize again the importance among the many secular readings of Certeau's project of giving due regard to his theological thinking" (Ward 2001, 502). As a major neoorthodox theologian and Regius Professor at Oxford, Ward astutely reads Certeau's walking in the contemporary city as an extension of his work with medieval mystical practices, and also in contrast and concert with Augustine's city of God: "Having elucidated the nature of this heterospacing [spaces without hegemony]—which makes all of us mystics for Certeau, if, as he enjoins, to be a mystic is to be unable to stop walking" (Ward 2001, 504). Indeed, a fellow Jesuit scholar remarks that the "whole oeuvre of Michel de Certeau is the story of the 'Abrahamic journey,'" marked by his own peripatetic ways:

> He moved rapidly, sometimes a little feverishly, from one place to another, always departing and in transit, as if he guessed that his days were already numbered. He never travelled, literally or figuratively, out of mere curiosity, still less by incapacity to settle in one place, but to learn something new and, much more, to share other experiences, the experience of others, out of passion for the human and the other.
>
> Moingt 1996, 479

Graham Ward argues that ultimately Certeau's work bears the impress of his Jesuit *charism*—a carefully chosen Catholic theological term meaning "a spiritual gift or talent granted by God to the recipient not primarily for his own sake but for the benefit of others,"[14] to avoid, I would guess, the more common and Weberian-infused form, *charisma*:

> Whatever Certeau's relationship towards orthodox Christianity (and its institutions) at the end of his life, there nevertheless remains the imprint of the Jesuit charism upon his writing. And nowhere is this more explicit than in his commitment to exploring the spoken voice. The Jesuit emphasis upon hearing the call of God (vocation) and the relationship between that calling, learning to listen, and being sent out under obedience, the emphasis upon the ingesting of Scripture as Word of God in order to weave its words into the tissue of one's life, the concern with social justice, an incarnate spirituality, and a gritty pragmatism which can operate within urban cultures: these marks remain on the body of Certeau's texts.
>
> 1996, 525

Is Certeau's walk really an ethnographic account? Oddly as Ward points out, there is really no city, nothing solid in those streets and that maddening crowd:

> First, the city, for Certeau, can only ever be a virtual reality. Its structures and organisations are mobilised both by time and subjective desire. To begin with, the city as place is always invested with a certain utopianism—reflecting the goal of human desire as it is fashioned by, and fantasises, in modernity: the ideal of transparency and control, manifesting its own rational system.
>
> 2000, 231

This may be about everyday life, but the act of walking becomes a meditation, as a kind of discourse or musing. Ethnography requires a lingering, settling down for a spell, really listening, and considering multiple levels of analysis. As much as Certeau calls for the now classic postmodern turn to particularity away from rationalized hegemony and toward the messiness of daily life, yet this combination of a theological perspective and Marxist tendencies means that these reflections are presented as statements about humanity with theological undertones—seemingly undoing a classic postmodern perspective as well as its emphasis on particularity.

Take Oneness for Example

So, what does happen in those heights? What is the interrelationship between a high-rise flat and a guru? On an October night in 2013, on the ninth floor of an HDB flat in Ang Mo Kio—high enough to qualify for Gehl's air traffic controllers or Certeau's voyeurs—members of the Oneness movement gathered for a puja to attain wealth and wellbeing. Oneness is based at the World Oneness University, a massive campus with temple and teaching facility in Andhra Pradesh founded and headed by "Amma Bhagavan"—Sri Amma and Sri Bhagavan (formerly known as Sri Kalki) in divine union. The worldwide organization, whose goal is nothing less than worldwide salvation, explains:

> Oneness, a spiritual organization, founded by Sri Amma Bhagavan seeks to alleviate human suffering at its roots by awakening humanity into oneness, wherein every individual feels connected to all that is. The central understanding of Oneness is that inner transformation and awakening into higher states of consciousness is not an outcome of a mere intellectual understanding but a neurobiological process in the brain, whereby one's experience of life is redefined at its core. This is achieved by Oneness Deeksha, which is a process of transfer of divine grace that initiates a journey into higher states of consciousness.[15]

I have chosen this example as one of the "extremes," with the kind of promises of global interconnectedness, "scientific" claims, and healing practices that would drive Carrette and King to distraction. Also notice the recurrence of "higher" in the discourse above. The group has grown in recent years. I had encountered them first in 2007 at their monthly satsang, then held in Little India; years later, celebrating the wedding anniversary of Bhagavan and Amma at the Ceylon Sports Club (June 2010); in a booth at the massive Suntec center as part of the Heart, Mind, Body Festival (June 2011); providing free food at a temple in Little India as *seva*, "service" (June 2012); and at a daylong "meditation and blessing" session in the group's new facilities, the Oneness Centre, a converted flat on the second floor of a HDB block in Ang Mo Kio, which a devotee had given over to Oneness for this use (2013). Finally, two days later, a group gathers for my prime example on October 13, 2013. "Visesha Sadhaya Aishwarya Pooja," guided by Oneness Guide Anand Dasaji at the World Oneness University in India, took place via Livestream in the HDB flat of a dynamic facilitator of the movement in Singapore. Recently, I found the puja still posted on Facebook accompanied by an image of Lakshmi (goddess of wealth) with shining backdrop of golden coins.[16] My field notes—shortened and edited—describe the evening billed as a Pooja (*pūjā,* worship offering) for the attainment of Aishwarya (*aiśvarya*, "wealth; riches; glory; abundance; prosperity"):[17]

Tonight, I went to the most amazing puja possible. It was in a fine HDB flat in Ang Mo Koi. In the center of the room was a large kalasha (brass pot) into which we were to eventually invoke the presence of Amma-Bhagavan. Gradually participants began to sit in a circle around this pot on the floor. Behind us and dominating the room was a large flatscreen monitor connected to a laptop computer in the corner where our hostess presided (Fig. 6.3). This was the "English" group and she had invited us to her house to translate because the director of the puja was to speak in Tamil. The group was small: three Chinese-heritage Singaporeans, two women and a middle-aged man, myself, and then an Indian woman and her, at first, unenthusiastic husband. Another young Indian-heritage man I had seen before was helping with the technology. I spoke with the middle-aged Chinese man who

Figure 6.3 Large monitor set to begin the Livestream session from World Oneness University in India.

was operating a new club for older people in the district, which was an important service to the neighborhood.

The amazing aspect of this puja: we were to be hooked up with Oneness groups from Malaysia and Brunei as well as Singapore via Livestream. The problem was that the hookup worked at first and then failed. Our leader in India, Anand, began by explaining that, although this puja was for the creation of wealth, the real problem for people was not lack of money but lack of good relationships. If we were having problems with money, really at the root were problems with our relationships, which we had to settle first. He seemed to be speaking to a young audience so we spoke about the relationship between mother and father but also husband and wife and friends. Then after some delightful fidgeting with the computer, the connection went out. During that waiting period we all began to giggle because the eerie noises that were emanating from the computer sounded like something from Star Trek. I took photographs of our leader on a computer desperately trying to solve the problem. I also have a seemingly incongruous photograph of a very traditional ritual brass pot in front of the computer. Finally, after about twenty minutes we decided to begin on our own, working with the leader via email and Skype.

But before we could actually begin, our coordinator needed to convey via email those special wishes from those who had asked for help. In spite of all of the lecturing about relationships, the formal requests included: May I make $100,000 a year in Australia; May I get my work permit in Singapore renewed; May I get the promotion that I have been wanting. I admit that the Protestant part of my soul was shocked but the Catholic/Hindu was not. The puja itself took about forty minutes.

First, we offered forty-nine coins that each of us had brought with us, with each offering we chanted a mantra so that we were saying the mantra forty-nine times. The next step was to chant the name "Amma-Bhagavan" as a mantra for twenty-one minutes. As we chanted, we threw a variety of substances onto the kalasha (Sanskrit, *kalaśa,* round brass pot, also sometimes copper or silver) which included rose petals followed by rice then turmeric and finally kumkum (red vermillion powder). Then, we all took Deeksha (*dīkṣā,* in Oneness, a special blessing) by stretching our hand palms down toward the kalasha. In this organization, clearly the guru and his consort are divine, in the sense that their presence can be invoked into the waters of the kalasha as in many temple ceremonies. Yet officially leaders say that you may worship any god of your choosing.

The coordinator, a very generous person, sustains a comfortably middle-class life but is not "crazy rich" as the surprise hit movie set in Singapore would put it.[18] Her HDB flat is in an older building with only fourteen stories. The design has four apartments off of each elevator entrance so there are multiple elevators in the complex. The plan gives a small set of families relative privacy with a little hallway outside to display plants or statuettes. Our hostess has arranged her plants with Ganesh images and her neighbor displayed plants with Chinese-style deities. The flats are very comfortable and livable.

Considering this complex, and even confounding, ritual event, the seeming incongruities abound beyond a cliché of the crossing of tradition and modernity. Rather, here are *crossings* that no one considered unusual. The juxtaposition of the very advanced computer system connected to a large display seemed natural with all of us seated on the floor in a circle with the ultimate Hindu ritual implement—the brass pot, which appears in very traditional temple rituals for the installation of a divine image (Fig. 6.4).[19] The questions I asked then and now: Where were we and to what were we connected, and how were those connections formed? There is little doubt that the ritual had derived from Hindu practice—and *via* the ritual, the living presence of Amma and Bhagavan had entered the kalasha in the middle of us all. But at the same time, via very up-to-date technology, we were equally connected to our leader in India at the Oneness campus and to small groups of devotees in Brunei and in Malaysia (I think it is telling that the exact locations of all of these other participants was never clearly disclosed nor of concern). Although we lost the digital connection, the feeling remained that we were doing this ritual in real time simultaneously with our affiliates in Malaysia and Brunei. The event at this home was multiethnic—although small—and in this sense very Singaporean.

What did Amma-Bhagavan offer? This was not the only unabashed ritual for wealth that I have attended in Singapore; in addition to Oneness pujas to Lakshmi the goddess of wealth and wellbeing, Rajayoga Power Transcendental Society (RPT) includes a form of visualizations to aid in the acquisition of wealth. Questions still linger here and remain important for the likes of Graham Ward, Carrette and King, and company. In some sense our leader in India did feel the need for some explanation. How can this unabashed puja for wealth be reconciled with concerns about commercialism and

Figure 6.4 The *kalasha* at the center of the puja, now covered in rose petals from our early round of offerings.

consumerism and spirituality—if indeed there is any need for reconciliation? And did the high-rise building itself enter as an actant in this process or in the social configuration of the event?

Living Vertically in Singapore

There is, in fact, little choice in Singapore with its total use of high-rise in the HDB flats. Here almost everyone lives in the same type of buildings, with the few private single residential houses at a premium. Interestingly Lee Kwan Yew's now contested family home and residence stands among the few surviving bungalows.[20] As the golden anniversary of independence passed, volumes celebrating this uniquely Singaporean institution began to appear, including a move by the government to include the food courts as "Hawker Culture in Singapore" on the UNESCO's Representative List of Intangible Cultural Heritage,[21] and a new appreciation for the HDB high-rises with the private publication of a stunning three-inch thick tome, rich in color photos and line drawings, *HDB Homes of Singapore*. The foreword by a former CEO of the HDB declares that the volume will "further convince Singaporeans that HDB flats are more than simply bricks and mortar." Mr. Liu goes on to extol the overtly price-saving simplicity of the bare walls and minimal division as ultimately giving "our residents opportunities to decorate their interior space over time according to their personal tastes and wishes ... the highly standardised flat became highly individual" (Miyauchi and Ogawa, 16). *HDB Homes* provides intimate views of wildly different interior living rooms and kitchens, yet treats the simplest of rooms painted bright blue with everyday furniture with the same aesthetic respect as the ultramodern steel-gray-painted flat with dark-gray sectional sofa, ceramic-tiled alcove and matching yellow-eyed gray cat with his own multistoried cat perch. With the exception of the "crazy rich," the HDB flats are home not only to multiple ethnic groups but diverse classes.

HDB Homes may celebrate the flats and present their homey interiors as private and idiosyncratic, nonetheless the buildings are monitored with soft but clearly present surveillance and social control. A more tempered discussion of the flexibility of the HDB high-rise design argues, "Our focus also emphasizes flux: vertical living involves processes of adaptation, contestation and appropriation as changing familial needs, norms and desires are reconciled within the socio-material constraints and affordances of high-rise homes" (Nethercote and Horne 2016, 1593). I heard a lecture on "Building Technology Innovation in Singapore's Housing and Development Board, 1960–1995" by Jane M. Jacobs on the struggles of the Housing Board to convince residents of the new high-rise regime to keep the elevators clear of trash and urine. This crucial new technology did not yet fit the social sensibilities of newly relocated high-rise residents. At one point, surveillance cameras were installed to prevent vandalism. Anyone, like me, who marvels at the civility and social grace of the denizens of these buildings remains unaware of the years of social engineering that accompanied the innovative engines of this new architectural technology—which the emerging field of socio-technical systems studies now reveals (Hughes 2004).[22] For those living high but not in the heights, daily life has taken on challenges and readjustments over the years. During my initial research in 2007, I spoke with a volunteer instructor for a course on the "basics" of Hinduism at the Hindu Centre, who also acted as a community liaison for the HDB flats. He mentioned arguments over the arrangements of flower pots and plants, including some falling on hallways below. I have also heard of hanging laundry dripping on neighbors' drying clothes downstairs. All of these issues are mediated in some way by the authorities—all is not as harmonious as the celebratory golden anniversary volumes picture.

So what role did the high-rise flat play in this process of sometimes fraught but enforced social interconnectedness? Here I return to Stephen Appold's perceptive study of community formation in Singapore's high-rise residences. Appold and the other editors of *High-rise Living* note that the government designed the HDB flats precisely over the dead bodies of old ethnic-based neighborhoods of old Singapore. By law, the population of each of these blocks must reflect the ethnic makeup of Singapore by percentages. But, as he concludes and I have also noticed, "Sharing physical space does not imply sharing social space" (2013, *kl* 4826). Rather, social groups tend to be confined to the family or groups sharing common ethnicity. What he does *not* see are precisely those interethnic spiritual groups claiming to move beyond ethnicity. However, his most important perception is crucial for an understanding of these groups:

> The residents of tall residential buildings, like others, are members of more extensive communities than neighbourhoods and towns. These communities are largely symbolic. Residents are also citizens and members of particular social classes. Tall residential buildings serve as very vivid symbols of both. Tall residential buildings, particularly those in large housing estates, have been used to create a feeling of membership in a larger community.
>
> *kl* 5004–5007

Appold points to the overwhelming middle-class character of the residential high-rise in Singapore; these are not estates of poverty but of prosperity. And owning such flats marks the resident *as middle class*, whether upper or lower. But more importantly, the residents of such high-rises have kept family and some extended ethnic belonging *but not as neighborhoods*—they identify with "larger" communities, the most important being the nation as a whole. The high-rise becomes emblematic as well as constructive of this change from particularity to generality.

Viewing the site of the Oneness event in the Ang Mo Koi high-rise residence, I see a building, whose very unadorned character becomes a *tabula rasa* for residents to decorate or fill at will. The high-rise, especially now, does not wear permanent clothing, not even the old rococo facades of its predecessor, the walk-up; it is like a manikin that can change clothing and be changed as needed.[23] Temples in Singapore are marked with identity; most are ornately decorated and unlikely to be mistaken for anything but what they are. But the high-rise building, precisely with its own lack of particularity, its own generalized persona, may suit these movements well. And I would say the same for many of the participants in this ritual. Our hostess is a businesswoman equally at home with computers and rituals. Her home is fully equipped with the latest TV and computer systems and she maintained an altar for Amman-Bhagavan in the same living room. I have helped her serve food at a temple in Little India as a social service and sat with her during several Deeksha sessions where "blessings" were bestowed. She moves with ease from her work to this puja and to other ritual occasions—both "traditional" and "spiritual." Those who were present are not monades—the gentleman who leads a community organization is at point here. Yet the goal of Oneness is oneness, a sense of unity, "wherein every individual feels connected to all that is."[24]

As Stephen Appold writes of the debate over high-rise, "Tall residential buildings are fodder for societal culture wars," I would argue that many of the most vocal critics of guru-led movements willingly engage in theological wars lurking behind the critiques of the evil high-rise. The high-rise residential building fits the underlying sensibilities of the global gurus—a super modern nonplace of fluctuating time and malleable space that conjures a different sense of sacrality, which does not privilege order or even orientation but focuses on personal development within newer forms of connectedness.

Appold appears to argue that the high-rise well suits the contemporary formation of community, and may well be active, an actant, in such new community formations which are *not* really residentially based. With the old notion of neighborhood gone (he implies, forever) the tall buildings fit the new nonlocal sensibilities—I would say nonplaces of the current world where symbolic belonging actually supersedes deeply emplaced connectivity to neighborhoods. Once again, Oneness provides a case study: I have followed the changing demographic, style, and location of the Oneness since 2007 and have witnessed the coevolving of practice and place—their move from using a function hall in a renovated shop house in the heart of Little India to the new center, a flat donated by a devotee within the HDB housing complex, and using devotees' high-rise residences. In October of 2007, I attended a satsang of the movement when the name Kalki was still used interchangeably with Oneness at a rented hall on the first floor of the North India Cultural Association on Cuffs Road. At that time the leadership was in different hands: an Indian-heritage thirty-something man wearing a Kennedy Space Center T-Shirt directed the process of setting up the room, and his elegant wife clad in graceful silk sari conducted the puja. Their contrasting choice of dress could be a metaphor for the mixing of styles here. On the one hand, my conversations with him and my friend Saro (who kindly introduced me to so many of these organizations early in my research) spoke of universality and the worldwide presence of Oneness, but the devotees who attended, their demeanor and dress, exuded a decidedly South Indian zest with the woman officiant speaking in elegant English but adding equally fine Tamil translations at key moments.[25]

Held during the festival of Navaratri, the nine nights devoted to the goddess in her many forms, this satsang fell on the second night of the celebration and so included a puja to Durga, the goddess as shakti (*śakti,* power). When I arrived in the hall in a renovated shop house, devotees had just set up an enormous gold-framed photo of Amma-Bhagavan seated on an ornate carved wooden gaddi; at their feet a devotee carefully set a coconut atop a brass kalasha on a silver pedestal (Fig. 6.5). Saro introduced me to the leader and I immediately asked how the group had formed. Clearly the organization was new, because he told me that those who had profound encounters with Bhagavan in India got together to "share their experience with others,"

Figure 6.5 In Little India, members revere a portrait of Amma-Bhagavan during a special satsang of Oneness in the early days of the movement in Singapore. I have blurred faces to protect the identity of participants.

who perhaps had not met him in person. Saro, along with my kind interlocutor, looked toward the portrait of this intense couple. They explained that this was not "just" a photo but could elicit a close relationship with the guru: "So when you are seeing him, you can take him to be whatever comes to you naturally. You can see him as a really divine person and you can have a relationship with that; or, you can see him and think, I would like to have a friendship so you can then have a friendship relationship ... what is more important is that you should *have* a relationship and ... open up your heart, meaning you should be able to talk about whatever is on your mind with him."[26] This kind of relationship, they both explained, becomes unique for each devotee, and the gurus give to each "what each is seeking." They affirmed all of this was very compatible to modern life. Then both stressed the importance of the "Deeksha"—a totally new practice to me at the time—to open the channels of the mind to a fuller experience of life. We had to cut the conversation short as the puja began. The officiant opened the puja with her explanation of the meaning and intent of the ritual. At this point, although I knew that we were firmly located in Little India and about to participate in a puja, we had *not* convened in a temple, for we sat together as a congregation and heard this well-articulated message:

The object of today's prayer is to liberate you from psychological suffering, fear, hatred, insecurity, inferiority, jealousy and anger and you will receive the blessing for inner peace and happiness also for good health and physical energy to carry out all activities in life. Durga Devi dispels psychological suffering and gives a boon for mental peace and happiness ... blesses us with love and courage. We can be instruments of God only if love and courage flowers within us. Some of us may think we have no psychological suffering but we need to know that if we have pressing problems in life it is a manifestation of our psychological suffering. In this puja Amma and Durga Devi will liberate the devotee from psychological suffering, she will also bestow mental peace and happiness which will help to achieve success in day-to-day activities.

She then asked us to fold our hands in prayer while she chanted effortlessly in Sanskrit with the intonations of a temple priest, but unlike a traditional priest—and especially unlike, as women rarely officiate at formal temple rituals—she explained each step as she proceeded, occasionally translating into Tamil with equal finesse. As is traditional, she first offered mantras (Sanskrit, *mantra*, a powerful sacred sound usually from the Vedas) to Ganesha (Sanskrit Gaṇeśa) to remove obstacles to our puja, and then chanted two rounds of mantras to invoke the divine presence of Durga into the kalasha. Now, as she completed other offerings, a group of enthusiastic women began to sing *bhajans* as the congregation joined them. The devotional songs became louder and more intense as the middle-aged lead singer neared ecstasy, her hands moving wildly to keep the beat, her face entranced (Fig. 6.6).[27]

Finally, the most innovative practice began, the giving of blessings, Deeksha, which I had not seen used in any other Hindu-based movements, although such a laying on of hands is not uncommon in Christian circles. Years later I attended Oneness events in which everyone took a turn giving Deeksha to all in their circle, but here the leader moved through the seated devotees as he performed the blessing on those who indicated their desire by bowing their heads. At first, he moved with the neon lights glaring, but soon the hall was darkened as his wife joined him in performing the Deeksha. A seriousness seemed to pervade the room; I did not feel the promised sense of joy or clarity but others clearly felt what I could not. After two hours of this fast-moving ardent satsang, the overhead neon lights came on and the session ended. As I walked home, like the others, I passed the noisy Toxic Bar and the general Saturday night din of workers literally spending their pay on wine, women, and song.

These two October pujas separated in time (2007/2013) and in place (Little India shop house/ninth floor of HDB flats) appear on what I could call a sliding scale of locatedness. In 2007, the portrait of Amma-Bhagavan rested in a cultural hall which was rented for the evening—the location was temporary because each month devotees had to remake the rather bare blue hall into a sacred space holding the powerful image of the Amma-Bhagavan. Nonetheless, we remained on the ground within Little India. The leader told me earlier that devotees found such ritual forms "comfortable" in this location, while he noted that, in the United States, such pujas would not be part of the satsang. However, even here we were not in a temple clearly identified and grounded in one of the few remaining ethnic neighborhoods in Singapore, but rather a building

Figure 6.6 Devotional songs, *bhajans*, bring some members of Oneness to near ecstasy in this Little India setting.

owned by an Indian cultural association dedicated to maintaining North Indian identity within this very South Indian enclave. So, at this point, like a stacked set of boxes, our location fits levels of the local within the global. Oneness remains a global guru-centered movement, *but* in Singapore fits *within* a government-designated ethnic Indian community—with its temples, its devotion, and its raucous diversions— yet convened *within* a shop house dedicated to the maintenance of a very particular ethnic identity.

However, by 2013, not only had the leadership changed hands but the spatial configuration re-formed. Just days before the puja, I attended a Deeksha and Meditation session at the new center now in the second floor of a typical HDB flat owned by a devotee and donated to Oneness for their use. Across the street stood a grand Chinese temple complex with glorious dragons guarding from the roof, and situated below us a convenience store. An unusual hand-lettered sign at the entrance read Singapore Oneness at the bottom and in Chinese at the top. To complement the Chinese, a carved wooden OM hung on the same brick-faced wall. Inside the dual presence of Chinese and Indian aesthetic continued. The ever-present framed photo of Amma-Bhagavan centered a lace-draped low table with a porcelain incense burner and prayer wheel. A set of silver paduka rested below the portrait and a wooden pair rested on a chair next to the altar (Fig. 6.7). Not only had Oneness left Little India for the diverse HDB world here, but the ambiance was decidedly Chinese-heritage as were the participants in a

Figure 6.7 The living room of an HDB flat now houses Oneness as Amma-Bhagavan's portrait and sandals occupy the furniture.

special Deeksha/meditation session held that afternoon and lead by Wes. In a tale of international interconnections, our enthusiastic young Chinese-heritage leader, trained as an accountant, had left Singapore to work in Australia while his sister studied there. On a business trip to Fiji, he attended a Oneness Deeksha resulting in a life-changing experience; with good luck he amassed the funds to fulfill his dream of studying at the Oneness University. This was his inaugural session. We had decidedly left the enclave of Little India for the high-rise world of the Singapore heartland, home to the majority of Singaporeans in the outskirts of the city center.

Sanskrit, Tamil, ecstatic devotional songs dominated the satsang in Little India with Deeksha added as the culminating event. By 2013, indeed we had ritual in the HDB flat: our hostess mentioned a session in Tamil somewhere, but here Singaporean English united the ethnically diverse participants. The program at the new center in the heartland stressed meditation, quiet reflection; Wes performed a very gentle Deeksha while we sat in place on Zen-like cushions to receive the blessings. While enthusiastic, none of these events exuded ecstasy.

Finally, in 2017, at a dinner in Little India with some of the key Oneness leaders, these members revealed yet another major change. Bhagavan had said that the time for using images, that is the *murti,* was over, and a new time had come when only Jyothi (Sanskrit, *jyotis,* "light from sun or fire"), as the goddess in her form as luminosity, should be used. I asked one of my fellow diners about her altar and she said that she still had the images of Bhagavan and Amma, but that when she next returns to India she will deposit them at the Oneness temple there and have only a picture of light on her altar. She explained that after all the gods are just a human creation, a way of understanding personality, but that need is over and Oneness members should now move beyond this.

So, in the case of Oneness, which initially seemed embedded both in the enclave of Little India and within a South Indian ritual idiom, the group moved into the high-rise heartland, both continuing the Tamil-style ritual forms but also emphasizing its Chinese- as well as Indian-heritage members with computer-aided multisited ritual, yet also now including meditation. As in the *pādukā* practice in Chapter 1 showed, a new form emerged, modeled on both meditation and devotion—with the Deeksha continuing. And finally, with the removal of all anthropomorphic images, only light would be honored on the altar. In the case of Oneness, the changing style seemed to accompany a move away from the shop house to the high-rise, with architectural context following changes in ritual and in embodiment—disembodied in some sense. The purposely flexible design, the enforced multiethnic environment, the move from particularity to generality, appear to fit the changing theology of Oneness.

Losing Ground

In his critique of high-rise living, Gehl could be accused of wanting to keep humans on the ground, within the norms of their physical limitations, which is not the global gurus' message and never the goal of yoga, and certainly not of Oneness. Sri Amma Bhagavan enjoins "inner transformation and awakening into higher states of consciousness," which enfolds worldly success and wellbeing. Every morning I receive a "Wake up to Wisdom" message from Sadhguru Jaggi Vasudev, who along with an eye to everyday concerns, often exhorts his netizens to move beyond bodily confines: "Once your mind becomes absolutely still, your intelligence transcends human limitations." Here concerns with human hubris—with going too high, with staying within bounds—are left on the altar of the many Towers of Babel rising higher and higher as they scrape the sky.

A series of books on the city published in the last decade continues to describe the urban world as a place of dislocation and discontinuity but *not* in the old sense of a lament—rather of excitement on the development of new ways of being and the emergence of new beings. Here the very constitution of personhood is in a creative relationship to new technologies. Terms like "post-human" (Braidotti 2014) or "actants" (Latour 2005) arise with the suggestions that humans can and do change their very constitutions. As Nigel Thrift now argues, with each new technology, persons reconnect with the things of the world in different ways, first with industrialization but now within this strange new urban world where "the individual" becomes "a bearer of all kinds of partial subjectivities which are bundled together, broken asunder and shuffled hither and thither by all manner of assemblages, and thus are constantly mixed in with all manner of objects such that the divides between subject and object (and inner and outer) are perennially not just confused … but perennially shifting" (2014, 3). Why fear Ward's "vague but phosphorescent spirituality" when such phosphorescence may characterize the new city with its ungrounded and unmoored denizens. Not only does architectural structure have *agency* but cities themselves are now "sentient," credited with "increasingly having their own forms of energy, tenacity and magnetism built out of forces of outstinct" (2014, 3). So, people who are living in a city are not people in any traditional sense: their "inscape" has changed, but *not* as Panikkar feared. Among these theorists there is no hopeless lament. In Singapore, planners openly embraced the high-rise to engineer a new kind of citizen: ordered, controlled, but also unbound from older identity formations. The global gurus, with their pujas and their practices and their media posts, also aim to re-form their devotees, indeed raising them from ethnic confines toward "boundlessness." Both are intertwined within a city-state alive with high-rise estates declared to be "more than simply bricks and mortar."

Templing Gurus in Little India

Walking down the heart of Little India on Serangoon Road from Albert Court Village Hotel to Lavender Street is a little over a mile. To stroll down to Race Course Road and then across passing the Tekka Center via Buffalo Road to Jalan Besar Road stretches less than a half-mile. Such is the length and breadth of the very walkable but densely populated area of this old ethnic enclave. For over a decade, most summers, I have walked these streets of Little India—literally not figuratively—as the heat and the dense crowds always make the area feel larger and the walk longer. Google Maps may claim that such a walk is possible in twenty-five minutes but only at 7:00 a.m. on a Sunday morning or using the back alley-ways—where the only real danger is tripping on a semiferal large-eared cat (now marketed and bred as Singapura).[1] Singapore's major Hindu temples open onto Serangoon Road—Sri Veeramakaliamman, Sri Srinivasa Perumal, Sri Vadapathira Kaliamman—all brightly painted with the traditional multistoried *gopura*, gateways, welcoming devotees—sometimes of Chinese or mixed heritage—and tourists, often from Korea or Japan (Fig. 7.1). Other temples, like Shree Lakshminarayan, are just a block away. The other major Hindu temples in Singapore are scattered over the island with the oldest, Sri Mariamman, actually located in Chinatown. But these, often very beautiful, temples, are bereft of the carts selling garlands and the step-down shops retailing prayer beads, small square copper-engraved yantras, and other articles needed for pujas, or the many tourist-centered shops with rows of deity images in plastic or plaster (Fig. 7.2); nor, is it possible to get a hot masala dosa (spicy rice flour crepe) on the way home. In short, such Hindu temples outside of Little India lack a sense of *place*, if *place* can be defined, as often suggested, as "a meaningful location"—a *locale,* with identifiable, often unique, constructions (Cresswell 2014, 14). Crossing the multilane Sungei Road from my hotel in Albert Court with the famous Sim Lim Square (four stories filled with the very latest technological equipment), I usually run as the signal light ticks off the seconds, over the road covering the old Rocher Canal with a new MRT line underneath. Then suddenly the border into Little India is immediate and visceral—by sight, sound, and taste.

Little India is about shopping for traditional clothing and eating familiar regional delicacies, but primarily Little India is the site of key *institutions*[2] for Singapore's Indian population, principally religious (with the possible exception of the Mustafa Centre[3]—conceivably a sacred site for the many shopping-crazed locals and visitors). Many of the religious structures are old and established, others newer, but all are *in some sense* settled into this place, usually sharing Tamil sensibilities and the Tamil language. While

Figure 7.1 Walking down Serangoon Road, a visitor soon encounters the Sri Veeramakaliamman temple gate with bright ornate sculptures.

Figure 7.2 Such shops cater to tourists but also to everyone seeking an inexpensive souvenir that could inhabit a self in their home.

some Indian families live in the HDB flats within or very near Little India, most South Indian-heritage Singaporeans travel here to shop, eat, and worship. Not only Hindu, but also major Tamil-Muslim, institutions are here. Nearby on Dunlap Street, walking toward Jalan Besar Road, rises the ornate multilayered Masjid Abdul Gafoor, whose call to prayer sounds over a portion of Little India five times a day. I woke to the recitation of the Qur'an when I stayed very nearby at the Perak Hotel and could hear the sermon in Tamil on Fridays. Painted pale yellow and trimmed in green, with a Victorian feel to its architecture, a Tamil flamboyance pervades this otherwise serious Islamic institution (Fig. 7.3). This mosque remains crowded as women walk glittering toward Friday prayers in black sequined full-length hijab. Sundays also bring the many migrant workers from South India to the area, carried by small lorries for their day off to shop, drink, and sometimes worship at the temples or the mosques. Long-settled Tamil Singaporeans also frequently flood the many temples. Here on Thursday nights, "guru night," another kind of devotee joins the permanent, and sometimes more makeshift, "spiritual" centers that also line the streets of Little India.

Figure 7.3 This was my view of the Masjid Abdul Gafoor from a landing near my room at the Perak Hotel across the street.

On Thursday evenings, devotees often attend the satsang at the Shirdi Sai Baba Centre[4] (also called the Shirdi Sai Worship Centre), taking the small elevator to the third floor of the community hall right next to the Sri Vadapathira Kaliamman temple, and then move a few doors down to join the lively *bhajans* at Sri Guru Ragavendra Society. A few blocks down on Hindoo Street, a framed photo of Mata Amritanandamayi looks out from a long room on the ground floor of yet another shop house-turned-temple, the Amriteswari Society, where devotees congregate early Sunday mornings. Across from the Mustafa in prime real estate, the oldest spiritual group in Singapore, founded in 1927, the Arya Samaj, also meets on Sundays (I have attended their satsang);[5] but their popularity has waned in recent years and they often rent their long-standing building to other organizations for special events. Other guru-centered groups have met in rented spaces in Little India as well; some of these have left the enclave, like Vyasa Yoga, Isha Yoga, the Sri Krishna Mandir,[6] and Oneness, mentioned in previous chapters. Also present is the Rajayoga Power Transcendental Meditation Society (RPT) in Singapore which meets on Fridays in a converted shop house across the street from the Sri Srinivasa Perumal. Their guru works from nearby Malaysia and has developed practices that include meditation and the cultivation of *siddhi* powers. Although located within Little India, the RPT falls as much outside as inside the enclave.[7] However, Shirdi Sai Baba, Guru Ragavendra, Amriteswari Society have a *presence* lasting over a decade that embeds them into Little India. These groups, although global in scope, are more *placed* in Little India, and by an interesting extension, into the Singaporean landscape; but, unlike their more prominent neighbors along Serangoon Road, they contain a sense of mobility and—at least in rhetoric—a purposeful practice of inclusion. The presence of the guru abides here, either as a framed photo or, as in the case of Shirdi Sai and Guru Ragavendra, embodied within a divine *murti* (Sanskrit, *mūrti,* image-body). All three are now served by a full-time priest. In short, these gurus are now "templed"—occupying a more concrete place and form, while their devotees continue to understand their practices as *spiritual* in ways distinct from the more formal worship at nearby Hindu temples. All of these spiritual institutions are a little over a decade old: many were just establishing their presence when I first sought such movements in Singapore, beginning in 2005 at the same time that *Newsweek* and the *Straits Times* reported on the worldwide spiritual-but-not-religious phenomenon. Now, with a new turn in spatial theory, the importance of *place* and *place-making,* even in Singapore, needs attention. As grand global gurus occupied the macrospace of the Expo center or Suntec City, these smaller groups—at least in their Singapore manifestations—took root in Little India. These *congregations*—this is the best term—rarely exceed a hundred people at a sitting, but their small numbers belie their importance in understanding Singapore in its full spatiality and sacrality.

Placing Little India

Little India is not wholly Indian nor does it neatly fit any classic sense of *place*—a much-used but ambiguous term, as Tim Cresswell observes: "no one quite knows what they are talking about when they are talking about place" (2015, 6). Cresswell's *Place:*

An Introduction[8] offers an extensive interdisciplinary evaluation and summary of the recent spate of interest not in the much-touted *spatial turn,* but rather in a realization of "a subtle shift of focus from space to place, with its rich cultural dimensions" (2015, 3). In the previous chapters, Singapore as a nation-state could have been termed a *place,* and the process of creating nationhood as *place-making,* but the *tabula rasa* scheme of the People's Action Party, the tearing down of old housing and the construction glorying in the ubiquitous and homogenous HDB flats, makes *place* a more difficult term for the whole of Singapore. However, the government via the heritage and tourist boards, openly developed Little India as a *place,* along with Chinatown with its spectacular new Buddha Tooth Relic Temple, and the "Malay enclave"[9] around Arab Street/Kampong Glam with the stunning Masjid Sultan. Neither *Visit Singapore* nor sites like *TripAdvisor* recommend a taxi ride or a stroll through the heartland of high-rises where most Singaporeans live. This is the irony of Little India: consciously *constructed* and maintained as a tourist site with enough covert and overt plays of power to satisfy any postmodern cultural analysist, the enclave functions at one level as a *place* of difference, an exotic site for those cycle rickshaws with whirling colored lights often filled with Korean tourists. At other levels, however, far more complex interrelationships exist between "insiders" and "outsiders" as T. C. Chang argues (2000). Designated as a conservation area only in 1988, but with initial discussions a decade earlier (Kong and Yeoh 1994, 249), the *Manual for Little India* suggested "the history of Little India is both colourful as well as alive ... such historic connections can best be highlighted with the establishment of a showhouse which will be a repository of artifacts, maps, drawings and photographs" (URA 1988, 30). Years later, the government ultimately inserted that stunning steel and glass house for memories—the Indian Heritage Centre—just off of Serangoon Road, meant for visitors and still regarded with indifference by locals. The tourist board maps the area with a number of suggested walking trails: the forty-minute *Serangoon in the 1900s* trail, or the one-hour *Walk of Faiths,* or the thirty-minute *Shop Till You Drop* (into one of the many recommended restaurants). Yet at the same time, Little India has grown organically—within regulations, of course—as did much of old Singapore. Like Chinatown and Kampong Glam, Little India is a cut-out from an old map of Singapore, left standing after the flood of progress washed away all of those overcrowded shop houses and infested kampongs from the rest of Singapore.

Little India's complexity as a *place* is matched by its complexity as an "ethnic" enclave. Fortunately, *Singapore's Little India,* published in 1982, offers not only a snapshot of the area less than twenty years after independence, but also a sophisticated discussion of the *concept* of an Indian ethnicity developed by the government along with an ethnographic account of the actual complexities of such an identity within Little India. Both historically and demographically, multiple ethnicities with Indian origins linked with differing languages characterized the population within the spatial boundaries of Little India: Tamils, Telegus, Malayalees, as well as North Indians speaking Hindi and related languages. Sharon Siddique and Nirmala Shotam understand *Indian* as a *conceptual category* defined by the government with its famous four, or CMIO—Chinese, Malay, Indian, and Others (often of European or mixed descent):

... these ideal types are in fact middle-range conceptual categories—suspended, as it were, between the higher conceptualization of the emergent Singapore national identity, to which it is assumed they will eventually be subsumed [this would change], and the lower particularistic ethnic categories which are recognized as breakdowns of the middle-range CMIO conceptual categories.

3

To move beyond these conceptual frames, Siddique and Shotam turn to a territorial dimension: "Communities have spatial as well as affective reference points" (4), they argue. Hence their concentration on Little India as marked by both *sentiment* and *locality*. Their conclusions prefigure my own, and what would become the spatial turn:

CMIO community space can be defined as an area wherein one of the constituent communities provides the definitive identity. This identity arises out of the community's actual physical dominance of the territory which is prerequisite for the development of a particular, recognizable, and unambiguous social-cultural and religious identity. The mental map of the area, including its boundaries, further reinforces that communality's dominance within these boundaries.

5

Implicit here, at least from the perspective of many passing years of spatial theories, the bounded territory also creates and forms the very sentiments that become an identity— in postmodern terms, constructed but then naturalized. In 1982, their interviews with visitors, especially young Indian Singaporeans, confirm that, "while well satisfied and even desirous of integrated housing, schooling, and employment, there is an expressed need to have a place within the larger island environs that is sensually their own" (88). Little India within this island urban setting in the early 1980s already was neither a clear ethnic territory, nor Hindu, but nonetheless an area dominated by an emerging *conceptual Indian* community. This will become important when considering the growing presence of guru-centered movements—hypothetically beyond race, ethnicity, or even religion—but nonetheless deliberately ensconced in Little India.

In the last few years, however, the environment of Little India has significantly changed both in appearance and in mood. When I returned to Singapore most recently, I was shocked to find my favorite mall at the edge of Little India, the Verge, boarded and partially dismantled, wrecking cranes hovering over its skeleton—with only rumors of its fate (Fig. 7.4). Here, small shops offered bangles and inexpensive clothing, travel agencies, and a very good grocery store with Chinese and general Asian goods, including household appliances. On asking, people remarked on its shabbiness—too old for a modern mall—but here many migrant workers from Tamilnadu used to congregate to purchase electronics, transfer funds, and arrange visits back to their homes, even though the ownership of stores was not always in Indian hands (Chang 2000, 355).

Until recently the government did not heavily regulate the whole area or update the facilities until a serious riot—one of the first in decades—occurred in December of 2013. An allegedly drunken Indian construction worker was removed from a minivan

Figure 7.4 The familiar wrecking crane begins its diabolical work on my favorite shopping center, the Verge.

on Race Course Road, then fatally run over as he staggered behind the van. Reacting to the tragic accident, over 400 migrant workers joined in burning police cars and pelting shop windows. Arrests followed with alcohol taking much of the blame, but, as the *Economist* pointed out at the time, "Neither the government nor the mainstream media has ventured to draw any link between the sudden display of rage and the dire state of rights for migrant workers."[10] A recently released official report argues strongly against such dissatisfaction, declaring: "Nearly every foreign worker who the COI spoke to— including those who were involved in the riot—testified emphatically that they were happy with their jobs and living quarters in Singapore, consistently rating Singapore as 'number one' among countries who receive migrant labour," although the report does acknowledge issues with some employers (Ministry of Home Affairs 2014, 45).[11] Evidence tells a different story of dissatisfaction over wages, and, even within the enclave, "Tamil migrant workers have found comfort and where they feel closest to home is Little India, yet they face exclusion from the residents and citizens there, making it an unhomely space for them (Hamid 2015, 6). The *Straits Times* headlined:

"5 years on from Little India riot: Businesses still in a slump but residents welcome less rowdy environment."[12] Little India remains under the Liquor Control Act which forbids sales after 7:00 p.m. Apparently this has resulted in fewer migrant workers in Little India to shop and play, but also an increase in what I had already experienced, annoyance with these workers especially among the settled Indian Singaporeans and newer high-tech or business émigrés.[13] The other visible results are those signs for the *Let's Keep Little India Clean* campaign and a general sense that more orderliness—I would say, gentrification—is necessary. None of this alters the crowding, but does transform the tone with more tourists and fewer migrant workers here for leisure. The tensions of Little India as a *place* are more palpable and public—the *space* between a quotidian South India style and a tourist Little India is wider and deeper as the specter of the rioting workers lingers.

Such tensions ironically force *experience*, not the cooler mode of meditation but louder more exuberant expression, a far more forceful and immediate sense of relationship between context and self. But Little India has always evoked more visceral sensibilities and remains a *place* in this sense—the kind of gritty unexpected walkways that Michael de Certeau would love—in contrast to the miles of HDB flats with carefully planned amenities. In Little India, pedestrians need to keep their wits about them to avoid a speeding taxi or a sudden stepdown in the iconic covered walkways fronting the rows of shop houses. HDB housing estates dot the enclave but the shop houses and old commercial streets seem to mitigate their impact. Unlike Orchard Street, Little India does not shield its inhabitants or visitors with a soothing umbrella of air-conditioned cool. Bodies are felt here; sight and sound seen and heard. Philosopher John Malpas's initial argument that "identity of persons is inextricably bound not merely to place in some general, abstract sense (which would be meaningless), but also . . . to those particular places, multiple and complex though they may be, in and through which a person's life is lived" (Malpas 2018, *kl* 698–701) remains both true and *not* true of Little India. That "fundamental intimacy of being with place" (*kl* 615) that creates *identity* for theorists like Malpas (à la Heidegger) again does and *does not* function for the many Singaporean Indians shopping, processing, worshipping, singing, or meditating here.

The enclave breathes *particularity*, speaks of heritage, exudes a history of migration and resettlement in its architecture, religious, domestic, and commercial structures. During the Thaipusam (Tamil, *Taippūcam*), ardent devotees carrying milk pots and kavadi *(Tamil kāvaṭi)*, often piercing their lips or backs, walk two miles from the Sri Perumal temple down Serangoon Road to the Sri Thendayuthapani temple just outside the enclave. These devotees embody very particular Tamil sensibilities and celebrate with a panache not seen in contemporary Tamilnadu. The often spectacular kavadi, with blinking lights and sense of showmanship, mixed doubtlessly with intense devotion (Fig. 7.5), allows the Tourism Board full scope to promote "a day of cultural adventures."[14] Yet Little India is rarely home to most Singaporean Indians, since only a small portion of the HDB flats can be owned by ethnic Indians as per the Ethnic Integration Policy,[15] and the private condos available remain very expensive. Those who participate in Thaipusam and who attend the temples here normally live their lives "in and through" the world of the HDB flats.

Figure 7.5 Each year that I have witnessed the Thaipusam, the kavadi become more elaborate.

The government of Singapore now encourages the maintenance of an ethnic identity at the same time that harmony and integration remain central. In education, Singapore's *bilingual policy* exemplifies the duality: English, to maintain a forte in international business and science, but the mother tongue to "access to one's cultural heritage, thereby strengthening one's values and sense of cultural belonging."[16] In the words of the founding prime minister: "Will we ever become completely homogeneous, a melange of languages and cultures? No. If we have only English and we allowed the other languages to atrophy and vanish, we face a very serious problem of identity and culture (Lee [2004] 2015). Likewise, Little India, along with the other ethnic enclaves, then, serves not only as a tourist destination but a living access to heritage, albeit with a cut-out, contrived quality, but *at the same time* an intense sensuousness. Here the tongue tastes the sweetness[17] of the Tamil language, even its divinity (Ramaswamy 1997, *kl* 474), and the spice of Indian food. It is *real*, but *authentic* is not quite the right term, especially today. In his summary, Creswell shows that past understandings of *place* in radical human geography "based on notions of rooted authenticity ... are increasingly unsustainable in the (post)modern world" (2015, 41). I see little evidence that the government projects worry about authenticity—not surprising in such a constructed macrospace—but rather about "celebration and appreciation," as the Indian Heritage Centre puts it.[18]

While there are other more radical voices, I will stay with Jeff Malpas's emphasis on *place and experience*. His focus on the interrelationship of *place* to the formation of the self seems to parallel the purpose of the enclave, to reinforce/rekindle/recreate *Indian*, mostly *Tamil*, identity, *but* in the full knowledge that all of this, like the bilingual policy, blends and bends time and memory. For Malpas, *place* tends to remain unconscious except "when we are displaced or disoriented and in the experience of nostalgia or loss, but also in contemplation . . . when we attend to that somewhere and are overtaken by a 'sense' of the place, by our own experience of it, by its very presence" (*kl* 1202–5). Such an experience of both displacements,[19] nostalgia, and the very presence of *this* place, fits the feeling of being-there in Little India. Most valuable here is Malpas's "Topography" and his emphasis on the intense interpenetration of place and persons without exception: "A region or place does not simply stand ready for the gaze of some observing subject. Instead, it encompasses the experiencing creature itself, and so the structure of subjectivity is given in and through the structure of place" (*kl* 1548–50). My own *subjectivity* remains challenged by the *presence* of Little India, perhaps because I share, ironically, the same sense of *place* and *displacement* that a recent émigré might feel or perhaps what a Singaporean-born ethnic Indian, who visits to family in Tamilnadu or to pilgrimage sites, would experience. Like many of its visitors, salespeople, and shopowners, I experience the *place* as someone long familiar with Tamilnadu, and viscerally know that this is *not* India, but at the same time can feel its presence. As an American, I have another layer of identity with its own challenges, but then I also share this stratum with several of my key interlocutors in the guru-centered groups who work for US-based companies, or took their degree in the same program at my alma mater, the University of Chicago, or travel the same routes to and from the US and Singapore. We meet in Little India. Adding to the layers, I first encountered Little India in 1974, when I stayed with my husband at the New Serangoon Hotel across from the Mustafa Centre on our long way back to the USA—it was the 70s—to Saigon, then via ship from Hong Kong to San Francisco. That hotel later collapsed killing thirty-three, the last of unregulated shoddy construction in the district, "considered one of the worst disasters in post-war Singapore."[20] At that time, Singapore existed as an independent country for little less than a decade. Yet, even then, coming from a year in Tamilnadu, Singapore's Little India afforded hamburgers and beer and a cosmopolitan feel. With all of this complexity, I will follow Malpas's directions for a topographic analysis, and my analysis will draw from my own affective experiences:

> The delineation of place can only be undertaken by a process that encompasses a variety of sightings from a number of conceptual 'landmarks' and that also undertakes a wide-ranging, criss-crossing set of journeys over the landscape at issue. It is only through such journeying, sighting, and re-sighting that place can be understood.
>
> *kl* 1657–1660

My sightings crisscross time and terrain from as early as 2005, continuous with the spiritual groups that I have followed here. I have watched a *process of emplacement* in these albeit small movements—a sometimes contested shift from emphasis on meditation or on singing *bhajans* to an emerging form of worship with an attendant priest and a more embodied presence of the guru. For some groups, the guru—considered a constant presence to his devotees but nonetheless without a living human body[21]—was formally embodied in a *murti*, an image-body/icon. Because some of my interlocutors wished to be named and others did not, my descriptions here will span time and keep all identities silent, but alive through my senses and consciousness.

Shirdi Sai Baba in Singapore

I met the first head of the Shirdi Sai Sanstana in 2006, a year after this small group of devotees had passed the hurdles of registering as a "society" with the government. A group of Sai devotees, mostly expats from North India, had approached this gentleman to help the Shirdi group because, as a Singaporean citizen, he could file the forms. At that time, the group met to sing *bhajans* to their guru in the Vadapathira Kaliamman temple on Saturday evenings. They wanted to remain in Little India rather than relocate to the "worship zones" allotted to new organizations by the Urban Redevelopment Authority which were mostly in industrial areas outside of the city center (the Sri Krishna Mandir eventually moved to such a location). He mentioned that some members were exclusively devoted to Sai and others also attended established temples, but all agreed that their new space would *not* hold any other deities but Sai and all the *bhajans* would be directed to him alone. When I asked him why Sai was becoming so popular (I had encountered ardent devotees while researching new Hindu temples in Chennai), his unambiguous answer was: "People find their prayers answered."

Within a year, when I returned to Singapore, the Shirdi Sai group had secured the third floor of a community center abutting the Sri Vadapathira Kaliamman temple. I soon attended their satsang session on Thursday night in August of 2007. The third floor seemed a temple in the making. The walls were white with three niches awaiting some decorative element. The floors were polished terrazzo with mats laid out for worship. A young man was decorating the altar where a picture of Sai stood surrounded by lights and hand-painted decorations, including a small umbrella on the top (Fig. 7.6). I approached him and he introduced himself; we were soon joined by another. Both were young men in their thirties. When I gave them my business card, my new friends were greatly disturbed at my title of Professor of Religion, which neither liked, preferring the term "spiritual." Both suggested that we change the name of our department from the Department of Religion to the Department of Spirituality. Now, in this era of spiritual-but-not-religious, their suggestion seems less eccentric!

Before the service, we began a discussion about the use of ritual for Shirdi Sai and his relationship to Religion and religions in general. At this early stage of the organization, opinions varied. This very articulate gentleman personally felt that Sai did not want a lot of ritual, nor any distinctions between the religions of his followers. Sai had accepted all religions and told people to come to him as they were—to a Muslim

Figure 7.6 Simple mats and a painted portrait of Shirdi Sai Baba await members at an early satsang in 2007.

he would discuss the Qur'an and to a Hindu the other sacred texts. Prior to 1918, the Muslim and Hindu followers were about equal, but then, after partition in 1947, Hindus began to predominate. He seemed genuinely concerned and said he had been arguing for a return to the spirit of the movement prior to 1947. He had read Sai's work and focused on his *teaching*s. He argued that Sai never claimed to be a god but rather a "mediator," to bring people to the divine. Throughout our conversation, this fervent disciple seemed troubled as he told me that one donor had paid for the current meeting area, and a marble image of Sai would soon come from India. The current organization would then disband and that family, recently come from New Delhi, would take control and manage this center as a temple. I could sense his disappointment and loss as he told me what Sai meant to him: "Like taking a taxi," he needed only one guru to drive him through life to the end. He found Sai at age 19 and his devotion continues.

That night the altar, decorated very simply, contained only the portrait of Sai. Our photos taken at the time show a combination of devotion but also meditation on line drawings of Sai in booklets that everyone held. Some devotees held their hands in a common *mudra* (hand gesture) for meditation with palms up, fingers open and thumb touching the index finger. After the service and the ending *āratī* with the prayers and chants in Sanskrit, I remarked how *Hindu* the observance seemed and perhaps how uncomfortable a Chinese person might be here. He agreed. He said that he wanted

Chinese to come and that he also wanted the prayers to be intoned in English *not* Sanskrit. He spoke about how Jesus spread, but only after many centuries; he thought that Sai might, too, spread over the world in time: his message was for the contemporary times. However, the disconnect between this young man's ideas and the congregation seemed to have widened. He studied Sai's teachings and envisioned Shirdi Sai Baba as an enduring powerful figure but not a deity in any traditional sense—indeed how could a Muslim continue with such a Sai? I wondered if he realized that the same issues of the status of Jesus troubled the early church. An alternate website for the Shirdi Sai Centre contains a disclaimer: "This is not the official website of the temple," and continues to advocate for pluralism, declaring, "Sai Baba is one of the greatest Sufi saints of our time and the debate on whether he was a Muslim or a Hindu is unresolved till this date."[22] The voice of those uncomfortable with their organization's metamorphosis into a temple lingers on the web and in the many translations and printings of the *Sree Sai Samartha Satcharita: The Life and Teachings of Shirdi Sai Baba*,[23] which I can recall serving for study sessions in Singapore.

Within a few months, I attended the consecration (*Prana Pratiṣṭhā*)[24] of a new lifelike marble image of Sai resting in state within a marble altar in the newly decorated center. New framed prints of Sai Baba now occupied the niches and more framed prints covered the white walls. As the new donor/patron of the temple explained (he remains anonymous here as in the public sites for the temple),[25] the space officially remained a spiritual center and not a temple as per government of Singapore designations, but nonetheless has a *murti* and a full-time priest from North India. A specialist in such consecrations had come from Delhi on that day to lead the ceremonies. The rites of installation proceeded in a hall of the temple downstairs—as I had witnessed many times in India for newly built temples—with the offerings poured into the holy firepits (*homa*), and the patron and his very devoted wife acting for the community in these rituals. When the energy shifted to the *murti* on the third floor (Fig. 7.7), the patron and his wife sat in the front row as the *bhajan* began. His wife rose and, with her eyes closed, began to sing. Watching her face as she sang, and even now looking at the photos, the devotion of this couple still stares out from these captured moments. My talk with him earlier confirmed this. At that time, they had recently shifted from New Delhi to Singapore. He first encountered Sai Baba when invited to Shirdi by chance in 1989. His visit did not produce an epiphany but rather an awed respect when he viewed the genuine simplicity preserved in Sai's living quarters. He thought that, unlike so many gurus seen on TV, Sai genuinely had renounced riches in his life. His wife became an ardent devotee in Delhi, holding meetings in their home. He emphasized how important giving was for Sai devotees and that the temple was only part of the work. This spiritual center fulfilled their sense of charity for the community.

Exactly a decade later, on my last visit to the temple to attend the evening puja, I arrived, but the center seemed well worn now. This was not Thursday, so only a few people dropped by, including one older woman alone, who seemed deeply troubled, and a family with the father later intensely listening to the chanting. I also spotted other women and a young girl glued to their cell phones in spite of a clear notice on the board that their use was prohibited. One woman was intently folding and then wrapping offerings of garments for the *murti* (there was a notice about that on the

Figure 7.7 Priest sits in wonder as Shirdi Sai Baba resides elegantly dressed and enthroned at the consecration ceremony in 2008.

website); she continued her work but kindly gave me permission to photograph. I noticed a new ritual had developed: the priest was there but each person came up to the white marble railing, kneeled down and touched the silver *paduka* in front of the *murti*, and took some holy oil in a container at the side to dab on their forehead. They rose then touched the feet of the life-size painting of Sai on the wall to the right, which looked to be the original portrait used prior to the marble *murti*. I saw the same continued reverence for the original printed portrait at the Sai Samaj in Chennai, which underwent a similar process with the installation of a large marble *murti* (Waghorne 1999, 224–36).[26] At about 6:30 p.m. the priest sat down next to the altar and began reading silently and very devotedly. He then rose and offered *ārati* as he chanted extensively with beauty and passion, but the sound level made it difficult for me to enjoy. I knew that this was not guru-night and I had seen the room totally filled on a Thursday a few years before. The most recent reports now appearing on a Facebook page for the center show great attention to the *murti* with increasingly elaborate clothing and stunning decorations, the posted photos including enthusiastic singing with live instrumentals and women devotees fashionably dressed.[27]

Both the practice of rituals and the worship of the person of Shirdi Sai began in his lifetime according to the *Sai Samartha Satcharita*. This book "akin to the Vedas for Sai devotees" (2004, vi) resembles the Christian Gospels in the mix of teaching, description of miracles, and reverence for a divine personage. The controversy, however, never abated over the use of Hindu rituals and over the person of Sai as guru *and* deity—as my earlier informant articulated so forcefully. In Chennai decades earlier, I visited a Shirdi Sai temple, which had only the *paduka* of Sai and still refuses to install a *murti* (Waghorne 2014a, 2014b).[28] Given the Tamil sensibilities of Little India, the work of a South Indian Tamil Brahmin born B. V. Narasimha Iyer, a successful lawyer whose personal tragedy led him to renounce his profession and rising political fortunes to seek a guru, remains key to this argument. Taking the name Narasimha Swami, the Hinduization *and* the emphasis on templelike ritual and worship of the saint of Shirdi are attributed to his prolific writing and organizational skills, as well as Sai's appeal to "middle-class Hindus engaged mostly in government occupations and in trade" (Srinivas 2008, 232). In 1939, Narasimha Swami founded the All-India Sai Samaj in Mylapore, a neighborhood in Madras (now Chennai)—an area studded with sanctuaries, some very famous. Initially only a large hall, the site developed into a temple with a large painted image of Sai, and finally added a marble *murti* in 1986, which I witnessed (Waghorne 1999). Narasimha's movement became, as the organization proclaims, *all-Indian*. Smriti Srinivas quotes from his claim that the Mahasamadhi (the death of the flesh-body of Sai) was a means of "starting a new era in Sai Bhakti and providing a special ethereal entity or Body that the entire people of India if not the world can be drawn to" (233). She concludes that Narasimha performed "an operation that allows Shirdi Sai Baba to be freed from locality and his physical body" and leaves behind "Baba's Sufi heritage" (233).

Karline McLain, in her close reading of Narasimha's work, adds the crucial religious-philosophical perspective (Narasimha experienced Sai through Advaita). From that perspective:

At the core of his understanding is the belief in the nondual nature of ultimate reality, whereby the self within is the same as God, which is also the universal All-Self. Shirdi Sai Baba is therefore not only the guru who leads one to that All, but is himself that All, which is located within us and all around us. Narasimhaswami would later expand upon this, arguing that when understood from this monistic perspective, Sai Baba was both formless and with form.

2016, *kl* 2150–3

As concerned about political unity in the struggle for independence in India, McLain shows Narasimha's continued sense of Sai as composite and yet One made him "the ideal figure to bring together members of multiple faith communities in India, especially its two largest communities, Hindus and Muslims" (*kl* 2225–6). The Sai enthroned at 555 Serangoon Road dwells in Little India, within multireligious and multiethnic Singapore. Here the arguments over Sai's status feel like a rerun of decades-old arguments with an active unofficial website still proclaiming Sai as "one of the greatest Sufi saints of our time,"[29] as he sits yet again within a defined locality with both Hindus and Muslims identifying as part of *Indian* (read *Tamil*) *heritage*.

However, the Shirdi Sai Worship Centre—as the current sign now proclaims—remains closer to what Siddique and Shotam term an *association* in their early study of Little India, *not* a *community*. Here they quote another sociologist[30] whose application of the term *community* actually comes close to its common use among anglophone Indians: a group primarily defined through "decent-related being and behavior" which includes customs and *religion* (2). An *association*, on the other hand, is voluntary and "exists within a system of goals"—so the early studies on the new urban landscape defined the emerging social formations. Already highlighting the enclave's blurring of these categories, *Singapore's Little India* nonetheless predates the growth of the spiritual movements—with two important precursors, the Arya Samaj remaining in, and the Ramakrishna Mission finally building outside, the zone. Groups like Shirdi Sai Worship Centre, by their classification as *societies* by the government, and by their common conceptions as "open to all," remain *associations*. However, by common consent and arrangement, this association tends toward North India. With the Hindi language

Figure 7.8 Devotees crowd the Shirdi Sai Center for a Thursday night satsang.

dominant here, the center also functions like an ethnic *community* as it looks out on the very Tamil-inflected Sri Vadapathira Kaliamman temple. Yet on a Thursday night, I see a mix of devotees and a system of worship that do not replicate the priestly services in the adjacent goddess temple nor in the multiplicity of its deities. Here in the Sai center, worship is now *worship* and less a meditation, but the veneration is done as a *congregation* (Latin *congregātiō*, "an assembling together; union, society, association"[31]), which in the more literal sense of the term reflects the Sanskrit *satsang* (*sat* + *saṅga*)[32] with everyone praying, chanting, and singly *together*, using the same printed folio of collected *bhajans*. This practice of using a common "hymnal"—for want of a term—continues through all of the transformations of this association (Fig. 7.8).

Sri Guru Ragavendra Society

After attending the satsang at the unfinished Shirdi Sai Worship Centre on that August evening in 2007, shortly after arriving in Singapore, I walked toward the MRT station past the grand Sri Perumal temple and heard passionate singing in Tamil emanating from a small wood-latticed pavilion in the side yard just next to the parking lot. I recognized the image of Sri Raghavendra (the society adopts a Tamil form and renders him, Ragavendra) from my work on new temples in Chennai, and quietly joined the group sitting at the back. At the front was an altar with a bronze *murti* of Raghavendra fronting a large, now iconic, poster of the saint seated in front of his Samadhi (*samādhi*, mausoleum, more usually called his Brindavan, from Sanskrit *vṛndāvana*)[33] with an image of a five-faced (Tamil, *pañcamukam*[34]) Lord Hanuman and huge white bull in the back; this dais was assembled anew each Thursday evening. The two officiants were not formally priests, although the main officiant was properly bare-chested with a saffron dhoti and wearing stunning mala (*mālā*, garland) of crystals and rudraksha (*rudrākṣa*) beads. He offered *āratī* as the *bhajans* began. I listened to the animated singing when a woman spotted me and began to talk. Suddenly, I was invited up and given a silver tray filled with marigolds and rose petals and told to follow and do whatever the other ladies did. I began to chant along and offered flowers with each emphasis—self-consciously at first but, as the singing became more infectious, I forgot myself. Now overly enthusiastic, I offered too many petals at one time so the ladies next to me kept filling my tray as I ran out. I felt totally welcomed although everything was in Tamil, including the announcements and bound xeroxed copy of the *bhajans*. Their language, however, was what I would call textbook Tamil, and I could follow much of the meaning. That evening when the satsang was over I asked for the yellow schedule I saw others holding. Someone quickly handed me this program for an upcoming special ritual for Guru Raghavendra on August 29 at 6:30 p.m., and encouraged me to come. I still have the bright yellow, red-trimmed program, with Tamil on one side and English on the other.

The society organized the elaborate three-day celebration, Aradhana (*ārādhana*, "worship") just two weeks later, to commemorate the 336th anniversary of the day that Sri Ragavendra entered into his tomb, sometimes called *mahāsamādhi,* to voluntarily cease bodily activity. I attended the second-day offering of milk to bathe the image body of the guru (Tamil, *pāl-apisēkam*). I joined a long line of women, most dressed in silk saris, all carrying a small pot of milk to the altar (Fig. 7.9). A priest in a bright orange and gold dhoti then poured the contents reverently over the bronze image of the saint. In neat rows of chairs, a large crowd of devotees sat outside the pavilion observing and chatting. Finally, they rose and entered the pavilion for *āratī* and the revealing of the elaborately decorated *mūrti (alaṃkāra)*. The officiants carried the fully clothed and ornamented image of Vishnu/Krishna (to whom Ragavendra was devoted) around the perimeters of the pavilion (we were adjacent to a Vaishnava temple).

The rituals followed many such celebrations as I have witnessed in temples throughout Tamilnadu—the offering of milk, the procession, devotees rushing to place their hands over the burning camphor flames, the formal temple music, and the dinner that follows. But as I talked with my fellow participants that day, several pointedly mentioned that Guru Raghavendra is not a deity. Later, when I spoke to one of the officers of the society, asking him why the society seemed to emphasize *bhajans*, he explained: "the more we chant, the more the power comes into the vigraha [Sanskrit,

Figure 7.9 I watch as the priest pours my offering of milk on the image of Sri Raghavendra.

vigraha, mūrti, the image body]," but then emphatically denied that Swami Raghavendra was God: "He is not God but the intermediary to God. We need the guru." A very committed devotee, who befriended me during my many subsequent returns for the Thursday satsangs, told me the very day that I first met her that Raghavendra was guru but not God. She explained that he was still living and working from his Brindavan, and thus was alive and promised to live more years. She cited a book on his life in which Raghavendra affirms that he is not Hari [Vishnu] but was sent to do his work.[35]

During the Aradhana someone handed me a xeroxed sheet telling the story of that special day when the saint entered his tomb plus a lovely holy-card, reminiscent of my Roman Catholic heritage, with the iconic image of the saint inscribed Sri Guru Ragavendra Society Singapore, with the date ROS 11.01.2005, and a prayer in Tamil and in roman script on the back. The sheet, clearly prepared for this day, although in English, relies on terms (informally) transliterated from Sanskrit, and presents the guru as a learned scholar—the historical Swami Rāghavendra (1601–61)[36] wrote commentaries on Madhava theology and was a musician and an ardent devotee of Lord Vishnu.[37] Here, Raghavendra tells his saddened devotees who had gathered to witness his leaving: "The Lord Sri Hari had sent me here to do his Noble work, that task is completed ... Do not feel sorry that I will disappear from your sight, I will be in Mantralaya in the Brindavana and take care of you all!" Seated in lotus position and his japamala (*japamālā,* rosery), he began to chant instructing his followers to build a tomb around his body when his chanting ceased. Soon his seated, now stilled, body was encased. This reverent retelling stresses the saint's devotion to Vishnu enjoining importance of learning especially the "Vedas, Upanishadas, and Shastra," affirming that all of the miracles performed by the saint are by the grace of Vishnu. The prayer on the holy-card reflected this moment as well. I discovered online many current renditions— some sung in recordings and on YouTube—of this same prayer, a verse (*śloka*) from the Guru Raghavendra Stotra. Legend tells that the saint's chief disciple Appanacharya composed this hymn of praise (Sanskrit, *stotra,* eulogium) in his desperation, some say, as he swam across a flooding river to have a final sight of his master just as the tomb encompassed him. "Millions of people across the globe, irrespective of their caste, country, religion or sex, burst into a two-lined stanza almost every day ... there is a crescendo of this every Thursday when people gather in large numbers in temples of Raghavendra Swamy," as one blogger explains.[38]

As I look at these now tattered sheets and at the still vivid laminated card, the Guru Raghavendra, presented on that day as an orthodox figure firmly within the Vaishnava lineage, breaks out of such a bordered box. Even the *śloka* on the card presents an amalgam calling Raghavendra both the upholder of Truth and Dharma but also the Kamadhenu (Sanskrit, *Kāmadhenu*), the bountiful cow and the Kalpavriksha (Sanskrit, *kalpavṛkṣa*) the wish-fulfilling tree.[39] The more I experienced his life among devotees in Singapore as I returned to see and sing over the next decade, the predominantly Tamil congregation remained Śaiva[40] and much less concerned with their guru's theology or his orthodoxy than with his living *presence* and his miraculous powers of healing.

Later in 2007, I had the opportunity to speak with the two most visible leaders, who remained consistently present at the satsangs over the years. Others joined our informal conversations, anxious to add their experience or opinions. A younger man, who seemed adept at organizing, told me that each year, if possible, the society organizes a fully planned group pilgrimage to the Raghavendra Brindavan, sometimes including other religious sites. He was then planning a trip that would include the five Chinese-heritage Singaporeans devoted to Sri Raghavendra who wanted to return to Mantralaya as well as the famous pilgrimage site, Sri Venkateshwara temple in the Tirupati, in the same state of Andhra Pradesh. During the conversation, others asserted that Raghavendra is a medium between the devotee and God, but it "does not matter which God—could be Kuan Yin." And then, again strongly emphasizing: "he is a mediator with the Almighty, not God."

In another conversation, the acknowledged leader told me about the origins of this society. Once Raghavendra devotees had another larger society. This gentleman had a bronze image made of Raghavendra in India and had raised funds for a more permanent site, but the area was in an outlying industrial zone "too far away and hard to get there" with poor public transportation connections, unlike Little India. Some members reorganized at this point but, without a place of their own, the new society rented the pavilion at the Sri Perumal temple. He first became devoted to Raghavendra when his mother became very sick for one year but got completely cured from breast cancer with prayers to the saint. He then went to India to Mantralaya to thank Raghavendra. His wife accompanied him and was also cured there from another ailment while there. He asserted the guru is "not punishing us, he knows what we need and is still alive" in his Brindavan. He told another story of healing: his employer was sick and he went to his house and prayed chanting to his guru 108 times. When the doctor arrived and found the man much improved, he asked, "Did anyone come and pray?" His employers are Chinese people, yet credited his prayers and Raghavendra for this miraculous recovery. This devoted leader kept the *murti* in his home, and brought this for the satsang. I have watched him carefully setting up the portable altar and decorating the Raghavendra's image for each session (Fig. 7.10). He did have priests sanctify the *murti*. This impressive gentleman now conducts the pujas which he learned as he watched the priests who had come. He wears a mala of beads especially designed to "cool" his body, meaning to make him fit to perform the puja. He affirmed once again, as he put it, that for him "Lord Murugan is God, Guru is Guru." He mentioned the nearby Shirdi Sai Baba, whose simple ways while in the body he respects. He remains concerned with any guru who claims himself a god. While he does believe that others have power—"something is there,"—he has only one Guru, Raghavendra.

Each time I returned to Singapore, I always joined the satsang, not so much to talk as to sing the *bhajans*—which remained at the heart of this devotional community. The many warm nights at the pavilion, looking at the Perumal temple and the seemingly incongruent skyline, now blend together. I took no notes, but increasingly gained some skill with various cymbals and clangs. From the pavilion, an expensive high-rise seemed to dwarf the glowing gopura of the temple, but, from the street, the old row of wildly colored shop houses always overwhelm the bland buildings behind rising like some crinkly grey backdrop (Fig. 7.11). However, when I returned in 2012, the society had left this bucolic site for their own rented shop house almost adjacent to the Shirdi Sai Centre on Serangoon Road.

Figure 7.10 The leader of the Sri Guru Ragavendra Society officiates during weekly satsang in the covered pavilion next to the Sri Perumal temple.

Already much had changed, with the reverence shifting to a larger brightly painted clay image now kept in the back of this long narrow building. A priest now decorated the sculpture (Fig. 7.12), while the leader still enthusiastically guides the *bhajans* in the slim hall, with the devotees arrayed along the walls and with some outside in chairs on the sidewalk. By the time of my most recent visit in 2018, the transformation seemed complete. The Ragavendra Society closely resembled a temple, with the bronze *murti* now consecrated, installed on the altar in a carefully demarcated alcove, and served by a professional priest (Fig. 7.13). Iron railings fronted the altar, separating a priestly domain from the lay. The brightly painted sculptural image of the guru now occupied a shelf construction on the right-hand wall. Even the singing had taken a more formal tone with more professional singers using a microphone and harmonium; the leader still continued to add his voice but I noticed that the seated devotees became an audience rather than enthusiastic participants. The old circle of song was gone, devotion shifted now to the altar. A father, kneeling at the altar, patiently taught his delightful young daughter to pray, while others gradually came forward to the priest (Fig. 7.14).

Figure 7.11 Looking out from the pavilion, the ever-present modern skyline fails to dwarf the glowing temple.

I spoke with a woman at the donation desk who advised me to buy two deepa (*dīpa*), which she then helped me light to offer to Raghavendra. I took these up and offered *āratī* with the priest showing me what to do, a bit bemused. Later, the same woman told me that the society only rented the building, and really wanted to build a permanent temple, but they need millions to do this in Singapore. Unlike earlier satsangs when devotees sang together for hours, I noticed that people came in, offered abeyance at the altar, but did not stay long as they likely were making the rounds of the temples on Serangoon Road that Thursday evening. At the altar, the ritual was clearly simplified from the more elaborate pujas at the adjacent Sri Vadapathira Kaliamman temple. Most devotees offered the clay deepa at the altar, waving it, as I had, before the consecrated bronze image of Raghavendra. Then, taking holy oil from the priest and anointing their own foreheads, devotees moved to honor the sculptural Ragavendra, touching his feet and placing their flaming deepa next to the donation box at his side. Much like the developing ritual regime at the Shirdi Sai Worship Centre, this temple for a guru now combined elements of more traditional temple ritual with priest and a consecrated

Figure 7.12 In the new shop house location, an elaborate plaster image of the saint begins to take center stage.

Figure 7.13 The society has a more permanent site very publicly spilling onto the sidewalk on Serangoon Road.

Figure 7.14 A father teaches his little daughter how to pray as the priest looks on.

image embedded in an altar, but continued the emphasis on communal singing, although with less fervor (at least to my eyes and ears). Here were elements of communal interplay combined with the come-and-gone personalism of a Singapore Hindu temple on Serangoon Road. I call the process "templing": the society becomes more emplaced within the Little India landscape. However, keep in mind that form of Raghavendra installed here is the same bronze image commissioned by the leader-founder, an *utsava mūrti*, the form used for festival (*utsava*) processions, that is, the portable form of a holy figure—in this case, once firmly declared as not-god, but now treated even more like a divine image body, a *vigraha*.

Amriteswari Society of Singapore

My earliest search for "spiritual movements" in Little India in 2005 led me to the door of the Amriteswari Society of Singapore in a converted shop house as I turned off

Serangoon Road onto Hindoo (the spelling still retains the British double-O) Road (Fig. 7.15). Nearing 7:00 p.m., I had heard that a *bhajan* session would begin soon, and remained and waited. Mata Amritanandamayi, as a rising female guru with an increasing global presence, had just garnered an intense full-length study published that same year, *Hindu Selves in a Modern World* by Maya Warrier. Here in Singapore, a conversation with several women as they prepared for the event confirmed that the society, registered in 1996,[41] had just purchased the entire building: "Amma" traveled here to opened the center just last year; they claimed about 300 members. I entered the narrow hall with Amma's portrait under an ornate green sequined umbrella. On a pedestal in front stood a photo of her feet. The entire altar was elegantly draped in purple and gold saris. As the devotees entered, we sat on the floor on woven plastic mats, long runners as I had seen in the Shirdi Sai hall. Finally, about seventy-five had assembled, mostly women of Indian heritage but with one Chinese Singaporean couple and one Euro-American scholar. As the *bhajans* began, an older woman assuming the role of the priest began offering flowers, first touching each to her heart and then throwing them at the guru's feet. We sang the *bhajans* together for about forty-five minutes. However, everyone was expecting the arrival of "swami," who finally walked through the parting crowd with some bowing at his feet, while one passionate woman,

Figure 7.15 The front door of the society as I first encountered the group in 2006.

who had given each of us roses, threw hers at his feet. I held mine, confused, as were others. Instead of the sermon that I had expected, Swami Purnamritananda Puri began to play a simple wooden flute with passion and obvious proficiency for twenty minutes. He offered flowers and *ārati* to her image, and the program ended. Everyone lined up excitedly to offer abeyances and to take prasad, in this case sweets, from his hands. Seeing me, he called me over and we began to talk, but it was so noisy that swami brought me upstairs to "Amma's Room" where she had slept during the dedication last year. In that brief interview he spoke of his own early life-changing encounter with her, and his dedicating his life to her service. To this day, the swami's presence on the web catalogs his worldwide workshops and talks seemingly with the same sense of irony and humor that I saw that first night.[42]

When I revisited in 2006 for an evening puja, the society had engaged an energetic and very learned young priest, whose insights I continued to value when I returned for a full year's research in 2007–8. As I once again opened the door, deposited my shoes in the hall, and then entered the hall, the priest was in the midst of a puja, which immediately felt pukka, more professional. He held a silver tray with two silver paduka, here for Amma. Chanting prayers in Sanskrit, he sprinkled water and roses one by one on the sandals, later telling me that he tried to do this nightly. Now Amma really seemed to be treated as Goddess, and this society now resembled a temple. When all ended I presented my card, told him my project and he invited to come on Sunday morning from 8:00 to 10:00 a.m. for the weekly satsang and especially for a special event on July 10th, Guru Purnima Day Puja, and then the following Wednesday for a talk, adding that, after all of this, "we can really go to town."

That morning of the Guru Purnima Day Puja[43] in 2006 became a rich experience. The morning pujas began at 7:00 a.m. and, when I arrived at about 8:30 a.m., the rituals were already winding down. I soon learned that in Singapore 7:00 a.m. actually meant 7:00 a.m. I counted about fifteen to twenty people, both men and women, young and old, seated on the floor. Most were dressed in saris or salwar. I spotted one young Chinese man with rudrākṣa beads and a very old Chinese lady in blouse and pants. For the final ārati, this white-haired Chinese lady and an Indian-heritage woman in a sari held the ārati tray together; I still have that arresting photo (fig 7.16). As was customary for the weekly Sunday Satsang, I joined the congregation in stepping up the narrow stairway to the community room for Prasadam (Sanskrit, *prasāda*, "graciousness," food presented to a deity or guru and then taken by devotees), always a filling South Indian "tiffin."[44] I sat next to two lively ladies in their middle years who offered that they had been devotees for over seventeen years. As one woman told me, after seeing Amma for the first time, she was immediately "gripped by her presence." However, that first encounter did not linger, but "I saw her again and the devotion became permanent." She found others who had similar experiences, and this group of devotees began meeting once a month in each other's houses, then once a week in various temples, and finally purchased this building three years ago. Again, they emphasized that, although the formal members of this society numbered about 300, Amma had many more devotees, "perhaps thousands in Singapore," who come out when she visits in person. This group does some charity work together and organizes Satsang and festivals like Guru Purnima, but they do not meet socially. I would hear this again and again in such

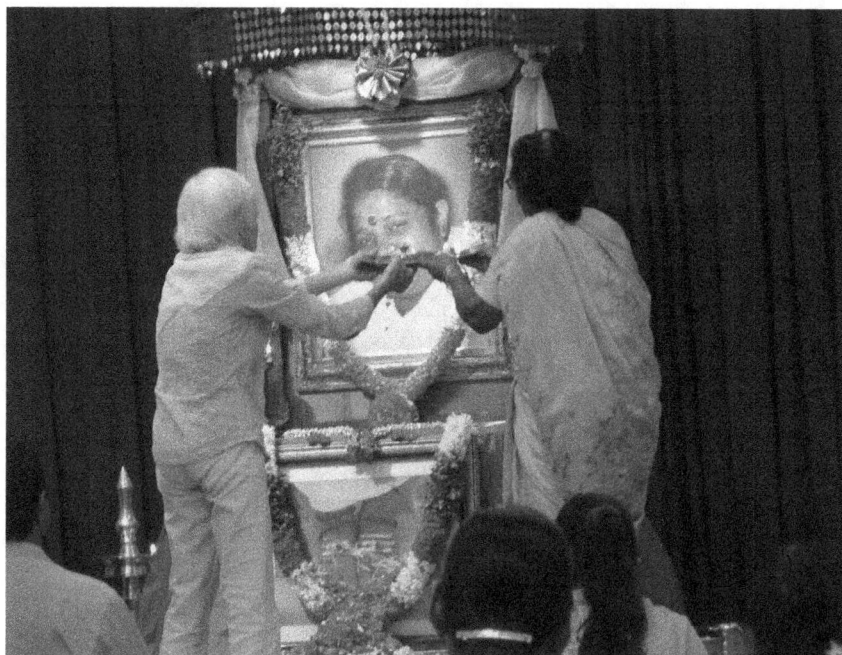

Figure 7.16 Two devoted members of the society offer *āratī* to the portrait of Amma in 2006.

groups in Little India. Maya Warrier confirmed this in her own study. Amma's congregations—at least here and in India—did not spill over into social friendships among devotees. Rather her devotees remained in close contact with family "geographically dispersed yet closely in touch through modern means of communication" such that in "their everyday life, these people saw little or nothing of their fellow devotees, and preferred to kept things that way" (2005, 12–13).

I spoke a bit later to the priest with the infectious smile as he was eating idly (scrumptious steamed rice flour dumplings). I asked him about his own work for the society and his views on spirituality and religion. His own daily routine included a three-hour *sādhanā* (Sanskrit, "accomplishment, performance, also worship"). He gave no details but such practices typically include chanting, meditations, and bodily exercises (the term is usually used within yoga traditions). He clearly was not an ordinary *pūjāri* (priest) that might serve in one of the temples on Serangoon Road. With a routine of daily pujas for Amma and his own practices, there was little spare time except the outside lectures he gave in schools and the class in the Gita he offered every Monday to a group of retired high-level lawyers, etc. The following year, I attended some of these sessions in which he recited verse by verse in Sanskrit, providing a translation and a commentary, taking on the role of pandit (Sanskrit, *paṇḍita*). I have witnessed many such religious "discourses," regularly listed in the newspapers in Chennai.

His insights on the difference between "spiritual" and "religious" provided a counterpoint to the usual critiques of spirituality. He explained that spirituality *transcended* religion, which he understood as focused on the "rites" of worship. For this priest, the temple was only a small part of Hinduism, and he was concerned that I not confuse or equate all Hindu practices with the temple: those "simple" practices, not the deeper or harder ones as in spirituality. Moreover, he understood religion to be associated with divisions, but not the spiritual. Amma and this society remained decidedly *spiritual*. I asked about the words I had heard in the *bhajans* that associated Amma with the Vedas; he said that all derived from the Vedas, the stories, etc., but the Vedas were too difficult for most people so that Amma, like many gurus, used singing of *bhajans* as another way to achieve the same thing: liberation. I began to talk about those who criticize spirituality as too individual or too commercial. We talked about money and the need for *artha* (Sanskrit, "wealth, property, money") to get things done; as he said, without money little can be achieved so that one must take care with gaining wealth, which must be obtained virtuously and put to good use. He offered why people misunderstand the relationship between money and spirituality: "they think spirituality means free," that a spiritual person can do anything they want, "so why should it cost any money." I also asked about another critique of spirituality, too much picking and choosing. Did Amma's devotees also worship at temples? And he said, of course, and some even go to other gurus. But he stressed that although one can take from many gurus, you must have your own discipline: "this in not shopping." On the seeming individuality of spirituality, I asked about the emphasis on communal worship that I had witnessed here, and he affirmed that when a group offers prayers it is more powerful than an individual and that this idea goes way back in Hindu history. He seemed to understand the difference for me to research and not become a devotee, but cautioned me to feel spirituality in order to talk about it—not to remain "in the books."

In the evening I attended the Guru Pada Puja, reverence to the guru's feet, "the only bond of love that is eternal and indestructible,"[45] as Amma explained online for a recent celebration of the ceremony in her ashram, Amritapuri in Kerala, where disciples bathed her feet in flowers. Here in Singapore that reverence was done to the photograph at the foot of the altar. In the evening the hall was packed with over a hundred people. I noted two other Euro-devotees and one young Chinese-heritage gentleman. I recorded the singing, which in spite of the Tamil and Sanskrit, has the cadence and quality of Christian hymns, and the congregational character of the worship felt like a Christian service. After the *bhajans* and chanting, a man and a woman devotee offered a lovely purple lotus to each of the congregation, as we queued in two lines, male and female, and offered our lotus at the lotus-feet of Amma. In general, the whole atmosphere exuded kindness. After the lotus offerings, and more *bhajans* taking another half hour, I felt embarrassed to leave early but I just could not keep awake at 9:00 p.m.—remember that time is upside down from New York City to Singapore—day is night is day and the massive jetlag lasts.

During my full year of research in 2007–8, my relationship with the Amriteswari Society of Singapore continued, but with some complications. I often attended the Sunday morning Satsang with a regular program—almost a liturgy but with less formality. Although very early on a Sunday morning, usually fifty to seventy people gathered to watch a simulcast from the ashram in Kerala, often with a discourse presented by a swami, one of Amma's closest retinue such as Swami Ramakrishnananda who spoke in a flowing mixture of Tamil, Malayalam, and excellent English, reaching the greater majority of his audience as he considered the problem of death. A PowerPoint appeared on the screen listing Amma's activities for the week at the ashram as well as notices of events for the Society in Singapore. Finally, the congregation sang *bhajans* in Malayalam with English translations, including some Hindi and Tamil hymns. The Society has a group of talented singers and musicians who performed so professionally that I mistook them for a prerecorded soundtrack. I noted that only a few devotees joined in the singing; mostly they kept time with their hands or moved their bodies in rhythm with the music although the words were printed on the overhead projector. The combination of the early morning hours, the sermonlike discourse, and the communal *bhajans* with printed words continued, perhaps incongruously, to remind me of years of morning chapel services at my Presbyterian college in Pennsylvania with a key difference: the focus of this devotion was a round-faced, sari-clad woman guru with tender eyes, still very much in the flesh in Kerala.

Over that year, the period following the formal Sunday satsang and the communal meal in the upstairs meeting room provided an opportunity to speak with the society members, sometimes at length, and sometimes for brief but revealing moments. On the whole devotees tended to chat sparingly with each other—and entering a conversation was not always easy, but I was often kindly aided by the leadership. Many of their stories of Amma spoke of crisscrossed continents and layered identities. A computer engineer, whose family was from Kerala, met her for the first time in 1987 when she had fewer devotees. He was a young man then and went to her for darshan when she came to Singapore. As he was waiting in line he thought that she might need money—such gifts to gurus are a Hindu custom. She hugged him and then he gave her an envelope with money, which she refused even when he pressed her. Then, seeing how hurt he was, said, "OK, give it to one of my people." He felt really put off; in his words, he thought, "OK, this is it, *hasta la vista.*" Then, years later, he was in Palo Alto setting up a company branch there, and was very lonely. He went into an Indian restaurant hoping to meet people and saw an announcement that this guru would be coming. He recognized her and decided to go. When he got to the darshan line, she nodded at him as he waited and, when he came up, she asked about Singapore. Then, throughout her talk, she kept mentioning her Singapore "son" and he felt like the star for the night! But now, considering this, he does not think Amma remembered him in the usual sense but rather that "she knows us, it's like computer data that she sees in us." I kept asking if it was like reading our minds and he said no, more like she has the larger universal mind and thus has access to our more particular souls. He married and continued in Silicon Valley for another four years but soon both he and his wife missed their extended families and returned to Singapore to work for an American company here. He had just set up in his business but missed the camaraderie at his old company. He also stressed that Amma is "above religion," which he saw to be moving these days toward narrow confines. But Amma accepts people of all religious backgrounds and does not care if you are white or Japanese, or even about caste. He pointed out that she was from the low fisher caste. He also told me a story of a Chinese man who was waiting in line to receive a mantra from Amma. She whispered one word in his ear. Then he was so pleased because this was exactly the same mantra a Buddhist guru in Taiwan had given him earlier, allowing him continuity. He agreed that for Amma the best term would be spiritual or spirituality which he definitely saw as different from religion. Our conversation ended with his sense that all over the world cities are lonely. There used to be only a few real cities—New York, London—but now all over the world there are many very large cities and these have many migrants and are lonely places.

In another significant conversation during lunch at the Singapore Cricket Club, a dedicated member of the Amriteswari Society shared his story where religions mixed within his own family in Kerala. His mother was Roman Catholic and his father a Hindu. There were no objections to the marriage and the children were raised in both traditions with both parents attending all of the rituals and celebrations. At one point he attended catechism classes and was very active in the Catholic youth group but he asked the priest why so many people would be condemned to hell because they were not Catholic (paralleling my own confrontation with a nun). The priest became angry and threw him out of the class. He never returned. He married a Hindu woman and identifies as a Hindu. While his brother, who married a Roman Catholic woman, is a Catholic. At one point he told me how wonderful it was to have Amma here now on earth and that sometimes, when he looks at her, he sees for a moment the Black Virgin of Guadalupe. He agreed that there is a confluence between Roman Catholic rituals and Amma's satsang, and noticed that Italians seem to be very comfortable with Hindu forms. His experiences are not uncommon in Kerala with its religious diversity. Hindu-Christian confluences with shared ritual styles and practices are common, although not without tensions (Dempsey 2001).

However, in spite of the many confluences in experience and common transnational movement, I did not always feel at home here, although I made my position clear as a scholar and not a devotee. In my dealing with other similar organizations there was always that sense that I could potentially be "converted," here in Amanda Lucia's sense of "creating a new spiritual *habitus*" (2018, 46).[46] That was not the case for this society. While attending a discourse by a visiting Swami Purnamritananda from the ashram in Kerala, whom I had met and interviewed in 2005, like many others, I took photos. However, I had purchased a small tripod for my Nikon Coolpix digital camera to avoid using flash. The swami thought I was video recording his talk and told me to stop, which was his right, but I nonetheless felt singled out because others where not only photographing but video recording. Later, as Amma began to add meditation to the end of her satsangs, which also became the practice in Singapore, another swami came to offer a course meditation developed by Amma, Integrated Amrita Meditation Technique® (IAM). The registered trademark meant that we all had to sign a confidentiality agreement, interestingly under the laws of California, not to reveal the technique to anyone including family members. Such agreements were common as I later attended the programs for Isha and Art of Living. However, once again my camera and recorder got me into trouble when the swami felt I had exceeded his permission to take photos just prior to the meditation. I has also turned on my recorder when he told us what we could say to others (so I thought it was public information). Once again, I was called out from the podium. I had been careful not to take any identifiable photos but shot from behind while the official photographer took full-faced photos and put them on the website.

I apologized in both cases and continue to regret the incidents. While none of this could overshadow the kindness of the society, nonetheless I continued to feel my otherness in this worldwide guru organization. However, conversation with others in Singapore, including with some members of this society and the larger organization, confirmed that the Amriteswari Society functioned *in part* as a Malayali-centered group—one place where this small community could come together in an ethnic Tamil-dominated area. Interestingly, Amanda Lucia notes a parallel case in the Paloma satsang in California which "functioned largely as an ethnic church" for Malayalee émigrés. However, in that place the gradual presence of more nonIndian "adopters" seeking spiritual rather than culture affirmation caused internal tensions (Lucia 2014, 196–7). In the Singapore satsang, only a very few devotees of Chinese or European heritage could be spotted, certainly with some other Indian ethnicities. In Little India and Singapore in general, Tamil remains one of the four official languages, but not Hindi or any other South Indian language. Here Tamil reigns in schools as *the* Indian language, in announcements for stops on the MRT and buses, and in official documents. However, unlike so many global gurus, Amma speaks only in Malayali. Hence the *bhajans* are mostly in that language and discourses from the ashram by her swamis may include English but always favor Malayali. Here, in a sense, the divine speaks in the language of Kerala, not Sanskrit or Aramaic or Arabic.

After a decade of turning my attention to other organizations, when I returned I wanted to reconnect with Amriteswari Society. Almost immediately after I arrived in Singapore in 2018, I awoke early on Sunday morning and took the long walk through the mostly deserted covered walkway along Serangoon Road to attend satsang at the Amriteswari Society. I remained for the full service to enjoy the Prasadam upstairs. In spite of my best intentions I arrived at 9:00 a.m., and the priest was not there and others led the program. When I entered to sit in the back, I noticed more rows of chairs with fewer people up front on the floor. The congregation, like me, was getting older and I saw mostly middle-aged people with only a few younger devotees. The rows of chairs with an aisle down the center felt even more churchlike than previously. I counted about thirty-five attending. The video projector was in full use with Amma up on-screen giving a discourse which seemed to be quite recent. Speaking in Malayali with English subtitles, which I could not see very clearly, I did notice that she had clearly aged along with me. After the discourse, *bhajans* began. The words were even more directed to her as *divine*—I have a screenshot of the words, but my impression of her divinity, however, was later corrected. Once again, I noted the limited enthusiasm of the singing: people knew the songs and responded but without gusto, at least to my ear. The *bhajans* were in Tamil, Marathi, Sanskrit, and Malayali. With the *bhajans* over, we had only three minutes of meditation: I remember a full thirty minutes during the last satsangs that I attended here in 2008. The meditation that I had seen added then now seemed truncated. Finally, the satsang ended with *āratī*. Afterward, I spoke with the same man who seemed to run the events in 2008. I asked him once again if most of the devotees here were Malayali and he confirmed this. Again, during the *bhajans* I finally realized that both the male and female singers were live, not recorded; they both had fine voices and the harmonium and drums sounded very professional.

The most important moments of the morning were brief conversations with two articulate women both in their fifties, just after engaging a man in conversation to find he had lived in Singapore for over thirty years and had an engineering firm and was a permanent resident, but not a citizen, of Singapore. After he walked away, somehow not wanting to talk any more, the two women come up to greet me. I told them that I was finishing a book on spiritual movements in Singapore and they were very pleased. I wanted their view on the differences between temples and this kind of organization, as well as their views on Amma as divine. I asked if she was God, and got the most engaging response: "God, we are all gods, there are so many but only she knows who she is and we do not." Further, when I began to ask about this style of service, they agreed that it was like a church *but* "we are very different in that we accept everyone [meaning any form of god] but the churches only Jesus." However, when I said that I meant *in style*, they agreed to the similarities. I began to ask differences between these practices and the rites in a temple. "Oh, we still go to the temple, but the temple is only a step," and they continued to explain that what can happen for an Amma devotee is that after going to the temple and being "ritualistic," then "we begin to ask is there more, beyond needs, then comes spirituality and Amma." At one point, trying to explain the differences, my conversation partners described ritual of the temple as active, always in motion, as she moved her hands in circles. Both were clear this was not a rejection of the temples, but as I tried to ask about the deities in the temples and Amma they were more hesitant. Both stressed that Hinduism has multiple gods and was ever-evolving, unlike Christianity; but then, when I mentioned the Catholic church and its constant inclusion of new saints, they were a bit perplexed. In some sense what I had seen as Amma's "divinity" was something far more than the presence and power of God/s within the temples.

This special status of the guru in relationship to the gods became clearer when I attended another Satsang the following Sunday. I arrived very early at 7:45 a.m. to be able to meet the priest again. I found him completing the decorations at the altar. He did not recognize me at first but later said he felt that he had met me before. I stayed through the entire satsang but had to leave to attend the first events of the International Day of Yoga. With the priest at the altar, the satsang included more direct adoration of Amma with offerings of flowers at her feet with Sanskrit *slokas*. At the end of the chanting, he offered a short discourse on the meaning of the guru which ended with his understanding of the nature of a "Realized Master." His discourse focused on "why we chant" a Sanskrit *sloka* (verse) frequently called the Guru Mantra, widely recited in many guru-centered movements. His short but complex discourse dwelled on light and darkness, sleep and wakefulness, and on consciousness. At the end he defined the nature and role of the guru:

> That which takes off the darkness at the heart of the disciple and spreads light which is nothing but the self-knowledge. If we worship guru, we start worshipping an external form. Guru's role is actually pulling us from māyā and pushing us to that real Self which is within. Pushing from outside and pulling from inside to that reality which is nothing but Supreme Light.

In the online website from the ashram in Kerala, a devotee directly asks, "Amma, who is greater, God or the guru?" Her answer is equally candid:

> In principle, God and the Guru are the same. But we may say that the Guru is higher than God. The Guru's grace is something unique. If the Guru wants, he can remove the effect of God's displeasure. But even God cannot remove the sin that comes from dishonouring the Guru. When you realise God, you can say that you and God are the same. But even then, you cannot say that you are the same as the Guru . . . It is the path shown by the Guru that led the disciple to the goal. The Guru will always have that special status.[47]

Here the priest in Singapore and Amma herself claims something more than divinity for the guru, rather a key role in the process of self-transformation. So here in Singapore, the desire for spirituality, unlike in California, was not confined to converts. To put this another way, in the midst of a society that identifies and is identified as a Malayali-centered community, nonetheless that inner self beyond social identity (the priest also made this point as he spoke that morning) continues to be invoked. Once again that much-touted need for a sense of *place* in the formation of the self depends on the understanding of "self": here in the Amriteswari Society, such a definition moves for many in the organization between an ethnic identity as Malayali related to *place* "with its rich cultural dimensions" (Cresswell 2015, 3) and a transcendent inner self beyond place.

The Microplace of Little India

Doreen Massey, an urban geographer whose essays on locality and globalization reoriented urban geography, called for a more "progressive sense of place" in the early 1990s. In the midst of the concern about globalization gnawing at the particular and the local, she worried "how to hold on to that notion of spatial difference, of uniqueness, even of rootedness if people want that, without it being reactionary" ([1992] 2018, *kl* 3126). She remained concerned that boundaries not be drawn too tightly around *places*. Her alternate vision of "what gives a place its specificity is not some long internalized history but the fact that it is constructed out of a particular constellation of relations, articulated together at a particular locus" and that its character "can only be constructed by linking that place to places beyond" (*kl* 3204). Here in Little India the official articulation within this particular locus involves the Tourist Board, the National Heritage Board, and the Urban Redevelopment Authority, and now the Indian Heritage Centre with its own narratives labeling the many artifacts in its collections. With their own articulation of *place*, not in narratives but in the style of their satsangs and the imaging of their gurus, spiritual movements can be viewed as stars on a map of the constellation forming Little India. Considering the last decade, the Shirdi Sai Baba Centre, the Sri Guru Ragavendra Society, and the Amriteswari Society have all moved toward what I have called *templing*—the process of embedding the organization into the landscape with a more permanent image of the guru, a more formal ritual program lead by a priest with training and a lineage, and a structure either owned or rented long-term by the leadership. Although not on the tourist list of temples in Singapore, nonetheless they are known locally and within the global movements with which they remain associated.

However, these movements, albeit with small numbers, add dimensions and complications to the sense of *locale* here—emplacements that are never fully placed in multiple ways. Each remains associated with an identifiable ethnic group—usually as much linguistic as racial—Sai with North Indian Hindi-speaking, Ragavendra Society remains Tamil in language and style, while Amriteswari Society a Malayali-dominated community. If the ethos/tone/presence of a place exerts influence, then I would say that *something* about Little India moves its denizens towards *templing* because sentiment and affective unity are not enough: some embodiment, some embeddedness, some sense of ownership to this locality abides here. However, with this *placement* and this *clinging* to ethnoreligious culture, *another* sense of place continues. In all cases the ashram or the samadhi holding the presence of the Realized Master moves the gaze back to India. However, the story of space and place does not end here. Crucially, in all cases, the nature of the *self*, the experiencer, opens to a space beyond place, the push and pull of the guru without and within toward other dimensions. Here, when Massey called for linking place "to places beyond," she never envisioned how far, or where, such beyonds may lead.

Notes

Preface

1 "Up To 34 Feared Killed In Indian Ship Fire." Associated Press, February 15, 1985. https://www.apnews.com/b6fb67b388edf60976ceb486bbac09de.

2 The National Library Board: SingaporeInfropedia has a complete article on the tragedy, "Hotel New World Collapse." https://eresources.nlb.gov.sg/infopedia/articles/SIP_783__2009-01-02.html.

3 An earlier article noted, "NEWSWEEK/Beliefnet Poll found that more Americans, especially those younger than 60, described themselves as 'spiritual' (79 percent) than 'religious' (64 percent). Almost two thirds of Americans say they pray every day, and nearly a third meditate." (Adler 2005).

4 The Tamil naming system does not fit well into our typical bibliographic form. Men and women are known by their own name often with the initial of their native town and their father's name in the case of men or unmarried women. After marriage a woman takes her husband's name often as her surname. Usually the father's/husband's name acts as a surname. So, in Chennai, I would be Mrs. Dick or Prof. Joanne. In the bibliographies that follow I respect how each most often choses to be named, so Nagah Devi daughter of Ramasamy is listed as Ramasamy, Naga Devi.

5 Completed her MA in Sociology in 2008 under the direction of Dr. Lai Ah Eng, "Ethnographic Accounts of the 'Sathya Sai Baba' Movement—A Spiritual Reform-Oriented Movement in Singapore: Identity Formation, Charity-giving & Rationalization Process."

6 For most of my dictionary definitions, I use my old and very reliable copy of *Tamil Lexicon*, University of Madras, 1936, and sometimes online sources which I will indicate.

7 https://www.hinducentre.org.sg/aboutus.php.

8 https://www.cnn.com/style/article/singapore-sustainable-tower-building-scli-intl/index.html.

1 Macrospaces and Microplaces

1 The government of Singapore at first depended on constructing a determined homogenized placelessness necessitated, so the PAP argued, by the racial and ethnic unrest that marked the nation's caesarian birth out of Malaysia. The city-state is a majority Chinese heritage city, precariously at the tip of Malaysia and just above Indonesia with old strong minorities of both Malay and Indian, mostly Tamil, denizens. A strong identity with *place*, in this context, meant associations with other homelands potentially, and once actually meant ethnic riots and a disassociation with the space of the newly independent Singapore—news photos of riots just before and just after Independence 1965 are harrowing. Creating new associations with this very

artificial homeland meant erasure of old ties with old homelands—the concern was real or, at least, felt to be real.

2   Is it really ground zero—really a *tabula rasa*? Others suggest that a "process of spectral return haunts" Singapore (Bishop, Phillips, and Yeo 2004, 9). The reconstruction of what was lost is ongoing.

3   March 7–18, 2016 at the National University of Singapore.

4   From the online website of An Atlas of Mirrors, https://www.singaporebiennale.org/sb2016/about-singapore-biennale-2016.php.

5   All photos from this exhibit are used with the kind permission of the curator Dr. Louis Ho.

6   *Jurong West Street 81, 2008*: "On a Sunday afternoon at 4:10 pm, 2008, artist Shannon Lee Castleman set up 16 video cameras in apartment blocks facing one another, on Jurong West Street 81. She asked residents in these buildings to simultaneously film and be filmed by their neighbours in the apartment directly facing theirs, while going about their daily domestic lives—with the resultant clips being completely spontaneous and unscripted in nature" (Siuli and Ho 2018, 66).

7   https://en.wiktionary.org/wiki/kampong_spirit.

8   http://www.dwellings.sg/community/little-pockets-heaven, September 9, 2015.

9   "Culling of 24 chickens in Sin Ming ruffles feathers." *Today online*, February 26, 2017, http://www.todayonline.com/singapore/sin-ming-chicken-culling-ruffles-feathers.

10 "Oral Answer by Ministry of National Development on culling of animals." Online PDF, "pq-oral-answer-by-ministry-of-national-development-on-culling-of-animals," February 20, 2017.

11 Here, because Isha's programs in Singapore charge a fee, they are therefore a business, Isha Pvt. Ltd., and now the organization as Isha Foundation has recently registered as a nonprofit but not yet a charity organization. Thus Isha, unlike many of the groups, is not a "society" under ROSES (Registry of Societies).

12 https://app.ros.gov.sg/ui/Index/index.aspx.

13 Isha Foundation Blog, February 2011 quoted in the story on the couple, https://www.ishayoga.sg/blog/-/blogs/sadhguru-sannidhi-initiation.

14 When I asked Thulasi to review a draft of this chapter, he gave permission to use his name and had no issues except that these practices with the Sannidhi are not accurately described as *worship* which is not the same path as devotion. He explained that in general the processes are "largely scientific so you do not need to worship anything, you just follow the process that been given to you . . . there is a certain method to it, you follow it with absolute technical precision it works, you don't need to look up to something . . . you just need to follow it as a process."

15 Sanskritdictionary.com/, *padaka*: "n. step; office, position; -krama, m. kind of gait; peculiar method of reciting and writing the Veda.

16 May 20, 2012.

17 For example, a compilation of critiques appearing online as "Severe Problems with 'Bhagavan Kalki's' Deeksha Oneness Movement. Compiled by Timothy Conway, Ph.D., April 2008." http://www.enlightened-spirituality.org/deeksha_oneness.html.

18 Very recently a long-time devotee told me that Bhagavan now enjoined that there should be no adoration or even display of his image—but more on that in a later chapter.

19 http://onenessuniversity.org/phenomenon-of-the-golden-orb/.

20 Kundalini (Sanskrit *kuṇḍalinī*) appears frequently in yoga and meditation movement, often imaged as a coiled snake rising from the base of the spine. "*kuṇḍalinī* ('the coiled

one'). An individual's power or śakti, visualized as a dormant serpent coiled at the base of the spine," W. J. Johnson, *Dictionary of Hinduism*. Oxford University Press, 2014, available online at http://www.oxfordreference.com.

21 http://www.onenessmovementflorida.org/ChakraDhyana.htm. These instructions are on a website from Florida but mirror our movement in Singapore.

22 Deviji reports the Global awakening mission fulfilled, and people awakened 1,830,000 as of February 21, 2014.

23 https://onenessuniversity.org/journey-into-oneness/.

24 Issues are also about money such as "Many long-time seekers are appalled by this charging of big money for 'spiritual services.' And many others are apparently content to throw this money at him, as his empire expands exponentially." Guru Ratings, Anti-links for Sri Kalki Bhagavan—www3.telus.net. Also, critics bemoan the emphasis on the "message towards prosperity and success," from "A Critique of the Indian Oneness Movement and its use of Western Success Coaching," http://mortentolboll.weebly.com/.

2 Statecraft and Cosmology: Making the Macrocosm in Singapore

1 YouTube video available as: "NDP themed MRT trains launches today (July 11)."

2 This is actually in the title of his seminal book, *Third Space: Journeys to Los Angeles and Other Real-and-Imagined Places*. I will return to Soja in detail in Chapter 5.

3 A recent publication honoring the HDB flats may well confirm this prophecy—the beautiful photographs of interiors of these flats show a deep creativity and, as the authors comment, "each and every HDB flat is a life in itself; it is a unique, artistic and sacred one" (Miyauchi 2017, 20).

4 Comment on the official coverage from the Prime Minister's Office of "Lee Kuan Yew State Funeral Procession 29 March 2015 (Part 1)" posted on YouTube https://www.youtube.com/watch?v=tiYDoNxa5Yk. See also Lee Kuan Yew State Funeral Eulogy 29 March 2015 (Part 2). https://www.youtube.com/watch?v=5rvcOIGHR4s.

5 I am not the first to use this term—a blog on the love of the story fiction by Cage Dunn also refers to mythophile. https://cagedunn.wordpress.com/tag/mythophile/.

6 *The Sacred Canopy* was also an argument about the secularization of modern society, but just a few year later Berger published *A Rumor of Angels: Modern Society and the Rediscovery of the Supernatural* in 1969. However, even today, it's *The Sacred Canopy* that remains associated with Peter Berger.

7 Such a reading takes no account of the whole sense of dialectics, and doubtless would be refuted by a careful reader of Marx. Eliade's deep anti-Communism fomented by his exile from Romania is at play here.

8 This introduction is by Hong Lysa, an independent scholar formerly in the Department of History, National University of Singapore.

9 Written and directed by Singapore filmmaker Tan Pin Pin, and available online as a DVD or as a download.

10 This now quaint delightful debate is available on YouTube from the Richard Nixon Foundation. https://www.youtube.com/watch?v=XRgOz2x9c08. I accessed it May 17, 2017, coincidentally on the anniversary of the debate in 1959.

11 See https://www.clc.gov.sg/research-publications/publications/urban-systems-studies. Currently there are nineteen Urban Systems Studies books in print and five booklets.

At the time I initially wrote this chapter, there were only nine! The books are available on the site for download as PDFs and the booklets can be purchased at www.amazon.com (digital and print).

12 Singapore was born in a massive crisis situation. Supposedly the divorce from Malaysia came shockingly and suddenly. Indeed, reading the *Straits Times* dated August 9, 1965, nothing appeared amiss concerning the union, with the headlines during parliamentary news from the capital city, Kuala Lumpur, even reporting on Lee Kuan Yew's possible exit as prime minister of Singapore. Then suddenly August 10 reported the startling news announced late on August 9: "Singapore is Out" following a "secret signing" (1) and "A dream shattered . . . now a parting of the ways" (10). In addition, this was the era of the US involvement in the war in Vietnam and the unshaken sense that communists were about to take over much of Southeast Asia—beginning at the time that the British declared the Emergency in their then colony of Malaysia from 1948 to 1960. Even more disturbing were the ethnic-religious riots in Singapore in 1964.

13 Smart's textbook, *Worldviews: Cross-cultural Explorations of Human Beliefs* (3rd ed. Pearson), is still in use and in print defines phenomenology as an empathetic approach within the study of religion.

14 In his insightful article, Robinson lists "1) Inoculation—admitting a little bit of evil in an institution so as to ward off awareness of its fundamental problems . . . 2) Removing history—making it seem like social phenomena simply 'exist' or are there for the viewer's gaze, eliminating both causality and agency . . . 3) Identification of the other with the self—projecting inner characteristics onto the other . . . 4) Tautology— treating the failure of language as expressing the essence of a thing . . . 5) Neither-norism—refusing radical differences between phenomena by combining them in a kind of middle ground . . . 6) Quantification of quality—treating differences in kind as differences in degree. 7) Statements of fact without explanation . . ." (2011).

15 At this point Cassirer had died and Susanne K. Langer translated the work and became the major voice for symbolism as the "new key" for philosophy. See Langer 1946.

16 https://withanopenheart.org/2013/01/04/the-story-of-the-lotus/.

3 Macrospaces—Guru Style

1 I received my ticket via email on January 10, 2017. I ordered this online and received updates with useful information up to the day of this very well-organized event.

2 https://www.facebook.com/events/154405298265665.

3 The term is usually used for formal religious festivals at Hindu temples, giving this a religious aura in an Indian context without naming this as such in the anglophone world.

4 See https://www.youtube.com/watch?v=IrGqd_fcI4k.

5 I have shared this chapter with Vijaya and use her name with permission.

6 http://singaporeexpo.com.sg.

7 https://youtu.be/I9oOes4N8mU "Sri Sri rubbishes Adiyogi Shiva and Sadhguru explains." *Sadhguru And* (video series within Isha). Published on February 26, 2018.

8 https://youtu.be/DcGcoiqGLBk.

9 "Chief Minister Edappadi K. Palaniswami, Puducherry Lt. Governor Kiran Bedi, and Union Ministers Vijay Goel, Bandaru Dattatreya and Pon. Radhakrishnan were among the VIPs present." *The Hindu,* February 25, 2017.

10 In a personal conversation with Jeremy Carrette during an American Academy of Religions meeting, he spoke adamantly about this misunderstanding—they were not condemning all spiritual movements but rather the overly tight connections with the commercial sphere of some. A careful reading of the last section of the books does make this clear. Nonetheless the book continues to be viewed as the major negative statement about contemporary spiritual movements.

11 For example, I recently received a notice from The Spiritual Life Council here at Syracuse, about interfaith dialogue. This group of chaplains from the various religious communities on campus preferred to discuss "different spiritualties," rather than Religions.

12 In India, Jaggi Vasudev remains close to the current prime minister Narendra Modi. For Independence Day 2015, he sent a blog message to his followers in India, "Every citizen should participate in shaping the future of this nation. May you know what it means to create something beautiful." *Wake up to Wisdom: Mystic Quote* (blog), August 15, 2017. https://pages.ishausa.org/index.php/email/emailWebview.

13 https://www.ascendas-singbridge.com/en/our-properties/singapore/light-industrial/techplace-ii/.

14 The invitation was for a Devi Darshan at the Sri Ruthra Kaliamman Temple in October 2017 and explained, "Linga Bhairavi is an exuberant expression of the Divine Feminine created by Sadhguru, representing the creative and nurturing aspects of the universe." Personal email from Isha Singapore dated September 19, 2017.

15 Given Singapore's location just below Malaysia and above Indonesia, concern about security in the context of religion is not surprising.

16 Sinha 2011 provides an extensive discussion of the history and workings of the Hindu Endowments.

17 In a talk at the Asia Research Institute, "Religious Education in Singapore: Exploring the Options," Charlene Tan, then an assistant professor in Policy and Leadership Studies, National Institute of Education, Nanyang Technological University discussed "the attempts by the Singapore Government to teach religious beliefs and practices in Singapore schools through Religious Knowledge (RK), Civics and Moral Education (CME), and National Education (NE)," published abstract, August 29, 2007.

18 During a recent month in Singapore in January–February of 2017, several people noted the growth of both organizations, not just in Singapore but worldwide, and especially in India where Prime Minister Modi affords Jaggi Vasudev and Sri Sri Ravi Shankar increasing influence. See the discussion of Sri Sri's massive World Cultural Festival on the banks of the Yamuna: "Sri Sri event: When rockstar gurus bring political rivals together." *Hindustan Times*, March 11, 2016. https://www.hindustantimes.com/india/sri-sri-event-when-rockstar-gurus-bring-political-rivals-together/story-hWOo6ISmLhxHpU3KNrG1LK.html.

19 "Together we achieve: Clap, clap, clap to wipe out mozzies." *Straits Times*, August 10, 2017. http://www.straitstimes.com/singapore/clap-clap-clap-to-wipe-out-mozzies.

20 Usually this term is written Satsang, but because the Isha ashram is in a Tamil-speaking area, the "t" is transliterated "th" to distinguish this from a hard "t."

21 I also refer to this event briefly in Waghorne 2014b, 293 in a different context.

22 Numerous videos are still available online and on YouTube through a Google search under "25th Anniversary of Art of Living."

23 http://www.artofliving.org.sg/index.php?option=com_content&task=view&id=185&Itemid=110.

24 http://picturesofjesus4you.com/gallery1portraits.html. For a fine discussion of the power of the Sallman images, see Morgan 1998, 124–51.

25 There is no one single defining image of the Buddha but the robes of monks in Sri Lanka are draped similarly yet in ochre or red and, to my knowledge, never white.

26 The Art of Living Website mentions Sri Sri Ravi Shankar at age 17 completing his "traditional studies in Vedic literature and a degree in modern science." http://www.srisri.org/biography/timeline. Gautier's description of Sri Sri's childhood in Tamilnadu makes it clear that he was from a Brahmin family where Sanskrit would have been used, but Jaggi Vasudev was decidedly non-Brahmin which, in South India, especially in the 1960s, was significant. Jaggi Vasudev gives a fuller account of his unorthodox studies at university but nonetheless mentions his immersion in European classics (Simone and Vasudev, 140–51). On Sri Sri Ravi Shankar's early traditional training, also see Gautier 2008, 17–34.

27 From a poster distributed throughout Tamilnadu. The event was reported via email to Isha members as "English Sathsang 24 June, 2008." http://www.ishafoundation.org/component/option,com_newscomponent/Itemid,242/act,view/id,1781/lang,en.

28 From a blog sent thought the Art of Living to archive individual experiences of the event on February 17–19, 2006. http://feb19.blogspot.com/, June 3, 2006.

29 The map appears at http://www.artofliving.org/worldwide.html.

30 The International Center of Art of Living is not a temple but the grand architecture gestures toward a closely related style resembling a Buddhist pagoda—I have not seen this in person. https://www.happinessretreat.org.

31 For another perspective and analysis of these satsangs, see my chapter "Alone Together" in *Place/No-Place in Urban Asian Religiosity* (Waghorne 2016, 71–90).

32 In some cases, during more formal interviews, participants did give me permission to use their names but I prefer for this description to preserved their anonymity. Again, to protect identity, I have not dated these events.

33 For another version of this garden visualization and discussion of this community, see my chapter "Alone Together" in *Place/No-Place in Urban Asian Religiosity* (Waghorne 2016, 71–90).

34 Because these quotes were taken from recorded conversations during formal interviews, I have edited the quotes only slightly from standard Indian or Singaporean English to usages more common in British or American English. In these cases, I am quoting by permission but not naming my interlocutors, since these were told to me as opinions or personal experiences. No one spoke as an official of any organization. In some cases, I am quoting anonymously from unnamed persons who spoke during events.

35 This process of testimonials also appears in similar organizations. The Art of Living has a "share your Sudarshan Kriya experience" video inset on the main website at one point with a woman lawyer from Canada attesting to regained health and wellbeing after taking the program.

36 While many different stories exist about the origin and even the reasons for this celebration, most emphasize Shiva's role as the ultimate guru—teacher even—to the deities, his revelation in the aniconic form of the linga alight with flames, and his cosmic dance of creation and destruction.

37 I shared a draft of this chapter with Tina via email; her comments interestingly were concerns for poor copy-editing—she works on Isha's publications—but also she expressed some consternation that I had compared Sadhguru with Guruji. She felt that such a comparison was like apples and oranges—just too different to put into the same comparative basket. I honor her concern—for someone who has taken Jaggi Vasudev

as the guru. The same is true of devoted followers of Sri Sri: there can be no comparison with a beloved unique spiritual teacher. This has always been an issue within religious studies scholarship: how to honor the sensibilities of insiders while writing with academic conventions of typologies and categories and generalizations?

38 With a faculty of "full-time volunteers dedicating themselves to nurture the blossoming of every child" as the website declares. http://ishahomeschool.org/faculty/.

39 "Isha Institute of Inner Sciences celebrates grand opening in the US," June 21, 2006. http://www.ishafoundation.org/component/option,com_newscomponent/Itemid,242/act,view/id,582/.

40 This is a South Indian transliteration using the way Tamil speakers would pronounce this, adding a "th" where the formal Sanskrit is a "t," and a "b" where the formal Sanskrit is a "bh."

41 Sadhguru terms them "A small, core group of people … initiated in a particular way which turns their energies in a completely different direction" than everyday life. http://isha.sadhguru.org/blog/yoga-meditation/demystifying-yoga/what-is-the-significance-of-brahmacharya/.

42 These are non-Brahmans who chant devotional hymns to Shiva (Peterson 1989, 55–75).

43 The Isha Ashram very kindly allowed us to photograph this event on the condition that we submitted the digital camera card to the director of publicity right after the event. She checked all photos and returned our card. The photos used here were approved.

44 A leading industrialist in the Coimbatore, who is also an old friend, had another side of Jaggi Vasudev to report. Most of his associates do not go to the ashram precisely because they remember Jaggi as a yoga instructor dressed in jeans and going from house to house offering classes. "He was a hippy," then suddenly he rose into a guru. My friend related the mystery of Jaggi's wife's death in 1997. When she died suddenly, her father filed a case of murder against Jaggi, who was acquitted—but the issue remains and occasionally shows up online. The story our friend told us does not completely mesh with stories Sadhguru has gradually revealed about his life. But many in Coimbatore, including some of his earlier disciples, remember him in the stage just before his mercuric rise as a major guru.

45 http://isha.sadhguru.org/us-en/rally-for-rivers-us-concerts/.

46 Owned by *India Today* as their online opinion, see "India Today Group launches Medium clone, DailyO." https://www.medianama.com/2014/09/223-india-today-dailyo/.

47 A Muslim by birth, he relates his story on the Art of Living BlogSpot, September 7, 2010.http://artoflivinglifestories.blogspot.com/2010/09/m-rajaque-rahman-arunachal-pradesh.html. He declares, "The truth that the true art of living transcends man-made barriers of caste, creed, nationality, and religion."

48 An environmental committee reported that the "entire floodplain area used for the main event has been completely destroyed, not simply damaged" and Sri Sri was fined but he refused to pay. "Sri Sri Ravi Shankar's World Culture Festival Destroyed Yamuna Floodplain: NGT Panel." The Wire, April 12, 2017. https://www.google.com/url?sa=t&rct=j&q=&esrc=s&source=web&cd=6&cad=rja&uact=8&ved=0ahUKEwjc7dHe35nbAhWFwFkKHWwHCyQQFghSMAU&url=https%3A%2F%2Fthewire.in%2Fenvironment%2Fsri-sri-ravi-shankars-world-culture-festival-destroyed-yamuna-floodplain-ngt-panel&usg=AOvVaw23MU2-JDKsITe4iWCkIQQt.

49 See "PM Narendra Modi's Spiritual Guru Dayanand Saraswati Gets Padma Bhushan."
    https://www.ndtv.com/india-news/pm-narendra-modis-spiritual-guru-dayanand-
    saraswati-gets-padma-bhushan-1270014.

50 "Unfortunate to link spirituality with religion." *The Times of India*, March 7, 2017.
    https://timesofindia.indiatimes.com/india/unfortunate-to-link-spirituality-with-
    religion-pm-modi/articleshow/57519923.cms.

51 Sri Sri Ravi Shankar's attempts are widely reported in the India media, sometimes with
    a sense of his naïveté or sometimes with appreciation: "How Sri Sri Ravi Shankar's
    image was sullied as a negotiator in the Ram Temple dispute." *DailyO*, February 18,
    2018; and sometimes deeply critical: "Sri Sri Ups the Communal Ante By Wading into
    Ayodhya's Murky Waters." March 7, 2018, *The Wire*, https://thewire.in/communalism/
    sri-sri-ayodhya-controversy.

52 "Sadhguru on Yogis | Favouring Shri Ravi Shankar's Act on Ayodhya Dispute."
    Interview Kalvakuntla Kavitha FICCI Hyderabad published on *Sadhguru And* (blog).
    Sadhguru says "you are a citizen of this nation, you have rights and responsibilities of
    being in this country." Published November 30, 2017, https://www.youtube.com/
    watc:?v=bXcvWIeSaMk.:

53 http://sanskritdictionary.com/?iencoding=iast&q=bhūmi&lang=sans&action=Search.

54 "Modi hails yoga day as a 'new era of peace': PM takes to the mat in New Delhi to
    celebrate ancient practice." *Straits Times*, June 22, 2015.

55 "Modi attacks Congress, says why does Kapil Sibal want to prolong Ayodhya case."
    ZeeNews, December 5, 2017. http://zeenews.india.com/gujarat/pm-narendra-modi-
    attacks-congress-says-why-does-kapil-sibal-want-to-prolong-ayodhya-case-2064240.html.

4 Yoga on the Move

1   The website provides a brief history, which predates the control of the BJP: "The
    Ministry of AYUSH was formed on 9th November 2014 to ensure the optimal
    development and propagation of AYUSH systems of heath care. Earlier it was known
    as the Department of Indian Systems of Medicine and Hemopathy (ISM&HO), which
    was created in March 1995. http://ayush.gov.in/about-us/about-the-ministry. Here the
    prime minister moved a department up to a ministry and hence a cabinet level
    organization. Important to recall that Mahatma Gandhi, longtime head of the Indian
    National Congress which became the Congress Party, strongly supported indigenous
    medicine.

2   Facebook India in Singapore (High Commission of India, Singapore) entry dated July
    14, 2018. The final version of the website listed almost 100 separate events at various
    times and all over the island giving Singaporeans a wide choice. See https://idayyoga.
    com/list-of-venues.

3   Carl Ernst argues for "an ambiguous relationship between Sufism and yoga," in which
    the issue of influence is complex today "because we are faced with an especially
    challenging problem arising from the gap between scholarly analyses of the history of
    religions and the way in which these traditions are appropriated in the global
    marketplace of contemporary thought, especially under the rubric of New Age
    spirituality" (2016, *kl* 5903–5).

4   Conspicuously absent were the many globally active guru-centered organizations that
    do use the term *yoga* but stress meditation over postural forms. For example,
    Shivarudra Balayogi, whom I met both in Singapore—and later in Monroe NY—

during a daylong retreat in Singapore taught us some postural practices but emphasized such exercises were preliminary to mediation practices which are central to the final goal of liberation. The Amritanandamayi organization also offered a session on "IAMs meditation," at the *Amriteswari Society* building on Hindoo Road, which I attended. This focused on meditation but not postural yoga.

5   A website connected to this saint-centered temple with the disclaimer, "This is not the official website of the temple and we do not carry any updated information on the temple happenings," nonetheless asserts, "Sai Baba is one of the greatest Sufi saints of our time and the debate on whether he was a Muslim or a Hindu, is unresolved till date—in his time, the devotees were both Hindus and Muslims." http://www.saisansthan.com.

6   https://www.puti.org/en/introduction-about-bodhi-meditation/.

7   Isha has programs in China and offers Inner Engineering in Mandarin.

8   https://yoga.ayush.gov.in.

9   *New York Times*, June 21, 2015. "International Yoga Day Finally Arrives in India, Amid Cheers and Skepticism" by Nida Najar. http://nyti.ms/1MYdNxx.

10 LinkedIn lists the director as Sadasivam Chinnathambi with a cameo photo standing with Prime Minister Modi. https://www.linkedin.com/in/sadasivam-chinnathambi-4a134515/#experience-section.

11 I have not mentioned all of the organizations here and I did not recognize several of those listed. Also, there were others missing with ties to India and Hindu-based spiritual practices perhaps not considered sufficiently close to yoga or unresponsive or uncorralled to be on this list. I did not interview anyone from the High Commission because of time. During my longer 2015 visit, I learned of the role of the High Commission in the process—late in my research.

12 May 11, 2015 the then new ambassador Arun Kumar Singh (served 2015–16) was present—the event was uploaded by the Embassy of India to YouTube. https://www.youtube.com/watch?v=Mz-ngUYCy3Y.

13 He went on to explain how careful they normally are to avoid distractions: "even if we are playing a video, we made sure that nothing on the walls are distraction, nothing should go behind that screen" to distract from Sadhguru's message.

14 https://vyasa.org/about-us/president. This very sophisticated website from the large campus in Bangalore includes discussion of charities, health centers, and yoga research facilities. The founder remains as president. A Ph.D. in Mechanical Engineering, he describes his personal journey "From NASA to VYASA" as his own decision to return to India to devote his research skills to yoga after years of working in prestigious institutions in the US and UK.

15 https://www.innerengineering.com/ieo-new/sadhguru/.

16 http://www.gardensbythebay.com.sg/en/attractions/bay-east-garden.html.

17 http://www.gardensbythebay.com.sg/en/book-a-venue/bay-east-bridge.html.

18 http://www.azpayalebar.com/#one.

19 My special thanks to Ricky Anupom Saikia for his permission to use his name, and for his quick response to all of my questions.

20 https://www.littleindia.com.sg/lisha-1.

21 https://www.indianheritage.org.sg/en/about-us/the-building.

22 The speech is available on YouTube in both Hindi and English at https://www.narendramodi.in/message-from-pm-modi-on-the-4th-international-day-of-yoga.

23 The organization has a Facebook page: https://www.facebook.com/friendsofnarpanipearavai/.

24 https://www.myactivesg.com/read/2016/6/activesg-holds-mass-yoga-workout-in-celebration-of-international-day-of-yoga.

25 http://www.visitsingapore.com/festivals-events-singapore/cultural-festivals/thaipusam/.

26 In Singapore this is officially the Krishna Mandir, the festival with a life-sized image of Swami Prabhupada, which connects this to ISKCON. I participated twice at Toa Payoh Stadium in July 13, 2008 and again on July 6, 2014.

27 The Singaporean group of the larger worldwide Mata Amritanandamayi organization https://www.amma.org.sg.

28 Email from Isha Singapore singapore@ishayoga.org sent July 19, 2018.

29 http://yogadork.com/2015/09/04/10000-yogis-wear-white-for-heavily-sponsored-yoga-event-in-central-park-photos/. The account appeared on Yoga Dork, under "public displays of yoga" with more accounts offering stories of yoga in airports, etc. http://yogadork.com/category/public-display-of-yoga/.

30 Her cases include the Ramakrishna Mission, Saibaba Sansthan, Brahmakumaris, Chinmaya Mission, Vivekananda Kendra, Amritanandamayi Mission, and Art of Living.

31 As the legacy of Swami Vivekananda, the mission has long offered yoga with the emphasis, in keeping with the swami's teachings, on meditation; I attended sessions in Chennai and have long participated in RK activities while there.

32 https://www.narendramodi.in/message-from-pm-modi-on-the-4th-international-day-of-yoga.

33 Interestingly, they did meet in England and Max Müller produced one of his rare forays into contemporary practice mentioning yoga. Writing on Vivekananda's master, *Râmakrisha: His Life and Sayings*, Max Müller classified the Bengali saint not as one of those "who hardly deserve to called Sa*m*yânsins, for they are not much more than jugglers or Ha*th*yogins," but as a true Sa*m*yânsin who "devote their thoughts and meditations to philosophical and religious problems" (1899, vi).

34 From Max Müller's *The Six Systems of Indian Philosophy*, 1899.

35 Miller 1996, 36.

36 She qualifies this: "Yogic 'conversions' are not emblematic of the typical sociology of religion conception of an individual's adoption of an exclusive affiliation with a new religious institution, but rather they are a process of self-transformation wherein the individual adopts a gradual process of change to newly found spiritual attitudes and ritualized behaviors that buttress their newly formed yogic selves" (2018, 46).

37 "'God is just a Stepping Stone' |Sadhguru" New Delhi April 2012. Meditator Sathsang published on February 27, 2015 on YouTube. https://www.youtube.com/watch?v=kF3vIkvhBWM.

38 A new book on Paramahansa Yogananda argues that this is not just for anglophone ears but deeper (Neumann 2019).

39 These are clearly references to the sites of the once-called Cradles of Civilization—the key is North Africa=Egypt, South America=Mayan. Note that southern Africa is not mentioned.

40 As in the much-debated Indo-European thesis. For an update on the heated Hindu nationalist response, see Bryant and Patton, 2004.

41 Interestingly, an article "Effects of Shambhavi Mahamudra Kriya, a Multicomponent Breath-Based Yogic Practice (Pranayama), on Perceived Stress and General Well-Being" calls the *kriya* "a protocol within the Isha Yoga lineage" (Peterson et al. 2017).

42 Here Sri Sri is *not* quoting from Patanjali but likely from another later Sanskrit source with roots in South India, referring to another form of Śiva as a teacher (more popular in Tamilnadu than Ādiguru)—Dakshinamurti (Dakṣiṇāmūrti). I found a reference, "Ishwara, Guru and Atman—All One. The Vedantic concept of the oneness of Ishwara, Guru and the Atman (jiva) is brought out by Sureshwaracharya in the Manasollasa. Ishwaro Gururatmeti Murti bheda Vibhagine, Vyomavad vyapta dehaya Dakshinamurataye namah. (There is no difference between the Guru, Self and God. Obeisance to Lord Dakshinamurthy who is the personification of the Supreme Self that permeates through Space)." https://www.advaita-vedanta.org/archives/advaita-l/2017-July/045855.html. Also https://www.advaita-vedanta.org/archives/advaita-l/2017-July/045854.html.

43 Questions & Answers, "What is the difference between God and an enlightened master?" December 8, 2011. https://www.artofliving.org/observation-brings-wisdom-and-you-need-sensitivity-observe.

44 "Sri Sri's Message On Guru Purnima 2012." July 3, 2012, North Carolina, United States. https://www.artofliving.org/sri-sris-message-guru-purnima. In this he quotes the full verses to "Ishwaro Gururatmeti Murti bheda Vibhagine" adding the praise to Dakshinamurti as well as the second stanza, *Vyomavad vyapta dehaya,* which he is translating here.

45 Here a very basic encyclopedic description seems to point to striking parallels: "In the wake of his critique of Cartesianism, Heidegger turns his attention to spatiality. He argues that Dasein dwells in the world in a spatial manner, but that the spatiality in question—Dasein's existential spatiality—cannot be a matter of Dasein being located at a particular co-ordinate in physical, Cartesian space. That would be to conceive of Dasein as present-at-hand, and presence-at-hand is a mode of Being that can belong only to entities other than Dasein. According to Heidegger, the existential spatiality of Dasein is characterized most fundamentally by what he calls de-severance, a bringing close. 'De-severing' amounts to making the farness vanish—that is, making the remoteness of something disappear, bringing it close" (Being and Time: 23: 139). Michael Wheeler, "Martin Heidegger." The Stanford Encyclopedia of Philosophy, Fall 2017 edition, Edward N. Zalta (ed.). https://plato.stanford.edu/archives/fall2017/entries/heidegger/.

46 Note again the recent conversation at the discussion group Advaita-L: https://lists.advaita-vedanta.org//lists/. See above, n. 40.

5 Reading Walden Pond at Marina Bay Sands, Singapore

1 This chapter is an updated version of my article, "Reading Walden Pond at Marina Bay Sands in Singapore," *Journal of the American Academy of Religion*, March 2014, Vol. 82, No. 1, pp. 217–47. I have also added new images. Used with permission.

2 All photos except Figure 5 are by the author and my photographer husband, Dick Waghorne. I use "In the Soup" with the permission of the Marketing Department of the ArtScience Museum with my thanks.

3 Affect theory emerged in recent years mostly within cultural studies (see Gregg and Seigworth 2010) but now has spread to other disciplines and has become a major theory. My colleague Gail Hamner helped to establish a unit within the AAR, "Religion, Affect, and Emotion," and continues to lead an active reading group.

4 On May 22, 2012, my thanks to Nick Dixon for the interview as well as for permission to quote him, and to Christine Kho, Senior Administrator, for all her help.

5 King Abdulaziz Center for World Culture is in the process of construction to mark the seventy-fifth anniversary of Samco, the state-owned petroleum company. Like the ArtScience Museum, an international architecture firm Norwegian Snøhetta designed an iconic building "meant to represent the interconnectedness of world cultures, with each individual element attached to 'the physical and spiritual heart of the building.'" See online report at *International Artmanager*, October 5, 2012. http://artsdb.net/news.php?id=567.

6 "Joining the dots: arts and culture role seen as helping creatives connect," *Otago Daily Times*, January 5, 2018. Available online at: https://www.odt.co.nz/news/dunedin/joining-dots-arts-and-culture-role-seen-helping-creatives-connect.

7 Although the museum's status as "for profit" stands in contrast to the prevailing sense of nonprofit organizations as somehow above the fray. This tax status has divorced, and perhaps disguised, these origins.

8 From personal email correspondence with a government official.

9 Earlier in 1998 the Singapore Urban Redevelopment Authority had partnered with the Harvard Graduate School of Design to consider designs for what would become the Marina Bay promontory. The results of this graduate seminar project were published (Machado, 1999).

10 A joint project by Grant Associates Landscape Design (http://www.grant-associates.uk.com) headquartered in Bath, and Wilkinson Eyre Architects (www.wilkinsoneyre.com) in London.

11 Interestingly, the CEO of the Los Vegas Sands Corporation is from a Ukrainian-Jewish family and was raised in the Dorchester neighborhood of Boston. He remains a committed supporter of Israel and accompanied Mitt Romney on his campaign trip to Israel in 2012. Moshe Safdie, with offices near Boston, was director of the Harvard Graduate School of Design during the 1980s. Safdie designed major museums and centers in Israel.

12 Safdie was the subject of an exhibition at the National Gallery of Canada in Ottawa, "Global Citizen: The Architecture of Moshe Safdie" (October 6, 2010–January 9, 2011). Walden Pond State Reservation is open to the public for swimming, and other recreation. http://www.mass.gov/dcr/parks/walden/.

13 My thanks to my former colleague Edward F. Mooney, an expert on Thoreau, for his reading of my sections on Walden and providing advice on secondary sources.

14 A propos, *the New York Times* reported the opening of the CCTV building in Beijing, "a contoured form that frames an enormous void at its center," by the Rotterdam- and Harvard-based architect Ren Koolhaas. The *Times* article declares: "The CCTV headquarters may be the greatest work of architecture built in this century" (Ouroussoff 2011).

15 The article by senior correspondent Cheong Suk-Wai was titled "Habitats of humanity" after Safdie's most famous structure in Montréal, Habitat completed in 1971 and featured on the cover of *Newsweek*, April 19, 1971.

16 The original plan called for fifty-five floors. I suspect that Safdie's geomancer may have recommended better numbers. Interestingly twenty-one is a key number in Chinese Buddhist *mala* or rosary worn round the wrist—the most intimate prayer beads are usually twenty-one or sometimes twenty-seven beads.

17 http://www.amusingplanet.com/2010/06/infinity-pool-at-marina-bay-sands-hotel.html. Apparently this infinity pool is not unique to the Sands: a web search showed

images of hundreds of this style of pool over the world. http://designbeep. com/2010/08/20/40-breathtaking-infinity-edge-pool-photos-around-the-world/. The new Marina Bay Pools appears the most spectacular. Recently the surprise hit movie *Crazy Rich Asians* (2018, directed by Jon M. Chu) ended with a swimming party in this pool!

18 YouTube "Tour of the National Gallery of Canada with Moshe Safdie 'The Port Holes'." On Gallery Channel of the National Gallery of Canada. Uploaded by ngcmedia on November 10, 2010.

19 Especially in the American consciousness, "Nature Religion" has played a significant role and added here to the tendency to critique the inhumanity of urban life.

20 This was reported in an article in *the New York Times*, "What Sheldon Adelson Wants," June 23, 2012. Adelson was the biggest single donor to the Mitt Romney campaign and gave millions to the failed campaign of Newt Gingrich.

21 First published as *La production de l'espace*. Paris: Anthropos, 1974.

22 I cannot do full justice to the complex corpus of Lefebvre's work as a philosopher, Marxist theorist, or lifelong social activist. But it may be possible to look at a few threads without unfolding/unraveling the whole patchwork. Admiring interpreters and ardent critics have fed off his highly suggestive, but intentionally unsystematic, style filled with "references to the incapacity of language, texts, discourses ... to capture fully the meaning of human spatiality," (Soja 1996, 57) leaving variant readings open.

23 Thoreau likely read German. A delightful old article imagines a conversation between Thoreau and his contemporary Schopenhauer (see De Armond 1932). Ralph Waldo Emerson, Thoreau patron in this endeavor, had an older brother who studied in Germany and may have had much of this material in his library, which Thoreau used.

24 Lefebvre enumerates this "conceptual triad": *spatial practice* (*le perçu*), *representations of space* (*le conçu*); he describes, *le vécu*: "Representational space is alive: it speaks. It has an affective kernel or centre: Ego, bedroom, dwelling house; or: square, church, graveyard. It embraces the loci of passions, of action and of lived situations, and thus immediately implies time. Consequently it may be qualified in various ways: it may be directional, situational, or relational, because it is essentially qualitative, fluid and dynamic" (Lefebvre [1974] 1991, 42). The interpretation of *le vécu*/*lived space*/ representational space is a point of contention for Lefebvre's readers. For Łukasz Stanek, this third is "the irreducible and singular lived experience" (2011, x), and for the editors of *Space, Difference, and Everyday Life*: "lived space ... a contradictory realm of alienation and liberation" (Goonewardena et al. 2008, 9–10).

25 *La poétique de l'espace*, Paris: Presses Universitaires de France, 1958, 169. Online at http://www.scribd.com/doc/38555222/Bachelard-Gaston-La-poetique-de-l-espace.

26 Perhaps Gaston Bachelard was discovered too early, and too easily associated with other phenomenologists of the 1960s, including Mircea Eliade, to retain that edginess that excites.

27 Asha Persson confronted Casey's insistence that a sense of grounding was central to the formation of space in a fine study of a yoga community in Australia. She suggests that yoga is a deliberate "practice of simultaneously securing a sense of place, or 'grounding,' and attaining a sense of space, or 'expansion'" and "emptiness and void are generally seen as positive states" (Persson 2007, 45, 49).

28 From L'Heureux's essay in *Singapore Transcripts*, "Exuberant Singapore," which he subtitles "a love story" (L'Heureux 2011, 8).

6 How Is a Guru Like a High-rise?

1 These theological overtones are missing from the most recent accounts of the marketing of religion as sociologists consider the same phenomenon. See *Religions as Brands: New Perspectives on the Marketization of Religion and Spirituality* (Stolz and Usunier 2014).

2 Although not credited on the title page, Gehl thanks "Karen Steenhard for the translation of the book from Danish to English" (Gehl 2010, *kl* 68–9), so this could be a translation issue except for the repeated instances of the same imagery.

3 The question of when the new-style guru emerged is often traced to Swami Vivekananda at the turn of the nineteenth century, but today he is often associated with the Hindu religion, unlike the contemporary gurus who also combine yoga with teachings (see Waghorne 2009, 125–9).

4 "Multi-user places of worship get the OK," *Straits Times*, January 13, 2016.

5 For example, a website offers help in locating house designers attuned to *Feng shui* in major US cities.

6 "A Bad Omen" in Cry Freedom (blog) dated June 14, 2006 just as the plans for the hotel were revealed, which stirred a controversy from geomancers with whom Safdie had worked. http://swordofdemocles.blogspot.com/2006/06/bad-omen.html.

7 In a recent presentation at the Singapore University of Technology and Design, "Building Technology Innovation in Singapore's Housing and Development Board, 1960–1995," June 12, 2018, Jane Margaret Jacobs introduced a major research project on this radical transformation, highlighting the elevator as not only a new technology but another kind of space.

8 http://432parkavenue.com.

9 http://432parkavenue.com/health-wellness/.

10 http://www.lodhaluxury.com/the-world-towers/lifestyle.

11 www.lodhaluxury.com/the-world-towers/.

12 www.burjkhalifa.ae/en/the-tower/vision.aspx.

13 http://highrise.nfb.ca/2013/10/a-short-history-of-the-highrise/.

14 Online New Catholic Encyclopedia www.encyclopedia.com/article-1G2-3407702279/charism.html.

15 http://www.onenessuniversity.org/index.php/about-oneness/welcome.

16 Facebook: NewEarth AwakenLove in Oneness. Message from Anand Dasaji from Oneness University, dated June 18, 2014. He apologized that the initial video was not available—this was dated to the event that I attended in Singapore. https://www.facebook.com/OnenessHawaii/posts/message-from-anand-dasaji-from-oneness-university-todays-sadhaya-natchathira-poo/308955735934056/.

17 http://www.hindupedia.com/en/Aiśvarya.

18 "Crazy Rich Asians" (2018) directed by Jon M. Chu.

19 The only missing traditional element was the *homa*, the fire pit, which I have seen set up for another guru in another event in a high-rise flat in Singapore (which is another story).

20 The founding prime minister lived at 38 Oxley Road until 2005 and stated that he wanted the house torn down, but a family dispute continues over the house's fate. One family member declaring about 38 Oxley Road: "[Lee Kuan Yew] wanted demolition unwaveringly, and stated his wish repeatedly in private and public. . . . He did not want his home made into a shrine. His legacy is Singapore itself and not his old house" (Bhavan 2018).

21 From the National Heritage Board, https://www.oursgheritage.sg/hawker-culture-in-singapore/.

22 Professor Jane M. Jacobs was on sabbatical year in 2018 with Lee Kuan Yew Centre for Innovative Cities at the Singapore University of Technology and Design, working with Dr. Belinda Yuen Research, director of the institute, on a project, "A history of building technology innovation in Singapore public housing" under the Chen Tianqiao Research Programme on Urban Innovation: Cities and Innovation. The lecture introduced me to the emerging field of socio-technical systems studies. See https://lkycic.sutd.edu.sg/people/visitors/jane-margaret-jacobs.

23 Some gurus also change clothes. The head of Isha Yoga, Sadhguru Jaggi Vasudev is described as follows: "At home in loincloth as much as he is in blue jeans, barefoot through the mighty Himalayas, or straddling a BMW motorcycle on the expressway, Sadhguru is the most unusual mystic that one can encounter. Marking a clear departure from mere customs and rituals, Sadhguru's scientific methods for self-transformation are both direct and powerful." http://www.ishafoundation.org/Sadhguru.

24 It is not my task to judge if all of this is, as one allegation charges, "a gigantic scam based on corrupt greed and empty promises by its heads, 'Bhagavan and Amma,' and tragic naiveté and New Age superstition by too many (but certainly not all) of its followers." However, I have found those in the movement to be far from naive. http://www.enlightened-spirituality.org/deeksha_oneness.html.

25 I attended another satsang the following month but my reception was inhospitable. I do not know the cause but my friend at that point had broken from the group and this may have affected my welcome. I was asked, then, not to record, but had been given permission earlier for this description to record and quote, though not to use any personal name. This was a decade ago but I have still chosen photos that would not reveal any identities. I mention Saro but not her full name. I stopped attending the Kalki satsangs at this point and waited. The new leadership welcomed my presence.

26 I have slightly amended the quotes here for clarity and more common Anglo-American English form. I have not altered the meaning nor the intent.

27 Again, I have taken care that no one could be clearly identified in this photo. In some cases, I have blurred faces.

7 Templing Gurus in Little India

1 "The streets of Singapore are the origin of this breed. They are nature's combination of both the ticked coat pattern and the dark brown color, both of which are indigenous to Southeast Asia. The breed was brought into the US in the early 1970s by Hal and Tommy." Unfortunately, fewer of these little cats are seen on the streets, I assume from yet another (misguided) government attempt to "clean up" Little India. http://www.cfa.org/Breeds/BreedsSthruT/Singapura.aspx.

2 The National Heritage Board has a "Walk of Faiths" in the official Little India Heritage Trail which also includes Church of the True Light, Kampong Kapor Methodist, Foochow Methodist Church, Angullia Mosque, Sakya Muni Buddha Gaya Temple, Leong San See Temple. The site includes a stunning downloadable map: https://roots.sg/Roots/visit/trails/Little-India-Heritage-Trail-Walk-of-Faiths.

3 http://www.singapore-guide.com/singapore-shopping/mustafa-centre.htm. Another center also named *Mustafa* is actually a mosque in Virginia.

4 The center has a Facebook page: https://www.facebook.com/pages/Shirdi-Sai-Baba-Centre/453316958043977, and is listed with the many Shirdi Sai Baba temples globally at http://www.shirdisaibabatemples.org/2010/02/shirdi-sai-baba-temple-singapore.html.

5 Very early in my research, in 2005, I met one of their officials who told me that their main function is to run Hindi Schools which provide the required second language for K-12 education, and had 1,400 students at that time. The *havan*, fire sacrifice, and sermon that I attended had less than ten people, but their website still lists the Sunday morning services. They remain the only organization that can legally convert people to Hinduism. The Arya Samaj in Singapore would be a project in itself.

6 This is devoted to Swami Prabhupada and claims to be the official Hare Krishna Temple in Singapore. Their new temple is now in Geylang, and they maintain an active presence in Singapore. But like the Arya Samaj, theirs would be a story in itself. I attended many events of the organizations and plan to share this in a separate article. https://srikrishnamandir.org/home/temple-information/.

7 The guru is native to Malaysia and has developed a program based on a fascinating combination of transcendental meditation with a very Tamilian turn back toward the cultivation of *siddhi* powers, often classified as occult but fully part of the ancient forms of yoga, and catalogued in Patanjali's *Yoga Sutra*. See Bryant 2009, 301–405. This group merits special treatment.

8 The first edition in 2004 was much smaller and the title was *Place: A Short Introduction*; but now, with 50% more text, the "short" was dropped. The 2nd edition ten years later attests to the expansion of *place* as key concept.

9 As termed by "Passion Made Possible," a group out of the Tourist Board/VisitSingapore.com. https://www.visitsingapore.com/see-do-singapore/places-to-see/kampong-glam/.

10 "Big Trouble in Little India," *The Economist*, December 11, 2013. https://www.economist.com/banyan/2013/12/11/big-trouble-in-little-india. Similarly the *South China Morning Post* reported: "Migrants' rights under spotlight in Singapore after Little India riot," December 19, 2013. https://www.scmp.com/news/asia/article/1386186/migrants-rights-under-spotlight-singapore-after-little-india-riot.

11 However, the report does go on to say, "That being said, while the COI is satisfied that foreign workers' employment and living conditions were not the cause of this riot, this is not to say that a riot may never occur on this basis. There is no doubt that there are some foreign workers here who face real difficulties in their employment or living situation, especially those employed by errant firms who might withhold their salaries, not maintain the standards of their accommodation, or refuse workers warranted medical leave" (46). One of my friends from Pudukkottai district, where many of the migrant workers originate, was not surprised by the behavior, having witnessed such unruly behavior at home.

12 December 7, 2018. https://www.straitstimes.com/singapore/five-years-on-from-little-india-riot-businesses-still-in-a-slump-even-as-residents-welcome.

13 Bars remain open and widely used by tourists and more affluent denizens—the migrant workers cannot afford the prices here and had relied on buying the much cheaper bottles of beers from local retailers, usually very small shops.

14 https://www.visitsingapore.com/festivals-events-singapore/cultural-festivals/thaipusam/.

15 https://www.99.co/blog/singapore/ethnic-integration-policy/.

16 "Bilingual policy" from online *Singapore Infopedia* Government of Singapore via the National Library Board. http://eresources.nlb.gov.sg/infopedia/articles/SIP_2016-09-01_093402.html. See also Lee KY 2012.

17 One of the definitions of Tamil (*Tamil̠*) is "Sweetness, melodiousness" (Tamil Lexicon, University of Madras 1928. 1756b). See also https://en.wikipedia.org/wiki/Tamil_language. I have heard proper human relationships also called *sweet* by Tamil friends.

18 The Facebook page tells "Our Story." https://www.facebook.com/indianheritagecentre/.

19 Here the Arya Samaj, which I mention below, according to a conversation with the treasurer and a new faculty member at the National University of Singapore, Rajesh Rai, who eventually published an excellent book on early Indian migrants in Singapore (Rai 2014), was the first to ease the transition of early Indian migrants to Singapore and to provide them with a spiritual home. Interestingly the group rejected conventional temple worship very early and, in this sense, laid the foundation of what we now call spiritual vs religious.

20 The official National Library Board's Infopedia maintains a report: http://eresources.nlb.gov.sg/infopedia/articles/SIP_783__2009-01-02.html.

21 In both cases, and for such saints, the body never decays and remains within the tomb—but can only travel in spirit.

22 http://www.saisansthan.com.

23 Original compiled in Marathi by Govind Raghunath Dabhokar-Hemadpant and published in 1930 according to a timeline at the end of my English edition (2004, 793).

24 February 5, 2008.

25 An article on the center in a devotional website, "Shirdi Sai Temple Information," told the story this way and, interestingly, at no time named the donor. So although I have permission to quote, I do not use names here: "The philanthropist is a major industrialist who recently moved to Singapore from India, and was looking to build a Saibaba temple. After some deliberation he decided to take the multipurpose hall on the 3rd level of an adjunct building in the temple premises, on a long lease. Since this place belonged to an existing temple it did not require any new permits. The interiors of the hall were quickly renovated to create a magnificent temple within a few weeks; a marble idol of Shri Sai Baba was procured from India and was formally installed at the temple on 5th February 2008." http://www.shirdisaibabatemples.org/2010/02/shirdi-sai-baba-temple-singapore.html.

26 I was present with my photographer husband, Dick Waghorne, for this installation at the murti at the Sai Samaj in Mylapore, Chennai on March 22, 1987.

27 https://www.facebook.com/pages/Shirdi-Sai-Baba-Centre/453316958043977.

28 Sri Shirdi Sai Baba Mandir, Shenoy Nagar, Chennai is "More or Less a Dhyana Mandapam for Sri Sai Baba with a Seating Capacity of 1000+ Devotees. No Statue has been installed in the temple premises." http://selaiyur-sairaja.blogspot.com/2011/12/11-shenoy-nagar-sri-shirdi-sai-baba.html. This is dated 2011. I first saw the temple in 1994–5, as part of my work then on newer temples in Chennai. I encountered more such rejections or limitations on ritual or divine images later in 2004, and again in 2009, along with building grand new temples for Shirdi Sai, including huge marble image bodies for the divine saint.

29 http://www.saisansthan.com.

30 Quoting from Joshua Fishman, "Language and Ethnicity" in *Language, Ethnicity and Intergroup Relations,* edited by Howard Giles (London: Academic Press, 1977).

31 https://latinlexicon.org/definition.php?p1=2012841&p2=c.

32 These terms mean joined or an association of the wise or true ones. http://
sanskritdictionary.com/?q=saṅga%22&lang=sans&iencoding=iast&action=Search.

33 *Samādhi* has two meanings: a state of meditative absorption, or a tomb holding the
bodily remains of a yogi who attained *samādhi*, whose body is so purified that it does
not decay and is considered still potent. In the case of Raghavendra, his tomb is
termed Brindavan/Vrindavan after the holy forest of Krishna of whom he was a
devotee.

34 This derives from Sanskrit but would be rendered as this in Tamil.

35 The book she recommended was *Sri Raghavendra: The Saint of Mantralaya*: a
translation of "Sri Raghavendra Mahimai." Translated by K. Lakshman from the
original in Tamil by Amman Sathitanathan. Chennai: Arulmigu Amman Pathippagam,
1996. This is available in the Library of Congress.

36 This is the date and the form of his name that the Library of Congress assigns to him
as an author.

37 The Library of Congress lists papers from a seminar held on his contributions to
philosophy. *Seminar on Sri Raghavendra Teertha's Contribution to Indian Philosophy
and Sanskrit Literature* at Bangalore, 27, 28, 29 October 1972. Summaries of papers
edited by K. T. Pandurangi. Bangalore: Prabha Printing House, 1972.

38 https://raghavendraswamy.wordpress.com/category/sloka/. The story is very much
alive online with various translations and retellings of the deep devotion of
Appanacharya.

39 Here I began with a blog which provided a useful vocabulary list although not a literal
translation, "Guru Raghavendra Stotra (Shri Poorna Bodha)—lyrics and meaning."
https://sarvotamah.blogspot.com/2015/09/guru-raghavendra-stotrashri-poorna.html.

40 South Indians, both in Singapore and India, are divided between two religious and
theological systems formed around the Lords Vishnu (Vaiṣṇava) and Shiva (Śaiva).
Most migrants to Singapore remain within the Saiva system.

41 The current website supplies this date. https://www.amma.org.sg/amriteswari-society-
singapore/.

42 https://www.amritapuri.org/on/purnamritananda. On YouTube, "Six Types of
Laughter: Swami Purnamritananda," December 24, 2017. https://www.youtube.com/
watch?v=7J5MWGwEI9Y His flute music is available on CD, https://itunes.apple.
com/ca/artist/swami-purnamritananda-puri/30244083.

43 This continues to be held globally each year. https://amma.org/groups/north-america/
ma-center-new-england-0/events/guru-purnima-friday-july-27th-2018. I missed the
event in 2018 having to leave just before.

44 Usually South Indian light vegetarian food taken for snacks or tea (in this case idly or
variously flavored rice). One of those flavors is only recently available outside of ethnic
South India areas, but now in London, New York City, and Washington DC.

45 https://www.amritapuri.org/on/gurupurnima. Message dated July 9, 2017 at
Amritapuri, Kerala, India.

46 Lucia makes a very convincing argument that spiritual, yoga-based movements, even
while eschewing terms like religion and conversation, nonetheless engage in a new
kind of proselytizing. What this means on the ground is an openness to the possibility
that even a researcher can begin to experience and see. Hence, I was always reminded
that even to write, spiritually requires *experience*.

47 "On Guru: Amma says." https://www.amritapuri.org/6820/on-guru.aum.

References

Preface

Adler, Jerry. 2005. "In Search of the Spiritual," *Newsweek*, August 28, 2005. Available online at: https://www.newsweek.com/search-spiritual-117833.

Appiah, Kwame A. 2006. *Cosmopolitanism: Ethics in a World of Strangers*. New York: W. W. Norton.

Babb, Lawrence A. 1986. *Redemptive Encounters: Three Modern Styles in the Hindu Tradition*. Berkeley: University of California Press.

Burton, Tara Isabella. 2019. "For Marianne Williamson and Donald Trump, religion is all about themselves." *Washington Post*, August 1. Available online at: https://www. washingtonpost.com/outlook/2019/08/01/self-centered-religion-shared-by-marianne-williamson-president-trump/.

Hee, Limin, Davisi Boontharm and Erwin Viray, eds. 2012. *Future Asian Space: Projecting the Urban Space of New East Asia*. Singapore: National University of Singapore Press.

Ramasamy, Nagah Devi. 2008. "The Satya Sai Baba Movement in Singapore: Its Service Mission and Philosophy of Communal Identity Construction." In *Religious Diversity in Singapore*, edited by Lai An Eng. Singapore: Institute for Southeast Asian Studies, National University of Singapore.

Siddique, Sharon and Nirmala Shotam. 1982. *Singapore's Little India: Past, Present, Future*. Singapore: Institute of Southeast Asian Studies.

Sinha, Vineeta. 2005. *A New God in the Diaspora? Muneeswaran Worship in Contemporary Singapore*. Singapore: Singapore University Press.

Sinha, Vineeta. 2008. "'Religiously-inspired', 'India-derived' Movements in Singapore." In *Religious Diversity in Singapore*, edited by Lai An Eng. Singapore: Institute for Southeast Asian Studies, National University of Singapore.

Waghorne, Joanne Punzo. 1976. "Images of Dharma: The Epic World of C. Rajagopalachari." Ph.D. Dissertation, Divinity School, University of Chicago.

Waghorne, Joanne Punzo. 2013. "Beyond Pluralism: Global Gurus and the Third Stream of American Religiosity." In *Religious Pluralism in Modern America*, edited by Charles L. Cohen and Ronald L. Numbers, 228–50. New York: Oxford University Press, 2013.

Waghorne, Joanne Punzo. 2014a. "Reading Walden Pond at Marina Bay Sands—Singapore." *Journal of the American Academy of Religion* 82, 1: 217–47 (March).

Waghorne, Joanne Punzo. 2014b. "Engineering an Artful Practice: On Jaggi Vasudev's Isha Yoga and Sri Sri Ravi Shankar's Art of Living." In *Gurus of Modern Yoga*, edited by Ellen Goldberg and Mark Singleton, 283–307. New York: Oxford University Press, 2014.

Waghorne, Joanne Punzo, ed. 2016. *Place/No-Place in Urban Asian Religiosity*. ARI – Springer Asian Series. Singapore: Springer.

Wallerstein, Immanuel. 1991. *Geopolitics and Geoculture: Essays on the Changing World-System*. Cambridge: Cambridge University Press.

Yuen, Belinda and Anthony G. O. Yeh, eds. 2011. *High-Rise Living in Asian Cities*. Berlin: Springer. Kindle edition.

1 Macrospaces and Microplaces

Appold, Stephen J. 2011. "Community Development in Tall Residential Buildings." In *High-Rise Living in Asian Cities*, edited by Belinda Yuen and Anthony G. O. Yeh, 149–77. Berlin: Springer. Kindle edition.

Augé, Marc. [1992] 2008. *Non-Places: An Introduction to Supermodernity*. 2nd ed. London: Verso.

Bishop, Ryan, John Phillips, and Wei-Wei Yeo, eds. 2004. *Beyond Description: Singapore Space Historicity*. London/New York: Routledge.

Corke, Ben. 2014. "What is Singapore like? Modern, clean and soulless." Blog Adore Travel, August 13. Available online at: http://www.adore-travel.com/travel-tips/what-is-singapore-like.

Dover, Danny. 2013. "Why I'll never return to Singapore". Blog *Lifelisted*, November 5. Available online at: https://www.lifelisted.com/blog/happens-everything-goes-right/.

Fisher, Gareth. 2016. "Losing the Neighborhood Temple (Or Finding the Temple and Losing the Neighborhood): Transformations of Temple Space in Modern Beijing." In *Place/No-Place in Urban Asian Religiosity*, edited by Joanne Punzo Waghorne, 109–29. ARI – Springer Series. Singapore: Springer.

Frost, Mark R and Yu-Mei Balasingamchow. 2009. *Singapore: A Biography*. Singapore: National Museum of Singapore.

Gibson, William. 1993. "Disneyland with the Death Penalty." *Wired*. September–October. Available online at: https://www.wired.com/1993/04/gibson-2/.

Koolhaas, Rem, and Bruce Mau. 1995. *S,M,L,X*. Edited by Jennifer Sigler. New York: Monacelli Press.

L'Heureux, Eric G., ed. 2010. *Singapore Transcripts*. Singapore: Center for Advanced Studies in Architecture, National University of Singapore.

Lee, Hsien Loong, 2010. "Speech by Mr. Lee Hsien Loong, Prime Minister, at the official opening of the Waterfront Promenade and the Marine Bay City Gallery, 18 July 2010, 9.30am at Marina Bay." Available online at: https://www.pmo.gov.sg/Newsroom/speech-mr-lee-hsien-loong-prime-minister-official-opening-waterfront-promenade-and.

Lincoln, Bruce. (1989) 2014. *Discourse and the Construction of Society: Comparative Studies of Myth, Ritual, and Classification*. 2nd ed. Oxford: Oxford University Press. Kindle edition.

Lingham, Susie, and Andrea Fam, Michel Lee, Joyce Toh, Suman Gopinath, Nur Hanim Khairuddin, John Tung, Louis Ho, Tan Siuli, Xiang Liping. 2016. *An Atlas of Mirrors*. Catalogue for the Singapore Biennale 2016. Singapore: Singapore Art Museum.

Mahbubani, Kishore. 2015. "Why Singapore Is the World's Most Successful Society." *Huffington Post* online August 18, 2015. Available online at: http://www.huffingtonpost.com/kishore-mahbubani/singapore-world-successful-society_b_7934988.html.

Maki, Fumihiko. 1964. *Investigations in Collective Form*. St. Louis: Washington University School of Architecture.

Panikkar, R. 1991. "There is No Outer without Inner Space." In *Concepts of Space, Ancient and Modern*, edited by Kapala Vatsyayan, 8–37. New Delhi: India Gandhi National Center for the Arts.

Pile, Steve. 2005. *Real Cities: Modernity, Space and the Phantasmagorias of City Life*. London/Thousand Oaks/New Delhi: Sage Publications. Kindle edition.

Prakash, Vikramaditya. 2002. *Chandigarh's Le Corbusier: The Struggle for Modernity in Postcolonial India*. Seattle: University of Washington Press.

Raban, Jonathan. (1974) 2008. *Soft City*. London: Picador.

Sinha, Vineeta. 2016. "Marking spaces as 'sacred': Infusing Singapore's urban landscape with sacrality." *International Sociology*, 31(4): 467–88.

Smith, Jonathan Z. 1982. "Sacred Persistence: Toward a Redescription of Canon." In *Imagining Religion: From Babylon to Jonestown*, 36–52. Chicago and London: University of Chicago Press.

Tan, Siuli and Louis Ho. 2015. *After Utopia: Revisiting the Ideal in Asian Contemporary Art*. Pamphlet from the exhibition at the Singapore Museum of Art, 1 May–15 October 2015, curated by Tan Siuli and Louis Ho.

Tan, Siuli and Louis Ho, eds. 2018. *After Utopia: Revisiting the Ideal in Asian Contemporary Art*. Catalogue with interpretive essays from the exhibition at the Singapore Museum of Art, 1 May–15 October 2015, curated by Tan Siuli and Louis Ho.

Vittachi, Brian. 2013. "Don't come home to soulless Singapore." *Singapore News*, Yahoo Blog. July 30. Available online at: https://sg.news.yahoo.com/your-view--don-t-come-home-to-soulless-singapore-050421809.html.

Waghorne, Joanne Punzo. 2014. "From Diaspora to (Global) Civil Society: Global Gurus and the Processes of De-ritualization and De-ethnization in Singapore." In *Hindu Rituals at the Margins: Transformations, Innovations, Reconsiderations*, edited by Tracy Pintchman and Linda Penkower, 186–207. Columbia SC: University of South Carolina Press.

Walmsley, Stuart. 2013. "Singapore – a soulless success." Blog. September 18. Available online at: http://stuartwalmsley.com/author/stu/.

Ward, Barbara. 1962. *The Rich Nations and the Poor Nations*. New York: W. W. Norton & Co.

Wee, C. J. Wan-ling. 2007. *The Asian Modern: Culture, Capitalist Development, Singapore*. Hong Kong: Hong Kong University Press. Kindle edition.

2 Statecraft and Cosmology: Making the Macrocosm in Singapore

Allen, Graham. 2003. *Roland Barthes*. Routledge Critical Thinkers. London: Taylor & Francis. Kindle Edition.

Barthes, Roland. (1957) 2012. *Mythologies: The Complete Edition, in a New Translation*. 2nd ed. Translated by Richard Howard and Annette Lavers. New York: Hill and Wang.

Berger, Peter L. (1967) 2011. *The Sacred Canopy: Element of a Sociological Theory of Religion*. New York: Open Road. Kindle reprint. Originally published, Garden City NY: Doubleday, 1967.

Berger, Peter L. 1969. *A Rumor of Angels: Modern Society and the Rediscovery of the Supernatural*. Garden City NY: Doubleday.

Borneman, John, ed. 2004. *Death of the Father: An Anthropology of the End in Political Authority*. New York and Oxford: Berghahn Books.

Buncombe, Andrew. 2014. "Have you heard about the film Singapore has banned its people from seeing? Well, you have now." *Independent*, September 16, 2014. Available online at: http://www.independent.co.uk/voices/comment/have-you-heard-about-the-film-singapore-has-banned-its-people-from-watching-well-you-have-now-9736530.html.

Campbell, Joseph. 1988. *The Power of Myth*. With Bill Moyers. New York: Knopf Doubleday Publishing Group. Kindle edition.

Cassirer, Ernst. 1925. *Sprache und Mythos, ein Beitrag zum Problem der Götternamen*. Leipzig and Berlin: Teubner. Later published as *Language and Myth*. Translated by Susanne K. Langer. New York: Dover Publications, 1946.

Cassirer, Ernst. 1946. *Myth of the State*. New Haven and London: Yale University Press.

Centre for Liveable Cities (CLS). 2014. *Land Acquisition and Resettlement: Securing Resources for Development*. Urban Systems Studies. Singapore: Centre for Liveable Cities, Government of Singapore.

Centre for Liveable Cities (CLS). 2015. *Built by Singapore: From Slums to a Sustainable Built Environment*. Urban Systems Studies. Singapore: Centre for Liveable Cities, Government of Singapore.

Centre for Liveable Cities (CLS). 2016a. *A Chance of a Lifetime: Lee Kuan Yew and the Physical Transformation of Singapore*. In collaboration with the Lee Kuan Yew Centre for Innovative Cities. Singapore: Centre for Liveable Cities, Government of Singapore.

Centre for Liveable Cities (CLS). 2016b. *Cleaning a Nation: Cultivating a Healthy Living Environment*. Urban Systems Studies. Singapore: Centre for Liveable Cities, Government of Singapore.

Centre for Liveable Cities (CLS). 2016c. *Urban Redevelopment: From Urban Squalor to Global City*. Urban Systems Studies. Singapore: Centre for Liveable Cities, Government of Singapore.

Choe, Alan F. C. 2017. "The Early Years of Nation-Building: Reflections on Singapore's Urban History." In *50 Years of Urban Planning in Singapore*, edited by Heng Chye Kiang, 3–22. New Jersey and Singapore: World Scientific.

Chua, Beng Huat. 1997. *Political Legitimacy and Housing: Stakeholding in Singapore*. London and New York: Routledge. Kindle edition.

Chua, Beng Huat. 2017. *Liberalism Disavowed: Communitarian and State Capitalism in Singapore*. London and Ithaca NY: Cornell University Press. Also published in Singapore by the National University of Singapore Press.

Cook, Alexander C., ed. 2014. *Mao's Little Red Book: A Global History*. New York and Cambridge: Cambridge University Press. Kindle edition.

Culler, Jonathan. 2002. *Barthes: A Very Short Introduction*. Oxford: Oxford University Press. Kindle edition. First published by Fontana in 1983.

DeBernardi, Jean. 2016. "On Daoism and Religious Networks in a Digital Age." In *Place/ No-Place in Urban Asian Religiosity*, edited by Joanne Punzo Waghorne, 91–108. ARI – Springer Asian Series. Singapore: Springer.

de Certeau, Michel. 1984. *The Practice of Everyday Life*. Translated by Steven Rendall. Berkeley, Los Angeles, and London: University of California Press. Kindle edition.

Eliade, Mircea. (1957) 1961. *The Sacred and the Profane: The Nature of Religion, the Significance of Religious Myth, Symbolism, and Ritual within Life and Culture*. Translated by Willard R. Trask. Harper Torch Books. New York: Harper & Row.

Goldberg, Philip, 2010. *American Veda: From Emerson and the Beatles to Yoga and Meditation—How Indian Spirituality Changed the West*. With Foreword by Huston Smith. New York: Harmony Books (Division of Random House).

Heng Chye Kiang. 2017. *50 Years of Urban Planning in Singapore*. World Scientific Series on Singapore's 50 Years of Nation-Building. New Jersey and Singapore: World Scientific. Kindle edition. Pages numbered as in the printed text.

Kuhonta, Erik M. 2017. "Exceptional Engineering: Singapore's Politically Acquiescent Middle Class." Paper presented at the panel "Challenging Authoritarianism in East and Southeast Asia." Association of Asia Studies Annual Meeting, Toronto, March 18, 2017.

Lee, Hsien Loong. 1995. "Speech By D.M.P Lee Hsien Loong At The 10th Anniversary Celebration of LaSalle-SIA College of The Arts and the Opening of Its Two New Buildings at the Mountbatten Campus," August 18, 1995. Singapore Government Press Release, Ministry of Information. Release No.: 44/AUG 15-1/95/08/18. National Achieve of Singapore.

Lee, Jan. 2016. "Hop on National Day Parade themed trains from Monday until mid-August." *Straits Times*, July 11, 2016. Available online at: http://www.straitstimes.com/singapore/hop-on-national-day-parade-themed-trains-from-monday-until-mid-august.

Lee, Kuan Yew. 1961. *The Battle for Merger*. Singapore: Govt. Printing Office.

Lee, Kuan Yew. 1998. *The Singapore Story: Memoirs of Lee Kuan Yew*. Singapore and New York: Prentice-Hall.

Lévi-Strauss, Claude. 1958. *Anthropologie structural*. Paris: Plon. Later translated into English as *Structural Anthropology*.

Langer, Susanne K. 1946. *Philosophy in a New Key: A Study in the Symbolism of Reason, Rite, and Art*. Cambridge MA and London: Harvard University Press.

Long, Charles H. 1963. *Alpha: The Myths of Creation*. Paperback reprint. Toronto: Macmillan. Originally published by New York: G. Braziller.

Long, Charles H. 1986. *Significations: Signs, Symbols, and Images in the Interpretation of Religion*. Philadelphia: Fortress Press.

Long, Charles H. 2018. *Ellipsis: The Collected Writings of Charles H. Long*. London: Bloomsbury.

Lynch, Gordon. 2007. *The New Spirituality: An Introduction to Progressive Belief in the Twenty-first Century*. London and New York: I.B. Tauris.

Mittler, Barbara, 2012. *A Continuous Revolution: Making Sense of Cultural Revolution Culture*. Cambridge, MA and London: Harvard University Press.

Mittler, Barbara, 2017. "'Shishile': Mao's Death and the Making of the Chairman's Two Bodies." Paper presented at the panel "Death Becomes Them: The Posthumous Lives of Fatherly Bodies. Part 1." Association of Asia Studies Annual Meeting, Toronto, March 18, 2017.

Miyauchi, Tomohisa, and Eitaro and Tamae Ogawa, 2017. *HDB Homes of Singapore*. Singapore: Keyakismos and Dominie Press.

Oliver, Paul. 2014. *Hinduism and the 1960s: The Rise of a Counter-Culture*. London and New York: Bloomsbury.

Plate, Tom. 2010. *Conversations with Lee Kuan Yew, Citizen Singapore: How to Build a Nation*. Singapore: Marshall Cavendish.

Poh, Soo Kai. 2016. *Living in a Time of Deception*. Edited by Hong Lysa and Souk Yee. Singapore: Function 8.

Robinson, Andrew. 2011. "An A to Z of Theory: Roland Barthes's Mythologies: A Critical Theory of Myths," *Ceasefire*, September 30, 2011. Available online at: https://ceasefiremagazine.co.uk/in-theory-barthes-2/.

Seng, Eunice. 2014. "Habitation and the Invention of a Nation, Singapore 1936–1979." Ph.D., Graduate School of Arts and Sciences, Columbia University.

Singleton, Mark and Ellen Goldberg, eds. 2014. *Gurus of Modern Yoga*. New York: Oxford University Press.

Subramanian, Samath. 2017. "How Singapore Is Creating More Land for Itself." *New York Times*, April 21. Available online at: https://www.nytimes.com/2017/04/20/magazine/how-singapore-is-creating-more-land-for-itself.html.

Tan, Netina. 2015. "Institutionalized Succession and Hegemonic Party Cohesion in Singapore." In *Party and Party System Institutionalization in Asia: Democracies, Autocracies, and the Shadows of the Past*, edited by Allen Hicken and Erik Martinez Kuhonta, 49–73. Cambridge and New York: Cambridge University Press. Kindle edition.

Thrift, Nigel. 2008. *Non-Representational Theory: Space/politics/affect*. London and New York: Routledge.

Vasudev, Jaggi Sadhguru. 2016. *Inner Engineering: A Yogi's Guide to Joy*. New York: Random House Publishing Group. Kindle edition.

Wasserstrom, Steven M. 1999. *Religion After Religion: Gershom Scholem, Mircea Eliade, and Henry Corbin at Eronos*. Princeton: Princeton University Press.

Wee, C. J. Wan-ling. 2007. *The Asian Modern: Culture, Capitalist Development, Singapore*. Hong Kong: Hong Kong University Press. Kindle edition.

3   Macrospaces—Guru Style

Aravamudan, Srinivas. 2006. *Guru English: South Asian Religion in a Cosmopolitan Language*. Princeton: Princeton University Press.

Aupers, Stef and Dick Houtman. 2006. "Beyond the Spiritual Supermarket: The Social and Public Significance of New Age Spirituality." *Journal of Contemporary Religion*, 21.2: 201–22.

Berger, Peter L. (1967) 2011. *The Sacred Canopy: Element of a Sociological Theory of Religion*. New York: Open Road. Kindle reprint. Originally published, Garden City NY: Doubleday.

Carrette, Jeremy and Richard King. 2005. *Selling Spirituality: The Silent Takeover of Religion*. London: Routledge.

Chua Beng Huat. 2017. *Liberalism Disavowed: Communitarianism and State Capitalism in Singapore*. Singapore: NUS Press.

Gautier, Francois. 2008. *The Guru of Joy: Sri Sri Ravi Shankar and the Art of Living*. Carlsbad CA: Hay House.

Goodchild, Philip. 2002. *Capitalism and Religion: The Price of Piety*. London: Routledge.

Goodchild, Philip. 2009. *Theology of Money*. Durham NC: Duke University Press.

Heelas, Paul and Linda Woodhead. 2005. *The Spiritual Revolution: Why Religion is Giving Way to Spirituality*. Oxford and Malden MA: Blackwell.

Heelas, Paul. 2008. *Spiritualities of Life: New Age Romanticism and Consumptive Capitalism*. Oxford: Blackwell.

Hefner, Robert W., ed. 2001. *The Politics of Multiculturalism: Pluralism and Citizenship in Malaysia, Singapore, and Indonesia*. Honolulu: University of Hawaii Press.

Lau, Kimberly J. 2000. *New Age Capitalism: Making Money East of Eden*. Philadelphia: University of Pennsylvania Press.

Lucia, Amanda. 2018, "Saving Yogis: Spiritual Nationalism and the Proselytizing Missions of Global Yoga." In *Asian Migrants and Religious Experience: From Missionary Journeys to Labor Mobility*, edited by Bernardo Brown and Brenda Yeoh, 35–70. Amsterdam: Amsterdam University Press.

Lynch, Gordon. *The New Spirituality: An Introduction to Progressive Belief in the Twenty-first Century*. London: I.B. Tauris.

Mahadevan, Narayanan. 2016. "Sri Sri event: When rockstar gurus bring political rivals together." *Hindustan Times*, March 11, 2016. Available online at: https://www.hindustantimes.com/india/sri-sri-event-when-rockstar-gurus-bring-political-rivals-together/story-hWOo6ISmLhxHpU3KNrG1LK.html.

Morgan, David L. 1998. *Visual Piety: A History and Theory of Popular Religious Images*. Berkeley: University of California Press.

Peterson, Indira Viswanathan. 1989. *Poems to Siva: The Hymns of the Tamil Saints*. Princeton: Princeton University Press.

Rahman, M. Rajaque. 2016. "Why Modi's Sri Sri Ravi Shankar connection is good for politics." *Daily O*, January 1, 2016. Available online at: https://www.dailyo.in/politics/modi-government-sri-sri-ravishankar-art-of-living-hinduism/story/1/8213.html.

Roof, Wade Clark. 1999. *Spiritual Marketplace: Baby Boomers and the Remaking of American Religion*. Princeton and Oxford: Princeton University Press.

Simone, Cheryl Jaggi Vasudev, 2008. *Midnights with the Mystic*. Charlottesville, VA: Hampton Roads Publishing.

Srinivas, Tulasi, 2010. *Winged Faith: Rethinking Globalization and Religious Pluralism Through the Satya Sai Movement*. New York: Columbia University Press.

Subramaniam, Arundhathi, 2010. *Sadhguru: More Than a Life*. New Delhi: Penguin.

Taylor, Charles. 2002. *Varieties of Religious Experience Today: William James Revisited*. Cambridge, MA: Harvard University Press.

Vasudev, Jaggi, 2003. *Mystic Musings*. New Delhi: Isha Foundation.

Viswanathan, Gauri. *Outside the Fold: Conversion, Modernity, and Belief*. New Delhi: Oxford University Press, 1998.

Ward, Graham, 2006. "The Future of Religion." *Journal of The American Academy of Religion* 74.1: 179–86.

Warrier, Maya. *Hindu Selves in a Modern World: Guru Faith in the Mata Amritanandamayi Mission*. Oxford: RoutledgeCurzon, 2005.

Williamson, Lola, 2010. *Transcendent in America: Hindu-Inspired Mediation Movements as New Religion*. New York: New York University Press.

Waghorne, Joanne Punzo. 2014a. "From Diaspora to (Global) Civil Society: Global Gurus and the Processes of De-ritualization and De-ethnization in Singapore." In *Hindu Rituals at the Margins: Transformations, Innovations, Reconsiderations*, edited by Tracy Pintchman and Linda Penkower, 186–207. Columbia, SC: University of South Carolina Press.

Waghorne, Joanne Punzo. 2014b. "Engineering an Artful Practice: On Jaggi Vasudev's Isha Yoga and Sri Sri Ravi Shankar's Art of Living." In *Gurus of Modern Yoga*, edited by Ellen Goldberg and Mark Singleton, 283–307. New York: Oxford University Press.

Waghorne, Joanne Punzo. 2016. "Alone Together: Global Gurus, Cosmopolitan Space, and Community." In *Place/No-Place in Urban Asian Religiosity*, edited by Joanne Punzo Waghorne, ARI – Springer Asian Series, 71–90. Singapore: Springer.

Wuthnow, Robert. 1998. *After Heaven: Spirituality in America Since the 1950s*. Berkeley: University of California Press.

York, Michael. 2001. "New Age Commodification and Appropriation of Spirituality." *Journal of Contemporary Religion*, 16.3: 361–72.

4 Yoga on the Move

Alter, Joseph S. 2011. *Moral Materialism: Sex and Masculinity in Modern India*. New Delhi and New York: Penguin Books.

Atmashraddhananda, Swami. 2010. *Pilgrimage to Kanyakumari and Rameshwaram*. Chennai: Shri Ramakrishna Math.

Bryant, Edwin F. 2009. *The Yoga Sutras of Patañjali: A New Edition, Translation, and Commentary*. New York: Farrar, Straus & Giroux. Kindle edition.

Bryant, Edwin F. and Laurie L. Patton, eds. 2004. *The Indo-Aryan Controversy: Evidence and Inference in Indian History*. London and New York: Routledge.

Chaturvedi, Shubham. 2015. "Unsung Heroes-Gwalior City, Anil Sarode: The Man behind 'Retired but not tired' from Gwalior City." *Real Bharat* (blog) dated September 23, 2015. Available online at: http://www.realbharat.org/unsung-heroes-gwalior-city/.

de Certeau, Michel. 1984. *The Practice of Everyday Life*. Translated by Steven Rendall. Berkeley, Los Angeles, and London: University of California Press. Kindle edition.

De Michelis, Elizabeth. 2004. *A History of Modern Yoga: Patanjali and Western Esotericism*. London and New York: Continuum.

Ernst, Carl W. 2016. *Refractions of Islam in India: Situating Sufism and Yoga*. New Delhi and Los Angeles: Sage. Kindle edition.

Foo, Choo Meng. 2016. *International Day of Yoga: Singapore 21st June 2016*. Morrisville NC: Lulu.com (self-publishing).

Gold, Daniel. 2015. *Provincial Hinduism: Religion and Community in Gwalior City*. New York: Oxford University Press.

Lucia, Amanda. 2018. "Saving Yogis: Spiritual Nationalism and the Proselytizing Missions of Global Yoga." In *Asian Migrants and Religious Experience: From Missionary Journeys to Labor Mobility*, edited by Bernardo E. Brown and Brenda S. A. Yeoh, 35–70. Amsterdam: Amsterdam University Press.

Miller, Barbara Stoler. 1996. *Yoga: Discipline of Freedom*. Berkeley: University of California Press.

Neumann, David J. 2019. *Finding God through Yoga: Paramahansa Yogananda and Modern American Hinduism*. Chapel Hill: University of North Carolina Press.

Newcombe, Suzanne. 2018. "Spaces of Yoga – Towards a Non-Essentialist Understanding of Yoga." In *Yoga in Transformation: Historical and Contemporary Perspectives*, edited by Karl Baier, Phillip A. Maas, and Karen Preisendanz, 551–73. 'Wiener Forum für Theologie und Religionswissenschaft' [Viennese Forum for Theology and the Study of Religions]. Göttingen: V&R University Press.

Pandya, Samta P. 2016. "Sudarshan Kriya of the Art of Living Foundation: Applications to Social Work Practice." *Social Work in Action* 28.2 (April):133–54.

Pandya, Samta P. 2017. *Faith Movements and Social Transformation: Guru Charisma in Contemporary India*. New Delhi: Rawat Publications.

Peterson, Christine Tara, Sarah M. Bauer, Deepak Chopra, Paul J. Mills, and Raj K. Maturi. 2017. "Effects of Shambhavi Mahamudra Kriya, a Multicomponent Breath-Based Yogic Practice (Pranayama), on Perceived Stress and General Well-Being." *Journal of Evidence-Based Complementary & Alternative Medicine* 22 (4): 788–97.

Shankar, Sri Sri Ravi. 2012. *The Yoga Sutras of Patanjali*. Santa Barbara CA: Art of Living Foundation. Kindle edition. Original title: "The Yoga Sutras of Patanjali Commentary on the Yoga Sutras of Maharishi Patanjali given by H. H. Sri Sri Ravi Shankar in December 1994 and January 1995 in Weggis, Switzerland."

Singleton, Mark. 2010. *Yoga Body: The Origins of Modern Posture Practice*. New York: Oxford University Press. Kindle edition.

Suri, Manil. 2015. "India and the Politics of Yoga." *New York Times*, June 19, 2015. Available online at: https://www.nytimes.com/2015/06/20/opinion/india-and-the-politics-of-yoga.html.

Tuan, Yi-Fu. (1974) 1990. *Topophilia: A Study of Environmental Perception, Attitudes, and Values*. 2nd ed. New York: Columbia University Press. Kindle edition.

van der Veer, P. 2009. "Global Breathing: Religious Utopias in India and China." In *Transnational Transcendence: Essays on Religion and Globalization*, edited by Thomas J. Csordas, 263–78. Berkeley, Los Angeles and London: University of California Press.

van der Veer, P. 2014. *The Modern Spirit of Asia: The Spiritual and the Secular in China and India*. Princeton: Princeton University Press. Kindle edition.

Vasudev, Jaggi Sadhguru and Arundhathi Subramaniam. 2017. *Adiyogi: The Source of Yoga*. Noida, Uttar Pradesh and London: HarperCollins.

Vasudev, Jaggi. 2014. "Who Is Shiva: Man, Myth or Divine?" Available online at: https://isha.sadhguru.org/us/en/wisdom/article/who-is-shiva-meaning.

Vasudev, Jaggi. 2015. "The Presence of Shiva – On the Trail of the First Yogi." Available online at: https://isha.sadhguru.org/us/en/wisdom/article/shiva.

Waghorne, Joanne Punzo. 2009. "Global Gurus and the Third Stream of American Religiosity: Between Hindu Nationalism and Liberal Pluralism." In *Political Hinduism*, edited by Vinay Lal, 90–117. New Delhi: Oxford University Press.

White, David Gordon. 2014. *The Yoga Sutra of Patanjali: A Biography*. Princeton and Oxford: Princeton University Press. Kindle edition.

Zavos, John. 2012. "Researching Public Hinduisms: An Introduction." In *Public Hinduism*, edited by John Zavos, Pralay Kanungo, Deepa S. Reddy, Maya Warrier, and Raymond Brady William, 3–21. New Delhi and Los Angeles: Sage.

5 Reading Walden Pond at Marina Bay Sands, Singapore

Albanese, Catherine. 1991. *Nature Religion in America: From the Algonkian Indians to the New Age*. Chicago: University of Chicago Press.

Albrecht, Donald. 2010. "Creating a Humanistic Architecture." In *Global Citizen: The Architecture of Moshe Safdie*, edited by Donald Albrecht. Bentonville: Crystal Bridges Museum of American Art (in association with Scala Publishers, Ltd. London and Skirball Cultural Center, Los Angeles).

Appiah, Kwame Anthony. 2006. *Cosmopolitanism: Ethics in a World of Strangers*. New York: W. W. Norton & Co.

Armstrong, Robert P. 1971. *The Affecting Presence: An Essay in Humanistic Anthropology*. Urbana: University of Illinois Press.

Bachelard, Gaston [1958] 1969. *The Poetics of Space*. Translated by Maria Jolas. Boston: Beacon Press.

Bachelard, Gaston. 1958. *La poétique de l'espace*. Paris: Presses Universitaires de France. Available online at: http://www.scribd.com/doc/38555222/Bachelard-Gaston-La-poetique-de-l-espace.

Bennett, Tony. 1995. *The Birth of the Museum: History, Theory, Politics*. London: Routledge.

Bennett, Tony. 2006. "Exhibition, Difference, and the Logic of Culture." In *Museum Frictions: Public Cultures/Global Transformations*, edited by Ivan Karp and Corinne A. Kratz, et al., *kl* 779–1123. Durham NC: Duke University Press. Kindle edition.

Bishop, Ryan, 2004. "The Vertical Order Has Come to an End: The *Insignia of the Military C³I and Urbanism in Global Networks*." In *Beyond Description: Singapore Space Historicity*, edited by Ryan Bishop, and John Philip and Wei Wei Yeo, 60–78. London: Routledge.

Carrette, Jeremy and Richard King. 2005. *Selling Spirituality: The Silent Takeover of Religion*. London: Routledge.

Casey, Edward S. (1993) 2009. *Getting Back into Place: Toward a Renewed Understanding of the Place-World*. 2nd ed. Bloomington: Indiana University Press.

Center for American Progress. 2011. "It's Easy Being Green: Happy Birthday, Henry David Thoreau." Online Newspaper, July 13. Available online at: http://www.americanprogress.org/issues/2011/07/ebg071311.html.

Cheong, Suk-Wai. 2006. "Habitats of humanity." *Straits Times*. June 16.

Chi, Jiwei. 1994. *Dialectic of Chinese Revolution: From Utopianism to Hedonism*. Stanford: Stanford University Press.

Cook, Maria. 2010a. "Safdie's World." *Ottawa Citizen*, October 2, 2010, online version in the National Library of Singapore.

Cook, Maria. 2010b. "Global architect; Born in Haifa, raised in Canada and based out of the United States, the 'not quite famous' architect, Moshe Safdie, has left his mark around the globe." *National Post*, 6 October.

De Armond, Fred. 1932. "Thoreau and Schopenhauer: An Imaginary Conversation." *The New England Quarterly* 5(1): 55–64.

De Michelis, Elizabeth. 2004. *A History of Modern Yoga: Pañjali and Western Esotericism*. London: Continuum.

Desjarlais, Robert and C. Jason Throop. 2011. "Phenomenological Approaches in Anthropology." *Annual Review of Anthropology* 40:87–102.

Emerson, Ralph Waldo. 1836. *Nature*. Boston: J. Munroe and Company.

Goodchild, Philip. 2009. *The Theology of Money*. Durham NC: Duke University Press.

Goonewardena, Kanishka, Stefan Kipfer, Richard Milgrom, and Christian Schmid, eds. 2008. *Space, Difference, Everyday Life: Reading Henri Lefebvre*. London: Routledge.

Harris, Neil. 1990. *Cultural Excursions: Marketing Appetites and Cultural Tastes in Modern America*. Chicago: University of Chicago Press.

Hefner, Robert W., ed. 2001. *The Politics of Multiculturalism: Pluralism and Citizenship in Malaysia, Singapore, and Indonesia*. Honolulu: University of Hawaii Press.

Heng, Chye Kiang and Low Boon Liang, eds. 2010. *On Asian Streets and Public Space*. Singapore: Center for Advanced Studies in Architecture, National University of Singapore.

Iyer, Pico. 2000. *The Global Soul: Jet Lag, Shopping Malls, and the Search for Home*. New York: Random House.

Jackson, Bill. 2011. "Singapore's Transformation in Education: The Creativity & Critical Thinking Initiative." *The Daily Riff*, November 14, online edition.

Karp, Ivan, Corinne A. Kratz, et al., eds. 2006. *Museum Frictions: Public Cultures/Global Transformations*. Durham NC: Duke University Press. Kindle edition.

King, Anthony D. 2004. *Spaces of Global Culture: Architecture Urbanism Identity*. London: Routledge.

Kwek, Mean Luck. 2004. "Singapore: A Skyline of Pragmatism." In *Beyond Description: Singapore Space Historicity*, edited by Ryan Bishop, John Philip, and Wei Wei Yeo, 112–24. London: Routledge.

L'Heureux, Erik G., ed. 2011. *Singapore Transcripts*. Singapore: Center for Advanced Studies in Architecture, National University of Singapore.

Langdon, Philip, 1995. "Asia bound." *Progressive Architecture*; 76 (3): 43–88.

Lefebvre, Henri. 1973. "Vers une architecture de la jouissance" (Toward an Architecture of Jouissance). Unpublished manuscript.

Lefebvre, Henri. (1974) 1991. *The Production of Space*. Translated by Donald Nicholson-Smith. Oxford: Blackwell.

Macdonald, Lise, ed. 2012. *Andy Warhol: 15 Minutes Eternal*. Catalogue for the exhibit at the ArtScience Museum. Pittsburg: The Andy Warhol Museum (with the ArtScience Museum).

Machado, Rodolfo. 1999. *Singapore's Marina Bay: Urban Conditions Recreated*. Project for the Graduate School of Design in collaboration with the Urban Redevelopment Authority. Cambridge MA: Graduate School of Design, Harvard University.

Mooney, Edward F. 2009. *Lost Intimacy in American Thought: Recovering Personal Philosophy from Thoreau to Cavell*. New York: Continuum.

Mooney, Edward F. 2011. "Thoreau's 'Concord River': Living Transcendentally on Currents of Time." Unpublished manuscript available at http://thecollege.syr.edu/people/faculty/pages/rel/mooney-edward.html.

Ouroussoff, Nicolai. 2011. "Koolhaas, Delirious in Beijing." *New York Times*, July 11. Online edition.

Panikkar, R. 1991. "There is No Outer without Inner Space." In *Concepts of Space, Ancient and Modern*, edited by Kapala Vatsyayan, 8–37. New Delhi: India Gandhi National Center for the Arts.

Persson, Asha. 2007. "Intimate Immensity: Phenomenology of Place and Space in an Australian Yoga Community." *American Ethnologist* 34 (1): 44–56.

Preuss, Simone 2012. "Singapore's Gardens By The Bay: A Stunning Feat of Green Design." *Environmental Graffiti*, June 26. https://www.huffingtonpost.co.uk/entry/stunning-feat-of-green-design_n_1628349.

Robinson, David M. 2004. *Natural Life: Thoreau's Worldly Transcendentalism*. Ithaca, NY: Cornell University Press.

Ryder, Katherine. 2011. "Can Singapore Engineer Creativity." *CNN Money*, September 13. Online edition.

Safdie, Moshe and Wendy Kohn. 1997. *The City after the Automobile: An Architect's Vision*. Toronto: Stoddart Publishing.

Safdie, Moshe, 2009. "On Ethics, Order and Complexity." In *Moshe Safdie II*, edited by Diana Murphy. Victoria, Australia: Image Publishing.

Simonsen, Kirsten. 2005. "Bodies, Sensations, Space and Time: The Contribution from Henri Lefebvre." *Human Geography* 87 (1): 1–14.

Smith, David C. 1995. *The Transcendental Saunterer: Thoreau and the Search for Self*. Savannah GA: Frederic C. Beil Publisher.

Soja, Edward W. 1996. *Third Space: Journeys to Los Angeles and Other Real-and-Imagined Places*. Oxford: Blackwell.

Soja, Edward W. 1999. *Thirdspace: Expanding the Scope of the Geographical Imagination*. Cambridge: Polity Press.

Soja, Edward W. 2000. *Postmetropolis: Critical Studies of Cities and Regions*. Oxford: Blackwell.

Stanek, Łukasz. 2011. *Henri Lefebvre on Space: Architecture, Urban Research, and the Production of Theory*. Minneapolis: University of Minnesota Press.

Syman, Stefanie 2010. *The Subtle Body: The Story of Yoga in America*. New York: Farrar, Straus, & Giroux.

Thoreau, Henry. (1854) 2010. *Walden; or, Life in the Woods*. Boston: Ticknor and Fields. New York: Barnes and Noble, Nook book.

Tuan, Yi-Fu. 1977. *Space and Place: The Perspective of Experience*. Minneapolis: University of Minnesota Press.

Urban Redevelopment Authority Singapore. 2005. *Marina Bay: Explore, Exchange, Entertain*.

Warf, Barney and Santa Arias, eds. 2008. *The Spatial Turn: Interdisciplinary Perspectives*. London: Routledge.

6 How Is a Guru Like a High-rise?

Appadurai, Arjun, ed. 1986. *The Social Life of Things: Commodities in Cultural Perspective*. Cambridge: Cambridge University Press. Kindle edition.

Appadurai, Arjun. 2016. *Banking on Words: The Failure of Language in the Age of Derivative Finance*. Chicago and London: University of Chicago Press. Kindle edition.

Appold, Stephen and Belinda Yuen. 2007. "Families in Flats, Revisited." *Urban Studies* 44.3: 569–89.

Augé, Marc. (1992) 2008. *Non-Places: An Introduction to Supermodernity*. 2nd ed. London: Verso.

Badger, Emily. 2015. "In the shadows of booming cities, a tension between sunlight and prosperity." *Washington Post*, May 4. Available online at: www.washingtonpost.com/news/wonk/wp/2015/05/04/.

Beauregard, Robert. 2015. "We Blame the Building! The Architecture of Distributed Responsibility." *International Journal of Urban and Regional Research* 39.3: 533–49.

Bhavan, Jaipragas. 2018. "They're at It Again: Lee Kuan Yew Home Must Be Razed, Younger Children Insist." *South China Post* [Hong Kong], April 3. Available online at: https://www.scmp.com/week-asia/article/2140139/theyre-it-again-lee-kuan-yew-home-must-be-razed-younger-children-insist.

Braidotti, Rosi. 2013. *The Posthuman*. Cambridge MA: Polity Press.

Britton, Karla Cavarra. 2010. *Constructing the Ineffable: Contemporary Sacred Architecture*. New Haven: Yale University Press.

Buchanan, Ian, 2001. *Michel De Certeau: Cultural Theorist*. London: Sage.

Carlson, Maria. 2006. "Looking, Listening, and Remembering: Ways to Walk New York after 9/11." *Theatre Journal* 58.3: 395–416.

Carrette, Jeremy and Richard King. 2004. *Selling Spirituality: The Silent Takeover of Religion*. London: Routledge.

Cooke, Dewi. 2010. "Living the high life or just skyscraping by?" *The Age*, April 10. Available online at: http://www.theage.com.au/victoria/living-the-high-life-or-just-skyscraping-by-20100409-rysr.html.

Davies, Allen. 2012. "Is high-rise living unnatural?" *Crikey*, June 27. Reproduced from *The Urbanist* (blog). Available online at: http://blogs.crikey.com.au/theurbanist/2012/04/29/is-high-rise-living-unnatural/.

de Certeau, Michel. 1984. *The Practice of Everyday Life*. Translated by Steven Randell. Berkeley, Los Angeles, London: University of California Press.

DeBernardi, Jean, 2016. "On Daoism and Religious Networks in a Digital Age." In *Place/No-Place in Urban Asian Religiosity*, edited by Joanne Punzo Waghorne, 91–108. Singapore: Springer, 2016.

Fisher, Gareth, 2016. "Losing the Neighborhood Temple (Or Finding the Temple and Losing the Neighborhood): Transformations of Temple Space in Modern Beijing." In

Place/No-Place in Urban Asian Religiosity, edited by Joanne Punzo Waghorne, 109–29. Singapore: Springer, 2016.

Gehl, Jan. (1971) 1987. *Life Between Buildings: Using Public Space*. Translated by Jo Koch, New York: Van Nostrand Reinhold. (*Livet mellem husene*. København: Arkitektens Forlag)

Gehl, Jan. 2010. *Cities for People*. Washington, DC: Island Press. Kindle edition.

Goodchild, Philip. 2002. *Capitalism and Religion: The Price of Piety*. London: Routledge

Goodchild, Philip. 2009. *Theology and Money*. Durham, NC: Duke University Press.

Graham, Stephen. 2016. *Vertical: The City from Satellites to Bunkers*. London: Verso.

Harker, Christopher. 2014. "The Only Way Is Up? Ordinary Topologies of Ramallah." *International Journal of Urban and Regional Research* 38(1): 318–35.

Harris, Andrew. 2015. "Vertical Urbanisms: Opening up Geographies of the Three-Dimensional City." *Progress in Human Geography* 39(5): 601–20.

Hee, Limin, Davisi Boontharm, and Erwin Viray, eds. 2012. *Future Asian Space: Projecting the Urban Space of New East Asia*. Singapore: National University of Singapore Press.

Houdart, Sophie. 2008. "Copying, Cutting and Pasting Social Spheres: Computer Designers' Participation in Architectural Projects." *Science Studies* 21.1: 47–63.

Housing and Development Board, Singapore. 1973. *Residents' Guide: Handbook*. Singapore: Housing and Development Board.

Housing and Development Board, Singapore. 1975. *Residents' Handbook*. 2nd ed. Singapore: Housing and Development Board.

Hughes, Thomas P. 2004. *Human-Built World: How to Think about Technology and Culture*. Chicago and London: University of Chicago Press. Kindle edition.

Jacobs, Jane M. 2018. "Building Technology Innovation in Singapore's Housing and Development Board, 1960–1995." Lecture at the Singapore University of Technology and Design, June 12, 2–18.

Jacobs, Jane M., Stephen Cairns, and Ignaz Strebel. 2007. 'A Tall Storey ... but, a Fact Just the Same': The Red Road High-rise as a Black Box." *Urban Studies*, 44.3: 609–29.

Jhaveri, Prakruti. 2016. "Exclusive: A Look the World's Tallest Residential Project—World Towers by Lodha." *Luxpresso* online July 5, 2016. Available online at: http://www.luxpresso.com/news-homes-real-estate/a-look-at-the-worlds-tallest-residential-tower-in-mumbai-by-lodha/16070554.

Korte, Annie-Marie. 2012. "Sacred Symbols of the City: Babel, Barbara and their Towers." In *The Sacred in the City*, edited by Liliana Gómez and Walter Van Herck. London and New York: Continuum.

Latour, Bruno. 2005. *An Introduction to Actor-Network Theory*. New York: Oxford University Press.

Latour, Bruno. 2013. *An Inquiry into Modes of Existence: An Anthropology of the Moderns*. Cambridge MA: Harvard University Press

Lau, Kimberly J. 2000. *New Age Capitalism: Making Money East of Eden*. Philadelphia: University of Pennsylvania Press.

Lee, Kuan Yew. 2000. *From Third World to First: The Singapore Story: 1965–2000*. New York: HarperCollins.

Lofton, Kathryn. 2017 *Consuming Religion*. Chicago and London: University of Chicago Press. Kindle edition.

Miller, Vincent J. 2005. *Consuming Religion: Christian Faith and Practice in a Consumer Culture*. New York: Continuum.

Miyauchi, Tomohisa and Eitaro and Tamae Ogawa, 2017. *HDB Homes of Singapore*. Singapore: Keyakismos and Dominie Press.

Nethercote, Megan and Ralph Horne. 2016. "Ordinary vertical urbanisms: City apartments and the everyday geographies of high-rise families." *Environment and Planning A* 48.8: 1581–98.

Olalquiaga, Celeste. 1992. *Megalopolis: Contemporary Cultural Sensibilities*. Minneapolis: University of Minnesota Press.

Panikkar, R. 1991. "There is No Outer without Inner Space." In *Concepts of Space, Ancient and Modern,* edited by Kapala Vatsyayan, 8–37. New Delhi: India Gandhi National Center for the Arts.

Rai, Rajesh. 2014. *Indians in Singapore, 1819–1945*. New Delhi: Oxford University Press.

Schaefer, Donovan O. 2015. *Religious Affects: Animality, Evolution, and Power*. Durham, NC and London: Duke University Press.

Stolz, Jörg and Jean-Claude Usunier, eds. 2014. *Religions as Brands: New Perspectives on the Marketization of Religion and Spirituality*. Farnham: Ashgate.

Thrift, Nigel. 2014. "The 'sentient' city and what it may portend," *Big Data & Society*, April–June 2014: 1–21.

Vidler, Anthony. 2001. *Warped Space: Art, Architecture, and Anxiety in Modern Culture*. Cambridge MA: MIT Press.

Waghorne, Joanne Punzo. 2009. "Global Gurus and the Third Stream of American Religiosity: Between Hindu Nationalism and Liberal Pluralism." In *Political Hinduism*, edited by Vinay Lal, 90–117. New Delhi: Oxford University Press.

Ward, Graham. 1996. "The voice of the Other." *New Blackfriars*, 77, 909: 518–28. From the Special Issue: Michel de Certeau SJ—The first collection of essays in the English language devoted to Certeau's work from the perspective of a theologian.

Ward, Graham. 2000. *Cities of God*. London and New York: Routledge. Kindle edition.

Ward, Graham. 2001. "Michel de Certeau's Spiritual Spaces." *The South Atlantic Quarterly* 100. 2: 501–17.

Wharton, Annabel Jane. 2015. *Architectural Agents: The Delusional, Abusive, Addictive Lives of Buildings*. Minneapolis and London: University of Minnesota Press. Kindle edition.

Yaneva, Albena and Simon Guy. 2008. "Understanding Architecture, Accounting Society and 'How Buildings Surprise': The Renovation of the *Alte Aula* in Vienna." *Science Studies* 21.1: 3–7; 8–28.

Yuen, Belinda and Anthony G. O. Yeh, eds. 2011. *High-Rise Living in Asian Cities*. Berlin: Springer. Kindle edition.

7 Templing Gurus in Little India

Anderson, Kay J. 1991. *Vancouver's Chinatown: Racial Discourse in Canada, 1875–1980*. Montreal and London: McGill-Queen's University Press.

Bryant, Edwin F. 2009. *The Yoga Sutras of Patañjali: A New Edition, Translation, and Commentary*. New York: Farrar, Straus, & Giroux.

Chang, T. C. 2000. "Singapore's Little India: A Tourist Attraction as a Contested Landscape." *Urban Studies* 37.2: 343–66.

Clothey, Fred W. 2006. *Ritualizing on the Boundaries: Continuity and Innovation in the Tamil Diaspora*. Columbia: University of South Carolina Press.

Cresswell, Tim. 2015. *Place: An Introduction.* 2nd ed. Malden MA and Oxford: Wiley-Blackwell. Kindle edition.

Dabhokar-Hemadpant, Govind Raghunath. (1930) 2004. *Sree Sai Samartha Satcharita: The Life and Teachings of Shirdi Sai Baba.* Translated into English by Zarine. New Delhi: Sai Press Pvt. Ltd.

Dempsey, Corinne G. 2001. *Kerala Christian Sainthood: Collisions of Culture and Worldview in South India.* New York: Oxford University Press.

Garbin, David. 2017. *Religion and the Global City.* Bloomsbury Studies in Religion, Space and Place. London: Bloomsbury. Kindle edition.

Hamid, Wajihah. 2015. "Feelings of Home Amongst Tamil Migrant Workers in Singapore's Little India." *Pacific Affairs* 88.1:5–25.

Henderson, Joan C. 2008. "Managing Urban Ethnic Heritage: Little India in Singapore." *International Journal of Heritage* 14.4: 332–46.

Kinnard, Jacob N. 2014. *Places in Motion: The Fluid Identities of Temples, Images, and Pilgrims.* New York: Oxford University Press. Kindle edition.

Kong, Lily and Brenda Yeoh. 1994. "Urban Conservation in Singapore: A Survey of State Policies and Popular Attitudes." *Urban Studies* 31: 247–65.

Lee, Kuan Yew. (2004) 2015. "In his own words: English for trade; mother tongue to preserve identity." *Straits Times*, March 17, 2015. Reprinted exempts for a speech on bilingualism, November 24, 2004. Available online at: https://www.straitstimes.com/singapore/in-his-own-words-english-for-trade-mother-tongue-to-preserve-identity.

Lee, Kuan Yew. 2012. *My Lifelong Challenge: Singapore's Bilingual Journey.* Singapore: Straits Times Press.

Lee, Sean and Ian Phau. 2018. "Young tourists' perceptions of authenticity, perceived value and satisfaction: the case of Little India, Singapore." *Young Consumers* 19.1: 70–86,

Lucia, Amanda. 2014. *Reflections of Amma: Devotees in a Global Embrace.* Berkeley: University of California Press.

Lucia, Amanda. 2018. "Saving Yogis: Spiritual Nationalism and the Proselytizing Missions of Global Yoga." In *Asian Migrants and Religious Experience: From Missionary Journeys to Labor Mobility,* edited by Bernardo E. Brown, and Brenda S. A. Yeoh, 35–70. Amsterdam: Amsterdam University Press.

Malpas, Jeff. 2018. *Place and Experience: A Philosophical Topography.* 2nd ed. London and New York: Routledge. Kindle edition.

Massey, Doreen. 1996. *Space, Place and Gender.* Cambridge and Malden MA: Polity Press. Reprinted 2007. Kindle edition.

Massey, Doreen. (1993) 2018. "Power-Geometry and a Progressive Sense of Place." In *Doreen Massey Reader,* edited by Brett Christophers, Rebecca Lave, Jamie Peck, and Marion Werner, *kl* 3038–204. Newcastle upon Tyne: Agenda Publishing. Kindle edition.

McLain, Karline. 2016. *The Afterlife of Sai Baba: Competing Visions of a Global Saint.* Seattle and London: University of Washington Press. Kindle edition.

Ministry of Home Affairs, Government of Singapore. 2014. *Report of The Committee of Inquiry into The Little India Riot on 8 December 2013.* Dated 27 June, 2014.

Narasimha, Swami, (born: B. V. Narasimha Iyer). (1978–1982) 2002. *Life of Sai Baba.* Chennai: All India Sai Samaj. (This volume brings together four earlier volumes.)

Rai, Rajesh. 2014. *Indians in Singapore, 1819–1945: Diaspora in the Colonial Port-city.* New Delhi: Oxford University Press,

Ramaswamy, Sumathi. 1997. *Passions of the Tongue: Language Devotion in Tamil India, 1891–1970.* Berkeley and London: University of California Press.

Siddique, Sharon and Nirmala Shotam. 1982. *Singapore's Little India: Past, Present, Future.* Singapore: Institute of Southeast Asian Studies.

Tuan, Yi-Fu. 1977. *Space and Place: The Perspective of Experience.* Minneapolis and London: University Press of Minnesota. Kindle edition.

Urban Redevelopment Authority (URA), Government of Singapore. 1988. *A Manual for Little India Conservation Area.* Singapore: Urban Redevelopment Authority. Online from the National Library Board. http://eservice.nlb.gov.sg/data2/BookSG/ publish/4/4d6c894a-0422-4725-a615-088e2badc5aa/web/html5/index. html?opf=tablet/BOOKSG.xml&launchlogo=tablet/BOOKSG_BrandingLogo_. png&pn=6.

Waghorne, Joanne Punzo. 1999. "The Divine Image in Contemporary South India: The Renaissance of a Once Maligned Tradition." In *Born in Heaven Made on Earth: The Making of the Cult Image in the Ancient Near East,* edited by Michael B. Dick. Winona Lake: Eisenbrauns.

Waghorne, Joanne Punzo. 2014a. "Saint Above (Beyond) Religion: Mapping Shirdi Sai Temples in Chennai." Paper presented for the panel "Urban Religion in India," The 44th Annual Conference on South Asia, Madison, October 22–5, 2015.

Waghorne, Joanne Punzo. 2014 b. "Santa Baba or Christmas Chennai Style." Paper presented for the panel "Shirdi Sai Baba: A Saint for all Seasons, for all Reasons in a Time of Indeterminacy," Association for Asian Studies annual meeting, Philadelphia, March 27–30, 2014.

Index

Entries followed by *f* indicate a page that incudes a figure.

9 781350 283305